INTOXICATING ZION

INTOXI CATING ZION

A SOCIAL HISTORY OF HASHISH IN
MANDATORY PALESTINE AND ISRAEL

HAGGAI RAM

STANFORD UNIVERSITY PRESS — STANFORD, CALIFORNIA

STANFORD UNIVERSITY PRESS
Stanford, California

Printed in the United States of America on acid-free, archival-quality paper

Library of Congress Cataloging-in-Publication Data

Names: Ram, Haggai, 1960– author.

Title: Intoxicating Zion : a social history of hashish in Mandatory Palestine and Israel / Haggai Ram.

Description: Stanford, California : Stanford University Press, 2020. | Includes bibliographical references and index.

Identifiers: LCCN 2020025589 (print) | LCCN 2020025590 (ebook) | ISBN 9781503613263 (cloth) | ISBN 9781503613911 (paperback) | ISBN 9781503613928 (epub)

Subjects: LCSH: Hashish—Palestine—History—20th century. | Hashish—Israel—History—20th century. | Drug traffic—Palestine—History—20th century. | Drug traffic—Israel—History—20th century. | Recreational drug use—Palestine—History—20th century. | Recreational drug use—Israel—History—20th century.

Classification: LCC HV5822.H3 R35 2020 (print) | LCC HV5822.H3 (ebook) | DDC 362.29/50956940904—dc23

LC record available at https://lccn.loc.gov/2020025589

LC ebook record available at https://lccn.loc.gov/2020025590

Book Design by Kevin Barrett Kane

Typeset at Stanford University Press in Minion Pro 10/14

In memory of my beloved and missed parents,
Zipora & Elimelech Ram

CONTENTS

PREFACE AND ACKNOWLEDGMENTS

While recommending the continued categorization of cannabis as illegal for recreational use in 1995, the Israeli Knesset (Parliament) voted to allow regulated access to medical cannabis for patients who were severely ill. This made Israel one of the first countries to legalize medical marijuana. Furthermore, by running a state-supported program of medical cannabis and cannabis research, Israel became world-renowned for pioneering cannabis cultivation and extraction technologies. Cementing Israel's reputation as "the holy land of medical marijuana," as *US News & World Report* recently put it, is the doyen or "grandfather" of cannabinoid research, Hebrew University of Jerusalem's professor of medicinal chemistry Raphael Mechoulam. In 1964 Mechoulam discovered and distilled the THC molecule, one of the active ingredients in cannabis; he has since explored its medicinal properties and has publicly called for the use of cannabinoids as therapeutic agents. These and other circumstances have combined to make Israel an international leader in cannabis research, fueled in part by the highest percentage of financial resources devoted to that pursuit by any nation—so much so that former high-ranking politicians (including two former prime ministers), retired military officers, police officers, business entrepreneurs, and even a Nobel laureate have recently joined Israel's thriving medical cannabis industry, eager to profit from the new bonanza.

Though the subject is intriguing and highly relevant, this book is not about the licit aspects of the medical cannabis industry in Israel, a recent phenomenon that is still in flux. Rather, this book explores the yet untold social history of the entanglement of interwar Palestine, and then the State of Israel, with cannabis as an *illicit* recreational drug. It focuses specifically on hashish—the drug made from the resin of the cannabis plant, and the most popular recreational drug in the Levant and in Palestine-Israel until marijuana largely took over the country in the 2000s. This study takes a leap backward to the early years of the twentieth century, when cannabis was first criminalized on the global stage, including in Palestine. It examines the repercussions of the drug's criminalization on the underworld of hashish traffickers and smugglers, hashish consumers, and drug enforcers, and also on public discourse on cannabis from the 1920s to the 1967 war. At the same time, this book demonstrates the links between the usage, trade, regulation, and cultural perceptions of the drug, and broader political, social, and economic histories.

The work on this book has spanned continents, and is the product of an intellectual journey that began a decade ago. This odyssey would not have been possible without the support, guidance, and collaboration of numerous colleagues, students, and friends, all of whom were involved in the project in one way or another: Akin Ajayi, Maya Lavie-Ajayi, Gadi Algazi, Yoav Alon, Ami Asher, Nir Avieli, Ami Ayalon, Rotem Bar-Lev, Eitan Bar-Yosef, Orit Bashkin, Deborah Bernstein, Arik Bernstein, Hillel Cohen, Elliot Colla, Bat-El Danzig, Noa Davidyan, Bat Chen Druyan-Feldman, Ran Edelist, Shir Fischer, Zachary Foster, Yoni Furas, Motti Golani, Jeanne Hadida, Yair Horesh, Ofri Ilany, Tami Israeli, Limor Lavi, Roy Marom, Raphael Mechoulam, Yossi Melman, Yoni Mendel, Mansour Nasasra, Galit Nimrod, Yoav Nur-Sela, Omri Paz, Omri Perlman, Shira Perri, Halleli Pinson, Elie Podeh, Itamar Radai, Zvi Rav-Ner, Amnon Raz-Krakotzkin, Rami Regavim, Avi Rubin, Amit Sadan, Cyrus Schayegh, Yehouda Shenhav, Sami Abu Shehadeh, Matthew Sparks, Joshua Stacher, Lior Sternfeld, Jonathan Stoppi, Ted Swedenburg, Daniella Talmon-Heller, Dalia Talmor, Alon Tam, Salim Tamari, Hamutal Tsamir, Raquel Ukeles, Aliza Uzan-Swisa, Peter Valenti, Avner Wishnitzer, Mahmoud Yazbak, Orit Vaknin-Yekutieli, Nimrod Zagagi, Jamal Zahalka, Amalia Ziv, Eran Zur (the musician), and Eran Tzur (the attorney). My dear friend and colleague Lynn Schler invariably kept me on my toes by continuously challenging me with critical comments and suggestions. I "hated" her for this, but in retrospect I am deeply indebted for her wise insights and suggestions for revisions. I am also grateful to the Herzog Center for Middle East Studies and Diplomacy at Ben Gurion University of the Negev and the center's director, Orit Vaknin-Yekutieli, for providing the funding for the preparation of the book's index. To Renaldo Migaldi, I want to express my appreciation for his meticulous copyediting of the manuscript. Likewise, the manuscript benefited greatly from being read by two anonymous reviewers at Stanford University Press, where editor-in-chief Kate Wahl, associate editor Faith Wilson Stein, and senior production editor Susan Karani worked with grace, patience, and speed.

I am especially grateful to Liat Kozma. Liat's research on drugs in Egypt, on the League of Nations, and on prostitution in the interwar Middle East and North Africa inspired my own perspectives and writing. Moreover, while many of us usually keep our primary sources close to our chest, Liat graciously shared with me the bulk of the sources she carefully collected from the Geneva-based League of Nations Archives, thereby saving me a great deal of time, and demonstrating rare kindness and collegiality. I am also indebted to Nomi Levenkron, an important expert on the regulation of prostitution and woman trafficking in 1950s and 1960s Israel, for keeping an eye out for sources relevant to my research while she was racing to complete her own dissertation.

As anyone who deals with histories of vice and drugs knows full well, the subject is elusive by nature and difficult to research, in large part because drug traffickers and drug users leave few traces, while the authorities who retain pertinent evidence are much too often uncooperative. Striking exceptions to the latter are two Israel Police superintendents: Shlomi Chetrit, commander of the Israel Police Heritage Center, and Ori Kossovsky, head of the Israel Police History Unit. Scholars in their own right, they both went out of their way to help me trace relevant sources for my research and expedite the process of declassification. My debt to both of them is enormous. The Knesset Archive's Gilad Natan made an equally special effort to help me with my sources, and I thank him for that.

For the greater part of my academic career, I have taught and written about the modern history of Iran. To be sure, making the transition to the history of vice and drugs in Palestine-Israel has not been free of difficulties, agonies, and anxieties. Yet one of the most intellectually and socially stimulating consequences of making this move was meeting, befriending, and working with a group of wonderful and talented historians of drugs, many of them belonging to the Alcohol and Drugs History Society (ADHS), of which I am now a proud member. My deep gratitude goes to Cecilia Autrique Escobar, Patricia Barton, Sarah Beckhart, James Bradford, Isaac Campos, Emily Crick, Alexander Dawson, Maziyar Ghiabi, Paul Gootenberg, David Guba, Timothy Hickman,

James Mills, Ned Richardson-Little, Lucas Richert, Stephen Snelders, Aileen Teague, Thembisa Waetjen, and Susannah Wilson. Being introduced to their research topics, which deal with various regions and temporalities, has shown me the extent to which drug history is truly a global phenomenon. I cannot overemphasize how much I have enjoyed their company, and how much I have learned from their wisdom and insights.

While working on this book, I participated in a research group at the Van Leer Jerusalem Institute, whose objective was to situate the Middle East in global history. It was during the group's monthly meetings, readings, and discussions that I acquired many of the tools and methods for doing global-cum-transnational history. Through these discussions I also received critical feedback on my own work. I am tremendously grateful to the group's participants: On Barak, Aviv Derri, Omri Eilat, Basma Fahoum, Hilli Greenfeld, Oded Heilbronner, Kfir Cohen Lustig, Tom Mehager, Shira Pinhas, and Relli Shechter.

Finally, I owe a great deal of gratitude to my spouse, Ilana Susie Hairston. It was her love and consideration, and her insistence not to take my anguish too seriously, that kept me going during the process of researching and writing this book.

INTOXICATING ZION

INTRODUCTION

Moshe's hands began to scrabble under the table. His friend leaned across to hide him from view. A long and swollen joint emerged between his fingers. He lit it, and with the same match lit a regular cigarette. He lowered his tiny stature to the point that he was almost entirely under the table. His lips clung to the hollow space of his clenched fist. He inhaled from the joint, to the point he could no longer hold it in. He then handed it to his friend [Meir], remaining bent and still. He tried with all his might to stop the smoke [from coming out of his mouth], until his eyes bulged and his neck swelled. Soon, he coughed, and the smoke spewed out of his mouth.

THIS PASSAGE ABOUT HASHISH (the drug made from cannabis resin), and others of its kind, appear in Shimon Ballas's (1930–2019) first Hebrew novel, *Ha-Ma'abarah* (The Transit Camp).[1] Published in 1964, thirteen years after Ballas immigrated to Israel from Iraq, the novel is now "considered a classic, a kind of a Guide to the Perplexed for generations of readers, teachers and students alike."[2] It tells the story of the residents of a fictional yet realistic Oriya transit camp in 1950s Israel, most of whom are immigrants from Iraq. The plot revolves around the residents' repeated futile endeavors to take control of their destiny by organizing and appointing a committee to articulate their grievances with the camp's authorities.

Ballas's fiction was informed at least in part by the history of harsh and discriminatory treatment meted out to residents of transit camps in the 1950s and 1960s by veteran Ashkenazim and the Jewish state in general.[3] Even so, it should by no means be interpreted solely as a monograph of weeping and lamentation.[4] Reflecting on the novel many years later, Ballas observed, "I did not write a grieving folkloristic exposition about discrimination. . . . The plot was designed to describe the reality of an uprooted community fighting to obtain its rights and confronting the government."[5] Indeed, the novel is quite subversive in its very nature, running against the grain of the prevailing Zionist (Ashkenazi) ideology of the time. Its subversive character stems in no small part from the fact that Ballas invariably identified himself as an *Arab* Jewish writer—a writer who never lost his sense of belonging to Arab culture even after being absorbed into Israeli society. This positioning, in turn, presented an enormous challenge to the hegemonic classes in Israel.[6] It is as though Ballas was telling his readers (to borrow from Batya Shimoni): "I am an Arab; I come from Arab culture, I speak Arabic, and I don't mean to apologize for it. . . . I am a proud Arab Jew."[7]

Indeed, *Ha-Ma'abarah* is replete with subversive gestures, by means of which Ballas celebrates, presumably to the chagrin of his anticipated audience, an entire repertoire of Arab culture and politics: its tastes, smells, and customs.[8] But even so, as the excerpt cited at the beginning of this chapter suggests, in the novel Ballas's perspective converges to a striking extent with that of his middle-class Ashkenazi readership with regard to one crucial habit: the matter of hashish smoking, commonly associated in 1960s Israel with a putative Arab or Mizrahi "backwardness." As we will see in this book, Jews in interwar Palestine kept away from hashish—the main illicit psychoactive substance circulating in the Levant at the time, and the region's most popular recreational drug—because they viewed it as a stereotypical marker of Oriental backwardness and barbarism. After 1948, as the migrant Jews of Middle Eastern and North African descent (or Mizrahim) were pushed to the margins of society, and themselves became associated with hashish smoking, the state authorities feared that the habit would lead to the Levantinization of Israeli society and viewed it as an indication of pre-modern, primitive ways of life.

Judging from the pages of *Ha-Ma'abarah*, it would seem that Ballas internalized these perceptions of hashish smoking and was reluctant to present alternative perspectives on the habit. Hence, he describes Moshe and Meir, two hashish-smoking characters in the Oriya transit camp, in miserable and pitiable terms: unreliable, unable to exercise self-control. In one instance Meir, after "drawing from a joint [*glulit*], . . . continued on his wobbly way, his head dizzy and his feet barely bearing him, as though they were trapped in iron chains." In another episode, the two men, after sharing a hashish cigarette, "laughed and fell into each other's arms. Moshe tripped and he stumbled, but his laughter did not stop."[9] Throughout the book, hashish smoking is portrayed as something so socially inferior and unwholesome that Moshe and Meir must indulge in their habit surreptitiously (not to avoid law enforcement authorities, as one might assume, as the police tended to stay clear of the transit camps). The novel's closing scene finds Yosef Shabbi, the main protagonist, sitting in the transit camp's coffeehouse, sunk into despair. He has been forced to acknowledge that all his efforts to improve the transit camp and its miserable conditions have failed. In the process, the coffeehouse is overwhelmed with the "stench" of hashish. The novel's despairing last sentence reads thus: "The sharp pungent smell [of hashish] entered Yosef's nose, a heavy smell. He closed his eyes and listened to the clamor."[10]

For all the novel's antiestablishment stance, then, it is worth pondering the fact that an engaged Arab Jewish writer of Ballas's stature would nevertheless portray hashish and hashish smoking in terms similar to those used by the very establishment he railed against.[11] One reason, by no means the least, is that Ballas's stance demonstrates the extent to which the displaced, racialized, and class-laden perceptions of the drug, the stuff of Oriental backwardness, had become entrenched in the imagination of Jewish Israeli society of the time. Writers and intellectuals in the Arab world also conceptualized hashish in negative terms of race and class, in much the same way as their recently departed European colonizers had done. This may go some way to explaining Ballas's antihashish attitudes. But then again, hashish has a very long history in the Arab world, as well as in the Ottoman and Persian Empires, dating back at least to the Middle Ages. Consequently, it has been the subject of debate and disputation for many centuries. In Palestine-Israel, on the other hand, hashish was a relatively new phenomenon, only emerging as an issue to be reckoned with in the interwar period between the collapse of the Ottoman Empire and World War II. And even then, hashish consumption—as opposed to hashish trafficking, which was much more extensive and troublesome for the pre- and post-1948 authorities—never reached "epidemic" levels as it did in, say, India and Egypt, both in many respects "cannabis-oriented culture[s]."[12]

THE STORY TO COME

This book's main objective is to return to the zero point of Palestine's hashish "problem," the interwar period; to follow the histories of the commodity chains and consumption of the drug and of antihashish regulation; and to chart its social life up to and through the first two decades of the existence of the State of Israel. This book traces the beginning of the hashish "problem" in Palestine to the 1920s, a period corresponding with the establishment of global anticannabis regimes and the creation of the mandate system in the Levant.

On the one hand, the era of the mandates in the Levant does not reveal a significant break from earlier times, as it was "indebted to the transformations that had taken place in the region beginning in the second half of the nineteenth century."[13] As a matter of fact, the illicit hashish trade that was introduced in the region in the course of the interwar years, and which persisted well after the establishment of the State of Israel in 1948, owes much to the survival of late Ottoman-based social and economic networks. On the other hand, the creation of the mandatory system can and should be viewed as a landmark event in the region. Not only did it mark the end of an Ottoman political, social, and religious order that had shaped patterns of public behavior for four centuries; it also introduced in the region a new political system of nation-states, a system that has lasted to this very day.[14]

Indeed, during and after World War I the entente powers—Russia, Britain, and France—began to stake claims to the "Middle Eastern spoils" that until that time had been Ottoman possessions. Britain and France were the powers with the most vital interests in the Levant. France based its claim on its role as protector of Lebanon's Maronite Christian population, as well as on its economic interests in the region, such as investments in railroads and silk production. For the most part, Britain's interests in the region lay in its "long-standing obsession" with the protection of the sea routes to India, especially the Suez Canal, and in ensuring investment and trade in the region.[15] In addition, due to wartime exigencies Britain contradictorily agreed (under the agreement with Sharif Husayn of Mecca and the French government) to establish an Arab state in the region, but at the same time, by virtue of the 1917 Balfour Declaration, also to "view with favor the establishment in Palestine of a national home for the Jewish people."[16] These contradictions were never resolved, and should go a long way toward explaining the enduring regional conflicts in general and the Israeli-Palestinian conflict in particular. Meanwhile, the League of Nations was created in 1920. Invested with the mission of preventing future wars and providing humanitarian and social aid on a global scale, the League consolidated these powers' regional interests, realizing them through the creation of the mandate states system.

> Franco-British dominance received the acquiescence of the League of Nations, whose founding Covenant, drawn up in 1919, recognized the need for mandatory powers to watch over the peoples of the Middle East "until such time as they are able to stand alone," ready for independent statehood. At the Conference of San Remo, held in 1920, the Allied powers confirmed this new status quo. The entirety of the *Mashriq*—as present-day Lebanon, Syria, Israel/Palestine, Iraq and Jordan are commonly known in Arabic—was now under British or French mandatory rule.[17]

In the final analysis, France received the mandate for the territory that now includes Syria and Lebanon, while Britain got the mandates for and largely invented the political units of Palestine, Transjordan, and Iraq. The mandate system was in many ways reminiscent of nineteenth-century imperialism, "repackaged to give the appearance of self-determination."[18]

The destination of most hashish supplies crossing the Levant via Palestine was Egypt, also an important actor in this book. Egypt had been under British occupation since 1882. While it was not a mandate state, the British had no intention of relinquishing it, considering it a vital asset for the defense of British imperial interests. As Sir George Ambrose Lloyd, Egypt's high commissioner in the years 1925 to 1929, stated to the House of Commons in 1929, "The only place from which the Suez Canal can be economically and adequately defended is from Cairo."[19] In fact, one reason why the British assumed the mandate over Palestine to begin with, though the administrative unit of Palestine had not formally existed since the twelfth century, was that they counted on the Jewish settlers to help them preserve the security of the nearby Suez Canal.[20]

More will be said about the mandate system and British Egypt throughout this book. What is crucial to state here is that dividing the Levant, or *Bilad al-Sham* (Greater Syria), into separate mandatory states created new boundaries and borders, which frequently cut across existing commercial, social, cultural, and political networks. "This meant new borders to cross (legally or not) and new regulation and immigration policies on different sides of these borders by different national and colonial governments."[21] These circumstances coincided with the establishment of unprecedented global and local controls over opiates immediately before and during the interwar years, and over cannabis in the 1925 League of Nations International Opium Convention (which resulted from the 1924–25 League of Nations Opium Conference). These two events—the creation of the Levant mandate states and the criminalization of cannabis—enmeshed Palestine for the first time in large-scale and illicit flows of hashish across its territory, with "commerce [becoming] smuggling and the newly defined crime of narcotics peddling [becoming] tainted . . . as an arch-evil crime."[22] As though to add insult to injury, these events also created or at least exacerbated the habit of recreational hashish smoking in Palestine.

The demand for hashish in the region survived the transition from the interwar British colonial era to Jewish statehood. There is much to be learned from the changing patterns of trade, consumption, and regulation during this transition alongside the changing "social life" of the drug, and to assess their meanings. This book follows the transition from Mandatory Palestine to the State of Israel from the perspective of hashish: an illicit commodity smuggled across borders; a substance that was traded, consumed, regulated, and endlessly debated; and a screen upon which people projected their desires and fears. The book's endpoint is the 1967 Arab-Israeli War and its aftermath, which dramatically transformed the patterns of illicit hashish flows and illicit consumption in Israel and in the Levant writ large.

This study can be situated in what Paul Gootenberg has called "the new drug history."[23] As Gootenberg explains, academic interest in criminalized drugs until the 1990s was largely limited to the biomedical and legal-criminological fields. When historians began to evince interest in the subject, they naturally mobilized the tools of their profession. They delved into previously untapped archives, analyzing a wide variety of sources using cross-disciplinary cultural and sociological methods. The goal was to understand and contextualize the modern origins of drugs with rich and complex social, cultural, economic, and political histories. In the process, these historians have opened up an immense and fascinating field of study, including new understandings of the political and cultural contexts within which substances became "drugs"; the underworlds of users and traffickers; the complex roles played by race, gender, and class in the construction of "addiction"; and the place of colonialism and nation-building projects in dispersing drug use and enforcing drug restrictions. Historical research of these topics has offered exciting observations about societies across the Americas, Europe, Asia, and Africa, demonstrating the links between the usage, trade, regulation, and cultural perceptions of criminalized drugs and broader political, social, and economic histories.

In line with this trend, there has been of late a barrage of monographs, articles, and dissertations on drugs (especially opiates and cannabis/hashish, but also coffee and tobacco) in different Middle Eastern and North African contexts and temporalities.[24] Yet to date no historical study of the manner in which these issues came into play in Palestine-Israel has been undertaken. Although we know quite a lot about the history of criminalized drugs, particularly cannabis and opium, in other parts of the British Empire and most notably India and Egypt, we know very little about this history in Mandatory Palestine.[25] Similarly, very little academic attention has been paid thus far to the links between hashish use, hashish trafficking, and regulation in the State of Israel.[26] This book is the first study to fully explore the history of hashish as a criminalized drug in Palestine-Israel, and it presents a window through which one can explore broader political, economic, social, and cultural change.

PALESTINE-ISRAEL, THE REGION AND THE WORLD

Although my study prioritizes the territorial space of Mandatory Palestine and the State of Israel, it seeks to explore the structured integration between this space and the Levant region as a whole, and sometimes Europe and North America as well, in issues relating to the flow, consumption, control, and social life of the drug. Thus, in this and in other respects, this book is a transnational study. It endorses the view that, "by assuming national perspectives, historians have often underemphasized connections that transcend state borders, settling for explanations that can be drawn from events, people and processes within particular territories."[27] This compartmentalization of history means that the parallels, entanglements, and connections that contributed to shaping the modern world cannot come into view.[28] Consequently, while this study does not seek to abandon national history altogether, it seeks to expand and thus "transnationalize" it.

This history thus adds to a vibrant body of historical scholarship exploring the links, flows, and circulation of pilgrims, laborers, credit, capital, commodities, and knowledge between disparate territories, as well as the "people, ideas, products, processes and patterns that operate over, across, through, beyond, above, under, or in between polities and societies."[29] More precisely, it explores the ways in which the Palestine-Israel of this era was situated in the region and the wider world, and how the region and the world reached deep into it, penetrating and shaping it in matters concerning the commodity chains, consumption, and understandings of hashish itself. This transnational approach also reflects a growing scholarly awareness that criminalized drugs and the practices, ideas, and persons associated with them are a part of larger connected realms of cross-border politics, economics, and culture that cannot be studied adequately if we privilege the state as the exclusive category of analysis.[30]

My transnational approach has been inspired by Cyrus Schayegh's compelling proposition, in his 2017 book *The Middle East and the Making of the Modern World*, that the region of Bilad al-Sham (also known as the Levant, or "Greater Syria," roughly coextensive with present-day Syria, Jordan, Lebanon, and Israel-Palestine) was intertwined through diverse sociospatial ties from the mid-nineteenth to the mid-twentieth century.[31] As Schayegh explains,

> In Bilad al-Sham, 1918 . . . was not a sharp break from the late Ottoman world. Rather, the entire 1920s were an Ottoman twilight. Here three factors were at play. First, the protracted process of integration shaping Bilad al-Sham from the mid-19th century was powerful enough to not simply vanish in 1918. . . . Second, the relative strength of the decades-long process of regional integration stood in contrast to the relative weakness of two new sets of actors. One set—and this is my second factor—was nationalist movements and elites, which were quite weak in the 1920s. Third, the other set of actors was the French and British imperial administrations which, running the Mandates on a shoestring, had neither the means nor the will to totally undo the late-Ottoman regional reality. They even recognized that reality . . . and thus strengthened the region's integration in some ways. What irony given their division of Bilad-al Sham![32]

In the 1930s too, as Schayegh maintains, the mandate-governed Bilad al-Sham countries "matured in a shared regional framework rather than simply along separate tracks."[33] Surely, Zionists of the "New Yishuv"—the organized Jewish community of Palestine, pre-1948—envisioned their nation-state project in separation from their Arab neighbors. Still, they "echoed region-wide patterns, and the Yishuv was an integral part of region-wide structures. . . . They could not, indeed did not want to, isolate themselves from Bilad al-Sham. They were a universe away from comparing their home to 'a villa in the jungle' as Israeli general-turned-politician Ehud Barak did in 1996."[34] Indeed, Palestine's initial and persisting entanglement in the webs of hashish smuggling and consumption cannot be completely understood unless we assess it within the framework of the sociospatial intertwinements of the Levant region during the interwar period.

Schayegh goes on to suggest that the consolidation of territorial (*watani*) identities in the Levant, beginning in the 1940s, signaled a decline in the region's spatial intertwinements; and that the independence of the region's mandate polities—Lebanon, Syria, Jordan, and Israel—during the latter half of the 1940s delivered a coup de grâce to any lingering possibilities of integration.[35] Still, as this book will demonstrate, the State of Israel remained utterly dependent—at least in terms of hashish commodity chains and hashish consumption—on regional-border-crossing networks and individuals. It was also dependent on the dynamics of supply and demand elsewhere in the Levant, the commerce which had survived the transition from British interwar colonialism to independence. In sum, by focusing on one specific commodity, hashish, and tracing its transportation, sale, consumption, regulation, and place in discourse in Palestine-Israel, I will be able to identify connections between people and places in the Levant that might have remained marginal had we embarked on a more traditional study, defined by national borders.

The imperative of interrogating Palestine-Israel's "methodological territorialism" also stems from the reversal of the course of the "psychoactive revolution," which led to stimulants becoming pervasive across human societies around the world, via transoceanic commerce and empire building between the seventeenth and the long nineteenth centuries.[36] The establishment of unprecedented global controls over opiates before and during the interwar period, and over cannabis at the 1925 Opium Convention, meant that neither Palestine-Israel nor any other country could be left to its own devices in matters concerning criminalized drugs.[37]

Until the mid-1980s, historical research into the League of Nations was dominated by political or diplomatic analyses, focusing almost exclusively on the rise and fall of the institution—"from the hopes that accompanied its foundation to its failure to prevent Japan's takeover of Manchuria, Italy's occupation of Ethiopia and eventually the Second World War."[38] Yet improved access to archival material in Geneva and other parts of the world, coupled with present-day concerns about international collaboration and human welfare, have redirected scholarly attention from the institution's dismal political failures to its more successful and lasting endeavors in addressing and alleviating social problems and worldwide criminal activities, such as the trafficking in humans and drugs.[39] A few studies have demonstrated the reverberations of the League's actions and decisions regarding drugs in specific Middle Eastern contexts.[40] I build on these studies in order to consider the repercussions of the League's antidrug outreach initiatives in Palestine and the Levant.

There is no doubt that the international legal structures prohibiting and regulating drugs during the interwar period were relatively successful. Likewise, there is no doubt that at the same time they drove the drug trade into the black market.[41] Hence, the interwar period should be viewed as a milestone not only in the history of drug regulation-cum-prohibition, but also in the history of international crime and criminality—of which drug trafficking and drug use were an integral part.[42] In his classic book *Nations and Nationalism since 1780*, Eric Hobsbawm makes a point about "the utter impracticability [in Europe] of the Wilsonian principle to make state frontiers coincide with the frontiers of nationality and language." Given the distribution of peoples, Hobsbawm argues, "most of the new states built on the ruins of the old empires, were quite as multinational as the old 'prisons of nations' they replaced."[43] What ensued was a world of newly demarcated sovereign nation-states, threatened by the specter of the mass movement of "alien"—that is, ethnic, linguistic, and religious—minorities across borders. Joining these were the circulation of goods (some of them illicit) and the rise of new communication and transport technologies—products of the long nineteenth century—which made such movements easier and faster.[44] The result was the moral panic about "international crime." Border-crossing drug traffickers, exploiting advances in transportation and communication to move and conceal their illicit commodities, were especially singled out as new types of international criminals.[45] Thus, the hashish traffickers who operated in Palestine and the Levant in general were but a local manifestation of the growing audacity and sophistication of criminal activity that was surging on a global scale.[46] That circumstance also informs the transnational approach of this book.

Debates about hashish before and after the establishment of the Jewish state in 1948 and the kinds of knowledge that were read into this drug in both polities also direct this book toward a transnational and transcultural approach. On this issue I follow Arjun Appadurai, who argues that, as the temporal and spatial distance between producers and consumers of commodities increases, knowledge about those commodities tends to become partial, contradictory, and differentiated:

As the institutional and spatial journeys of commodities grow more complex, and the alienation of producers, traders, and consumers from one another increases, culturally formed mythologies about commodity flow are likely to emerge. . . . [Such mythologies] acquire especially intense, new, and striking qualities when the spatial, cognitive, or institutional distances between production, distribution, and consumption are great. . . . The institutionalized divorce . . . between persons involved in various aspects of the flow of commodities generates specialized mythologies.[47]

The knowledge about cannabis—mainly technical, but also medical, social, and aesthetic—that was received and negotiated in interwar Palestine and in Israel was the kind of knowledge that accompanied complex, long-distance, intercultural flows of commodities as suggested by Appadurai. This knowledge, colonial in the main, traveled to Palestine and then to Israel from India and Egypt, where the British had contended with cannabis-oriented peoples long before arriving to Palestine; but the knowledge emerged mainly from the League of Nations in Geneva, whose role was fundamental to shaping displaced, mythical ideas about cannabis around the world and, as will be seen, in Palestine-Israel as well.[48]

THE SOURCES AND THEIR LIMITATIONS

A transnational topic requires conducting archival research in several locations. Indeed, besides works of fiction and press reports in Arabic, English, and Hebrew from the interwar and post-1948 periods, my sources include archival records from multiple localities: Israel (i.e., the Israel State Archives, the National Library of Israel, the Central Zionist Archives, the Haganah Archives, the IDF Archives, the Knesset Archives, and the Israel Police Heritage Center); Europe (i.e., the United Kingdom National Archives; the Middle East Center Archive at St. Antony's College, Oxford; and the League of Nations Archives, Geneva); and the United States (i.e., the National Archives and Records Administration). For the pre-1948 period, these archives privilege the perspective of the colonial authorities (i.e., the British in Palestine and Egypt, and the League of Nations). For the post-1948 period, they privilege the perspective of the Israeli authorities (e.g., the Israel Police, the Ministry of Foreign Affairs, the Ministry of Health, the Israel Tax Authority, and the Ministry of Justice).

In most of the sources listed above there is a dearth of in-depth information about drug users and drug smugglers themselves, and their relationships and social backgrounds remain murky at best. These limitations are acknowledged by most social historians, recognizing that the people they study "either did not know how to write or, if they did, left no writing behind, which is among the reasons why the historical record is so maddeningly unfair."[49] With regard to the history of drugs specifically, Franz Rosenthal, in his classic and still very useful study of hashish in "medieval Muslim society," complained: "We do indeed hear rather much about the manifold ways in which hashish affects the user, but truth and fiction are hard to disentangle. We have no first-hand report of bona-fide hashish eaters setting down their experiences in writing with clinical detachment."[50]

What was true for the researcher of vice in the medieval Middle East remains true for the researcher of vice in the modern Middle East. With the possible exception of the works of fiction consulted, the sources used in this study all lack the voices of the main protagonists themselves—that is, the very people involved in the flows and consumption of hashish. This is understandable, because these groups of people would understandably not have been overly keen about leaving written records of their activities. On the contrary, they tried their best to conceal all traces of their activities, and many would have paid "a premium, in cash and violence, to keep their affairs from coming to public attention."[51] Indeed, while state officials, journalists, physicians, and diplomats—to name but a few—spoke about drug dealers, drug users, and the effects of drug intoxication, the dealers and users themselves remained silent.[52] What is more, even when the sources provide information about hashish offenders, this information, often terse and nondescript, does not lend itself to in-depth analysis. Such, for example, is the nature of press reports from the era, and of reports prepared by the British authorities, the League of Nations, and the Israeli police force. These limitations are exacerbated by the fact that "many of the more recent documents [on drugs] have remained classified or are heavily redacted." That is, the authorities, who retain pertinent evidence, are often uncooperative.[53] The scholar of the criminal underworld must therefore gather shreds of evidence from the mishaps, the arrests, the prosecutions, and so on. On the whole, however:

> When the cultivator grows unbeknown to local authorities; when the smuggler successfully delivers his or her package to its destination; when the dealer distributes without raising the suspicion of his colonial overlords; and when the user lavishes the rapacious savor of a turbid and [thick] cloud of hashish smoke in the privacy of his or her own home—the scholar will most likely never know about it.[54]

CHAPTER OUTLINE

This book is organized chronologically, each chapter highlighting changing patterns of illicit trade, consumption, and control in Mandatory Palestine, and in the State of Israel during the 1950s and 1960s. Chapter 1 explores the international and regional context of the creation of the Levant hashish trade during the late Ottoman and interwar periods—a trade that hardly existed before that time. This transregional illicit trade, the result of newfangled international and local antidrug regimes and not the cause of them, extended from Lebanon and Syria in the north (the countries of production) to Egypt in the south (the country of consumption).

Located between Lebanon-Syria and Egypt, this state of affairs entangled Palestine for the first time with extensive hashish flows across its territory, and led to the territory becoming the largest way station for hashish in the region during the interwar period. Chapter 2 examines the extent to which hashish smuggling across Palestine to Egypt posed a serious challenge to the British colonial authorities. In parallel, it examines the journeys of smuggled hashish commodities across Palestine, and how different kinds of hashish traffickers endeavored to overcome the barriers preventing the safe delivery of their cargoes to their final destinations in Egypt. These barriers included the new mandatory political borders with customs and police outposts, and police controls within Palestinian territory itself.[55] Preoccupied with other priorities and burdened with budgetary restrictions, Palestine's police force was practically powerless, unable to take any meaningful action to halt the huge supplies of hashish being trafficked across Palestine.

The burgeoning expansion of hashish smuggling operations, traversing Palestine from north to south, had crucial repercussions for the culture of hashish smoking in Palestine. With some of the Egypt-bound consignments left behind for the local market, the Levant hashish trade sparked a significant increase in hashish consumption in the country. This issue is explored in chapter 3. Increased supplies crossing Palestine from the early 1930s onward meant that hashish smoking among the working-class Arab population of the territory increased as well, with hashish-serving venues (e.g., coffeehouses, hashish dens, and brothels) proliferating across many towns, especially port cities. The situation sometimes seemed out of control, with many individuals wandering the streets of these towns in a state of hashish-induced intoxication. Here, too, the British authorities seemed unable to enforce their ban on the use of hashish.

Chapter 3 thus demonstrates the extent to which, "in transit countries, the problem often spills over to the local population because service providers to the illicit drug industry (such as groups that organize transporting the drugs) are often paid in kind."[56]

Chapter 4 explores the attitudes of Palestine's Jewish community toward hashish in general and hashish smoking in particular. With some exceptions, newer migrants to Palestine from eastern Europe kept away from hashish-related activities, whether trafficking or consumption. The same was the case with veteran Sephardic and Ashkenazi Jews, despite the fact that this population was interspersed across the local landscape, and was rooted in Ottoman and Arab culture and customs. Drawing on interwar colonial knowledge and Orientalist fantasies of various kinds, which they amended to match their own circumstances, Palestine's Jews viewed hashish as an abominable Oriental vice, liable to assimilate them into the Levantine environment to an unwanted degree. For them, hashish smoking posed a threat to the integrity and future of the Zionist project in Palestine.

The establishment of the Jewish state in 1948 did not end the flows of hashish across the newly independent territory. On the contrary, enduring Egyptian demand, coupled with the structural capacity of Lebanese producers to provide ample supplies of the drug, ensured the survival of the Levant hashish trade *after* 1948. With Israel's post-1948 borders—often porous and poorly demarcated—superimposed over existing smuggling routes, and with the Israel police force suffering from shortages of manpower, equipment, and infrastructure, the trade was not radically disrupted. The resilience of hashish smuggling across Israeli territory was also sustained by preexisting pre-1948 border-crossing trade networks. However, significant changes from the interwar period were also apparent: the entering of Jews into the transregional hashish trade (often cooperating with "Arab gangs" within and beyond Israel), the rising audacity of hashish smugglers, especially across the Negev desert, and the alleged involvement of the Israeli army in the hashish trade with Egypt. These and other trends of continuity and change in the transition from Mandatory Palestine to the State of Israel are addressed in chapter 5.

Chapter 6 explores the history and public discourse of hashish consumption among Israeli Jews after 1948. I argue that this public discourse was replete with pre-1948 colonial understandings of hashish—an Oriental drug not befitting the requirements of modern (read: Western middle-class) life. At the same time, these understandings were translated to immediate post-1948 demographic and political realities: the expulsion and flight of much of the Arab population of Mandate-era Palestine in the Nakba, and the country's repopulation by Jews, many of whom came from the Arab world and North Africa (also known as Mizrahim). For some of these Jews, hashish smoking was part of a cultural heritage, shared with their Arab neighbors in the countries of their birth, which they brought with them to Israel. For others, hashish smoking was a habit they acquired due to their ethnic and socioeconomic marginalization in Israeli society. Although hashish smoking in Israel during the first two decades of that nation's existence remained limited to no more than a few thousand Mizrahim, it rekindled a moral panic about the Levantinization-cum-Arabicization of the Jewish state. It also contributed to further marginalizing and criminalizing Mizrahim in Israeli society.

Tying together the various perspectives discussed in this book—the movement of hashish supplies across and beyond Palestine-Israel, the culture of hashish consumption, the efforts to control drugs, and the discourses in which these things were all embedded—the conclusion argues that, despite evolving circumstances and changing regulatory regimes, the hashish trade continued unabated, with new outlets emerging continuously along with the rising number of hashish users. At the same time, the conclusion to this book offers a brief, albeit first of its kind, exploration of these issues *after* 1967, elucidating why that year should be seen as a major watershed in the history of hashish in Palestine-Israel, and one that merits a separate study.

1

THE DRUG TRADE IN THE LEVANT

IN 1982 THE ISRAELI ARMY invaded Lebanon. It remained in partial control of the southern border region until 2000, when the army was finally redeployed to the internationally recognized border separating the two countries. Israel's occupation of southern Lebanon, nearly two decades long, opened wide—or, rather, reopened—the gates for hashish, which flowed from Lebanon into Israeli territory, and from there to Egypt.[1] As a young man from the Lebanese town of Marjayoun explained to an Israeli journalist in 1984:

> The Israeli invasion was the best thing that ever happened to the hashish business in Lebanon. Until then it was dangerous to deal with it. Great risks. It was especially dangerous when the drugs were transferred through Syria, Jordan, the West Bank to Egypt. Too many hands, too many partners, small profits. The sea was no less dangerous. The Israeli navy was reaching Tyre and Sidon in recent years, and closed the option of reaching Sinai by sea.[2]

Clearly, this young Lebanese man overstated the case. The illicit flow of hashish from Lebanon to Egypt, across the territory that now constitutes the State of Israel, is hardly a new phenomenon in the modern history of the Levant region. In fact, such movement of hashish supplies across the region can be traced back to the late Ottoman era, and specifically to the period of the British Mandate.

In this chapter, I go back to the early twentieth century to explore the creation of the Levant hashish trade. Events during this period enmeshed Palestine-Israel in that illicit trade on a huge scale, for decades afterward and possibly until the present day. My principal argument is that this transregional trade was a classic example of unintended consequences. Among other things, these hashish flows emerged from the incipient drug regulatory systems established in the period immediately preceding and after World War I. This turned Palestine into a critical link in the hashish supply chain stretching from Lebanon and Syria in the north to Egypt in the south, when previously it was not; and it generated a sharp rise in hashish consumption in the territory, where previously hashish smoking had been marginal at most.

PSYCHOACTIVE SUBSTANCES IN THE LATE OTTOMAN PERIOD

The use of intoxicants of various kinds was commonplace in the Ottoman Empire. Indeed, "a wide range of intoxicants were available in the Ottoman Empire, particularly Istanbul, and . . . they were consumed by various groups of the population."[3] The main mind-altering substances used in Ottoman society were opium (*afyun*) and its derivatives (e.g., laudanum), as well as cannabis or hashish (*esrar*).[4] Not unlike many European leaders, statesmen, and notables of their time,[5] Ottoman sultans, qadis, imams, and muezzins indulged in the pleasures of wine and opium. Members of Sufi orders, too, ostensibly "antinomian" and "sober," consumed opium and hashish during religious rituals and on other occasions.[6]

The consumption of intoxicants was not restricted to the upper echelons of the Ottoman state, however; reports record that ordinary people, the "lower classes," also spent their leisure time in coffeehouses, consuming large quantities of opium and oftentimes hashish as well.[7] William Biddulph, a preacher to English merchants in early-seventeenth-century Aleppo, reported, for instance, that "Turkish" men would congregate in coffeehouses, "more common than Alehouses in England, [to take] Opium which maketh them forget themselves, and talk idle of castles in the air, as though they saw visions, and heard revelations."[8] Drugs also served a wide range of medicinal purposes and could be procured from any shop or street vendor, especially herbalists (*attar*) and opium specialists (*afyoncular*).[9] A similar state of affairs prevailed in early-modern Iran,[10] and in early-modern Europe where sedative substances were "transmitted to the infant along with the milk," so that "from infancy to old age, narcosis ruled supreme."[11] So much for the "denial of coeoevalness" between East and West.

Neither Ottoman legal texts nor the Ottoman penal law explicitly prohibited the use of psychoactive substances. Even though their use was always frowned upon because it was considered immoral and a danger to the fabric of Islam, it was by and large tolerated.[12] Hatice Aynur and Jan Schmidt put it thus:

> Although from the outset there was a taboo on the consumption of [drugs] in Islam . . . loopholes in the taboo were found and time and again Muslims did (and do) drink wine and ate, and later smoked, opium and cannabis. . . . Because of the ongoing consumption of all of these substances, Muslims had to come to terms with the taboo in one way or another.[13]

Even if the beliefs and doctrines of Islam were hardly "the *deus ex machina* of strict drug prohibition,"[14] a 1725 sultanic decree nevertheless forbade the use of hashish,[15] and the Grand Vizier thus "dispatched circulars to all [the provinces] . . . prohibiting sternly any further cultivation of or indulgence in this pernicious but fascinating drug."[16] In the mid-nineteenth century, the Ottoman state—perhaps with an eye to deflecting European criticism of the alleged decline of the Ottoman Empire—undertook legal reforms to regulate the flow and use of certain intoxicants.[17] As old habits die hard, however, these measures failed to root out hashish consumption.[18] The Italian princess Cristina Trivulzio di Belgiojoso, exiled from Italy to the Ottoman Empire between 1850 and 1855, wrote detailed travelogues about her encounters there. These provide a colorful testimony of the open nature of hashish use in late Ottoman Syria. Noting that there were several Damascenes "for whom the smoking of hashish was the principal source of pleasure, even their principal occupation," the exiled princess continued:

> The use of this narcotic is widespread in Syria. If you meet a man whose eyes are dull and unsteady, whose face is lean, lips pale and thin, be assured that you are facing a hashish eater or drinker. If you see two such men facing each other at the table of a café, blowing clouds of smoke at each other without saying a word, you can be sure that those two types are in the middle of a hashish orgy. If anyone offers you some sweets or some sherbet be careful: there may be hashish hidden in it.[19]

The princess's flagrantly Orientalist perspective should be treated with caution, even if hashish use was indeed commonplace in prewar Syria.[20] However—and whether or not we give her account the benefit of the doubt—there is ample reason to believe that demand for hashish in late Ottoman-era Egypt was far greater. Given that the Levant hashish trade was, by and large, the product of this demand, I now turn to late Ottoman-era Egypt, to address the hashish question there.

EGYPT AND THE HASHISH QUESTION

Egypt has been intimately associated with hashish since the Middle Ages.[21] So ubiquitous is its identification with the drug that "with a mixture of affection and mild contempt Egyptians as a whole are widely referred to as the '*hashisheen*' across the rest of the Arab world, in recognition of their fondness for the drug."[22] The Egyptian lower classes turned to this substance partly as an alternative to forbidden wine, but also—and more practically—because hashish was cheaper to procure and easier to produce than wine.[23] The use of hashish became so rooted in the cultural practices of the era that occasional campaigns by the Egyptian authorities against its cultivation, trade, and consumption invariably failed.[24] These futile campaigns against the use of hashish in pre-modern Egypt were driven rarely by jurisprudential reasoning, but rather by the association of the substance with lower-class habits and sensibilities, and hence with dirtiness, immorality, and criminality.[25] Interestingly, however, religious scholars (*ulama*) often allowed believers to use cannabis, or any other generally disapproved substances, if these were deemed necessary for medicinal purposes.[26]

The first ban on hashish in Egypt in the modern era was enforced by the officers of the Armée d'Orient during the short-lived French occupation of that Ottoman province between 1798 and 1801. The ban was intended to deter French soldiers from indulging in local cannabis products, after a considerable number had picked up the habit after arriving in Egypt. A universal ban on hashish products soon followed, after a French general personally observed rampant addiction among French soldiers and Egyptians: "The prohibition was absolute, as the importation, manufacture, sale, and consumption of hashish were forbidden under threat of severe punishment."[27] Still, what had been an inherent characteristic of local Egyptian traditions and customs since the early thirteenth century could hardly be quelled conclusively by virtue of this brief occupation. This may explain why Egypt's Khedival rulers found it expedient to reinstate the ban on hashish cultivation and importation in a series of decrees promulgated over the course of the 1860s and 1870s.[28]

This ban had little effect. "Neither the rulings of jurists nor the decrees of rulers seemed to have much effect on hashish consumption. Many Egyptians had already developed a proclivity for the drug, and paid little heed to the moralizing of muftis or bureaucrats."[29] Because of the persistence of hashish use, the budding *Westernized* Egyptian middle classes, the *effendiya*—for whom hashish use by the urban working classes tarnished Egypt's image as a modern and progressive nation—were extremely hostile to the drug.[30]

When the British occupied Egypt in 1882, they adopted the existing ban, albeit reluctantly and against their better judgment. The British experience in the Raj, on which many of their policies in Egypt were based,[31] had taught them that the entrenched nature of practices like hashish use rendered prohibition impossible. Indeed, throughout its long-lasting rule over India, the world's largest producer of and market for cannabis narcotics during that era,[32] the British Raj repeatedly attempted to suppress cannabis, to no avail. India's vast territory, its teeming population, and the fact that the smoking of cannabis and opium had played a crucial role in Indian religious, medicinal, and recreational practices for centuries—all these made prohibition an ineffective mechanism. Hence, the British in India adopted a policy of "control and restriction" rather than prohibition, per a report prepared by the 1893–94 Indian Hemp Drugs Commission (IHDC), which stated: "The policy advocated is one of control and restriction, aimed at suppressing the excessive use and restraining the moderate use within due limits."[33] To this end, the commission called for the creation of a regulatory system that would levy a tax on hemp drugs, license cultivation and retail activities, and restrict the amount permitted as legal possession.[34]

Likewise, the British in Egypt believed that prohibition would be "neither necessary nor expedient," as the IHDC report put it. For example, in a 1894 report, Consul-General Evelyn Baring, later Lord Cromer, noted that hashish was so widely used in Egypt that it would be next to impossible to stop hashish from being smuggled into the country and locally consumed.[35] Similarly, in 1905 Cromer advised his foreign secretary that, "so long as the demand and the supply exist, it is almost impossible to prevent evasions of the law; no sooner is one route closed to the smuggler, than another is opened up."[36] Before arriving in Egypt, Cromer had been private secretary to the viceroy of India; one may surmise that he was acquainted with the cannabis debate there. It is more than likely that he had India in mind when he weighed in on the implausibility of eliminating hashish use and the hashish trade in Egypt.

Lord Herbert Kitchener, the British consul-general in Egypt in the years immediately preceding World War I, was another veteran of the British Raj. In a 1914 report of his own, Kitchener reproduced Cromer's observations verbatim to dispute the wisdom of the hashish ban in Egypt. Hashish, Kitchener went on to say, is consumed in Egypt "not by a small class of men given to vice," as conventional wisdom would have it, "but very generally by the population as a domestic medicine." Moreover, he added, while a small number of Egyptians did (ab)use hashish to the extreme, it was equally true that "a great section of the population habitually employ small quantities without any evil effects, and probably with a considerable amount of benefit." Had the use of hashish been confined to "a small class of intemperates," the prohibitive measures undertaken by the Egyptian government would in all probability be successful; "but it is . . . its general use which renders prohibition impossible." To illustrate his point, Kitchener urged the British foreign secretary to imagine what would happen if a prohibition on alcohol were to be enforced on the British Isles: "The amount of smuggling which would take place would be beyond the power of any Government to restrain." For a system of absolute prohibition to work effectively, he concluded, there must be "a large measure of general support." This, Kitchener stated, did not exist in Egypt at the time.[37]

The British, then, opposed the imposition of an absolute ban on the use of hashish in Egypt, against the wishes of the emulative, "self-civilizing, self-colonizing [Egyptian *effendiya*] elite," whose opposition to the substance was, as noted earlier, uncompromising.[38] In 1892, Alfred Caillard Pasha, the British general director of customs in Egypt, put it thus:

> In view of the impossibility of suppressing the contraband trade on haschisch . . . I [suggest] . . . the desirability of removing the prohibition against the importation of the drug. . . . It has been abundantly proved that the vice of haschisch smoking cannot be suppressed by legislation, whereas by a system of licenses it may be kept under control to some extent.[39]

The debate between the Egyptians and the British over the advisability of prohibition played itself out during the 1924–25 Opium Conference of the League of Nations, which took place in Geneva. The conference debated the extension of global controls over a wider range of drugs including, for the first time, cannabis (or "Indian hemp"), at the insistence of the Egyptian delegation.[40] In these deliberations the British leaned toward the Indian delegation's view, opposing the Egyptian proposal on the grounds that there were "social and religious customs which naturally have to be considered, and there is doubt whether the total prohibition of drugs easily prepared from wild growing plants could in practice be made effective"; "the plant . . . is based upon long tradition that has been traced back as far as the Vedas. The use of the hemp drugs . . . is largely of a quasi-medical nature."[41] Caught between the conflicting Egyptian and Indian positions, the British delegation, and eventually the conference's other delegations as well, opted for a compromise solution: "The wording of the convention made it clear that the sale of cannabis to countries which do not ban it (primarily India, but also Tunisia and Morocco, where it was monopolized), would still be permissible."[42]

It may also be true that the British were not inclined toward supporting a ban on cannabis products because during the interwar period they simply considered it as a comparatively harmless drug—certainly not as harmful as "white drugs," heroin and cocaine. During the interwar period, hashish receded to the background in Egypt as "white drugs" took center stage as the country's main "plague."[43] Thomas Wentworth Russell—better known as Russell Pasha, Cairo's chief of police, and later the illustrious head of Egypt's Central Narcotics Intelligence Bureau (*Maktab al-mukhabarat al-ʾamm li-l-mawad al-mukhaddirat,* or CNIB) between 1929 and 1946—recalled in his memoir that in the wake of World War I, "the roughs and the cackling laughter of the hashish dens . . . [gave] place to the emaciated shadows of heroin addicts slinking about round the offal bins."[44] Given that out of a total population of 14 million, nearly half a million "were now slaves" to heroin, "the drug that nearly killed Egypt was heroin," not hashish, he asserted.[45] Russell's associate, Baron Harry D'Erlanger, concurred:

> It was no longer a question of a little mild hashish-smoking which had for many years been the pet failing of many members of the poorer classes; nor even of extremely excessive hashish-smoking on the part of roughs and other shady characters. The effects of this indulgence have been described over and over again by earnest and observant travelers, horrified and not a little frightened by the "bared teeth and glassy eyes" of sinister-looking natives under the influence.[46]

Indeed, as heroin and cocaine gradually became subject to national and international regulation and control during the interwar period, many of the European manufacturers prohibited from selling these drugs in their home countries exported them to Egypt in massive quantities.[47] The result: China and the United States aside, Egypt was the one country that suffered an outbreak of heroin use between the wars.[48] To tackle the problem, in 1925 the Egyptian government promulgated new legislation prohibiting, in addition to cannabis, the import, sale, purchase, and possession of heroin, cocaine, raw opium, and their derivatives.[49] In the process, the Anglo-Egyptian authorities "stiffened drug-related penalties, imprisoned thousands, and urged European capitulatory countries to collaborate in their anti-drug war."[50]

As a matter of fact, what prompted the establishment of Egypt's CNIB, with Russell as its head, was the desire to eliminate the traffic in heroin and cocaine, not hashish.[51] Russell's idea was to raise the retail price of heroin and cocaine so as to make them inaccessible to the urban poor and the *fellahin*— "the backbone of the country," as Russell described them.[52] The campaign was largely successful, with heroin entirely out of the reach of the *fellahin* by the latter half of the 1930s.[53] The campaign seemed to have been such a success that by 1939 Russell was prepared to declare: "To-day we are a normal Oriental Country where addiction and traffic exist, but where, for the present, addiction has ceased to be a national problem."[54] The decline in heroin imports, however, was offset by an equal increase in the flow of opium (from Turkey) and hashish (from Syria-Lebanon) into Egypt—both arriving via Palestinian territory.[55]

At his annual appearances before the League of Nations as Egypt's representative on the Opium Advisory Committee (OAC), Russell repeatedly inflated and lamented the hashish problem in Egypt, and frequently amplified stories of the CNIB's accomplishments with cannabis prevention.[56] Yet, despite his passionate endorsement of the anticannabis agenda—which no doubt forced governments into action against that drug, while also providing the CNIB with valuable funds and resources—at other times he elegantly repudiated the claim that hashish was causing real damage to Egyptian society. For instance, in a 1930 report to the League, he stated that hashish was "the vice of the city slums and did comparatively little harm," adding: "In the villages there were a few hashish smokers who were looked upon rather as a joke . . . in the same way as the village 'drunk' is regarded in the English village."[57]

Nor was Russell shy in speaking out against the proposition, widely accepted during the interwar period, that hashish intoxication, especially among "Orientals" and other "unruly" populations, was conducive to criminal behavior and frenzied insanity.[58] At the fifteenth meeting of the OAC, held in June 1938, Russell, representing the Egyptian government, took care to communicate his "personal impression that hashish addiction was not leading to any particular crime wave." On the contrary, he observed, the hashish addict "was a tiresome type of individual," not the kind that would make a dangerous criminal. Hence, "it would not be true to say that much serious crime was due to hashish addiction."[59]

In making his case against these conventional wisdoms, Russell was prepared to confront, head-on, the infamous and all-powerful Harry J. Anslinger, founder of the US Federal Bureau of Narcotics (FBN) and its director from 1930 to 1962. The United States was not a member of the League of Nations; but Anslinger, maintaining an extraofficial presence as an observer on the OAC, consistently called for an uncompromising system of international drug control based on prohibition. In the United States proper, "mushrooming fears of drugs were blatantly manipulated by Harry J. Anslinger . . . who raised antidrug discourse to the shrill tone of Dr. Strangelove's fictionalized anticommunist phobia of 'bodily fluids.'"[60] Anslinger's exceptionally blatant and racially charged antimarijuana crusade extended throughout his thirty-two-year career. He linked marijuana use—mostly by Mexicans, blacks, and other minorities in the US South and Southwest—with "murders, suicides, robberies, criminal assaults, holdups, burglaries, and deeds of maniacal insanity," as he put it.[61] The terms "killer weed" and "reefer madness," which invoked the supposed evils of marijuana, owed their provenance to Anslinger's campaigns throughout the 1930s, which were aided by the media and the movie industry.[62] In keeping with these ideas, in 1937—the same year in which the Marihuana Tax Act, first federal law against cannabis, had been enacted in the United States—Anslinger informed the OAC that several "cases of violent crime in the USA in 1936 . . . were directly traceable to the use of cannabis."[63] A year later he informed the OAC, "The drug [marijuana] maintains its ancient, worldwide tradition of murder, assault, rape, physical and mental deterioration . . . [and] its use is associated with dementia and crime."[64] Russell, however, would have none of this. He quickly dismissed Anslinger's claim with a sarcastic observation: While indeed "hashish addiction could be extremely dangerous," in most cases hashish addicts tended to lapse not into a state of "homicidal insanity," but "into a state of jovial idiocy."[65] Russell was not alone in such a lenient position regarding cannabis. Claude Scudamore Jarvis, the British governor of Sinai from 1923 to 1936, likewise contended that hashish was no "more of an evil than the hangover one got from mixing whisky and champagne. If it made the hard life of the *fellahin* more bearable, so be it."[66]

Hence, the British in Egypt—as opposed to Egypt's middle classes—did not consider hashish a social ill that required total eradication. Even Russell, the country's highest British antinarcotics official, treated conceptualizations of the drug as a pathway to insanity and criminality with a large dose of skepticism.

LEBANON, SYRIA, AND PALESTINE STEP IN

Despite considering hashish to be the lesser evil and opposing its prohibition, by the turn of the twentieth century the British in Egypt had become deeply worried about the uncontrollable trafficking of hashish into the country, thereby retaining the ban on hashish which Egypt's rulers had imposed before the 1882 British occupation. Egypt's long borders, the ingenuity and audacity of smugglers, the corrupt practices of the Egyptian law enforcement forces, the lack of resources, and, last but not least, the demand for the drug by Egyptians—all these, as the British complained continuously, rendered the task of cutting off incoming hashish supplies practically impossible to achieve.[67]

Traffickers and smugglers brought hashish to Egypt in small vessels, dropping their contraband away from the shore, west of Alexandria or east of Port Said.[68] Bedouin—allegedly "warlike, abstemious . . . treacherous and lazy,"[69] but also "thoroughly well acquainted with the coast where it [was] contemplated to land hashish"[70]—would pick up hashish consignments and transport them across the desert, on camels, to Cairo and Alexandria.[71] With time, "the old practice" of running large quantities of hashish in one convoy was abandoned in favor of "concealing small quantities of hashish on the person and in the luggage of passengers arriving by steamer at Alexandria and Port Said."[72] That is why we learn that hashish arrived in Egypt in "small quantities carried on the person; inside the soles of boots, hats, by women simulating pregnancy, etc."[73]

Without its customary English understatement, Britain frankly expressed its exasperation with the Egyptian state's inability to contend with, let alone eliminate, the flow of hashish. In his dispatches to London, for instance, Cromer did not mince words in bemoaning the setbacks encountered year after year. In 1900 he wrote, "It is almost hopeless to expect that the importation of hashish can be altogether prevented. The most that can be done is to render its acquisition difficult as possible."[74] A year later, he reiterated: "Egypt is plagued with hashish. . . . It is almost hopeless to expect that the use of hashish by the population of Egypt will ever be wholly discontinued."[75] Likewise, in 1905 he wrote: "The use of this drug still continues to exercise its baneful effects on the population of Egypt. . . . The campaign against the use of the drug continues, but . . . it cannot be said to be very successful."[76]

At the turn of the twentieth century, cannabis products were still legal across much of the globe, with the exception of Egypt. By the 1920s the Egyptian market had emerged as the primary focal point of an international contraband trade in hashish.[77] Hashish was smuggled into Egypt from a number of countries (e.g., India, Cyprus, Romania, and Turkey), but its main source country was Greece, where cannabis was grown in small islands in the archipelago. The Greece-Egypt route took the form of boats sailing across the Mediterranean passing through Cyrenaican ports.[78]

This illicit trade created a windfall for many a hashish trafficker. Hence, Henry De Monfreid, a notorious early-twentieth-century French soldier of fortune as well as a smuggler of hashish, arms, and other contraband to Egypt, reminisced succinctly: "I knew only two things—that [cannabis] was grown in Greece, and sold very dear in Egypt."[79] For Egyptians and British colonial officials this was not merely a matter of lucrative entrepreneurship, but cause for grave concern. "The whole of the hashish consumed in Egypt comes from Greece," Cromer complained in 1906. He added, "It is difficult to do very much more than we already do in Egypt. What is wanted is that Greece should prohibit the cultivation of hashish."[80]

In keeping with Cromer's advice, the British mounted continuous pressure on the Greek government to ban hashish cultivation, so as to "stop the introduction of hashish [in Egypt]."[81] The parties reached a partial understanding in 1913, the Greeks agreeing "to restrict in various ways the cultivation and sale of hashish," as Lord Kitchener informed his foreign minister.[82] The Greeks also permitted Egypt to "execute . . . search warrants where Greek subjects were suspected of smuggling this drug."[83] Clearly, this was intended to partially remedy the pernicious effects of the Ottoman Empire's capitulations system, under which foreigners in Egypt could only be prosecuted by their respective consulates—in effect, placing them above Egyptian law. The Egyptian market for hashish was dominated by a powerful cartel of Greek merchants.[84] It was in reference to them that de Monfreid reminisced, "For the love of smuggling, the Greeks are the first nation in the world, bar none."[85] The 1913 agreement limited the ability of these merchants to conduct their hashish businesses with impunity. It was a crucial stepping-stone in the eventual abolition of the Greece-Egypt hashish trade.

In the meantime, as mentioned earlier, the 1925 League's Opium Convention imposed global controls over cannabis. This cast further doubt on the feasibility of hashish cultivation in Greece. The convention went into effect in 1928; four years later, in 1932, Greece finally prohibited the cultivation of cannabis, thus putting an effective end to the traditional smuggling route to Egypt.[86] The final death blow to the Greece–Egypt hashish route was dealt by the 1937 Montreux

Convention, which abolished the capitulations, allowing for "only one law [to be] applicable to narcotic offences, whether committed by Egyptian or by foreigner."[87] In a retrospective account, Russell details the "enormous difficulties" that the capitulations put in the way of the fight against the drug trade:

> Had it not been for the protection that the foreign trafficker derived from them, the narcotic problem in Egypt would never have reached the magnitude it did. . . . Even when the goodwill and co-operation of the Consulates and the Consular Courts had been obtained, the traffickers of many foreign nationalities had the great advantage of having nothing to fear from their Consular courts beyond fines of a few pounds and a few days' imprisonment, owing to the inadequacy of the penalties for narcotic trafficking in their various national legislations.[88]

It is no surprise that when the 1937 Montreux Convention was completed, Russell crowned it as "the year's event of the greatest importance."[89]

In a generally informative study of Lebanon's entanglement in the international drug trade, Jonathan Marshall observes rather vaguely, and without providing any context, that "decades ago [Lebanon] became one of the world's major exporters of opiates and hashish to international markets."[90] No doubt the origins of cannabis cultivation in Lebanon-Syria remain vague, and there are claims that it was introduced there at some point during the Ottoman era.[91] In his reports to the League of Nations in the late 1920s, however, Russell Pasha was able to provide a specific context for Lebanon's emergence as a major exporter of hashish. He recalled that when he first entered the service of the Egyptian government in 1902, "hashish came [to Egypt] entirely from Greece." He went on to disclose that "in about 1907, certain persons began the experiment of growing it in the Lebanon district of Syria." As Greece gradually came around to curtailing the cultivation of hashish in the course of the 1920s, Russell added, "the cultivation in the Lebanon increased enormously and reached an annual production of fifteen hundred to two thousand kilos." That hashish, he concluded, "was and is almost entirely exported to Egypt."[92] Hence the creation of the Levant hashish trade, extending from Lebanon-Syria in the north, across Palestinian territory, to Egypt in the south.[93]

|In the next chapter I will consider the repercussions of this trade for Palestine; but first, a few notes on the hashish question in the French-mandated Levant hashish producer states are in order. The cultivation of cannabis, as well

as the preparation of and trade in hashish, was prohibited in the Levant states under the French Mandate, as indeed it had been in all mandated territories.[94] However, the French government suggested that anticannabis measures in Syria-Lebanon had gone "further than the Opium Convention of 1925, which merely prescribe[d] control," not prohibition.[95] This claim derived from one of the very few things that international forces agreed upon in matters concerning drug policy: enforcement ought to be the primary responsibility of *producer* countries. To be sure, this claim was also linked to the need to respond to mounting pressures from consumer states, Egypt in particular.[96]

Yet anticannabis enforcement was never one of the stronger elements of French governance in the Mandatory Levant. For one thing, a drastically shrinking colonial budget after World War I encumbered effective police action against cannabis cultivation, production, and commerce, preventing the French from maintaining the strong presence in the Lebanon-Palestine border zone that was necessary to stave off hashish smuggling across it.[97] Another major impediment to drug control was "endemic corruption that left only a small segment of officialdom untouched."[98] This circumstance undercut state institutions, as well as the legitimacy required to combat drug trafficking and other illicit activities. Significantly, many of these officials, French as well as Lebanese politicians, had powerful stakes in the hashish trade, as people who owned or were in de facto control of the land on which the cannabis was cultivated.[99] In 1929, Russell Pasha described the repercussions of this situation in these terms: "The peasant who grows the crop does so by orders of the big notables who own the land, and who are mostly the powerful members of the local republican governments."[100] A decade later, a CNIB report to the League of Nations again stated: "Big landowners, ministers, deputies and notables were sowing hashish . . . hasten[ing] to follow the example of the Government officials in the hopes of making a small profit."[101]

For their part, the French were not always prepared to come out against the livelihoods of cannabis-cultivating peasants under their rule;[102] to their credit, they were sometimes quite frank in acknowledging this position. For instance, in 1929 the French authorities in Lebanon explained why they had failed to act on Egyptian demands to eradicate cannabis fields, stating: "For the inhabitants of certain districts [in Lebanon] the cultivation of Indian hemp . . . [is] a source of income which could not easily be replaced in a single season."[103] Another reason cited by the French was the opposition that they had encountered from Lebanese landlords and peasants alike. For instance, in the Beqaa Valley's Baalbek District, the policy of destruction met with tacit but effective opposition from the large proprietors, who not only refused to destroy their crops, but used their influence to prevent the peasants of their own and of the neighboring villages—from entering their land and cutting down the prohibited hemp.[104]

Given the above, it is not at all surprising that by the 1930s, Lebanon's annual production of Egypt-bound hashish reached fifty to sixty tons.[105] This was the final straw that broke Russell's patience with the French. Consequently, he issued a personal complaint to the League of Nations regarding Mandatory Lebanon's enduring failure to fulfill its obligations regarding control, using the League "to internationally shame Paris."[106] At the same time, he urged the French delegate to the League "to use his influence with his Government to change the Syrian law by making it an offence under the Law to possess a substance whose cultivation, manufacture and transport is already forbidden. . . . It is quite useless for one country to fight [the distribution of hashish] and a neighboring country to tolerate it."[107]

Obviously embarrassed by Russell's uncharacteristically harsh denunciation, the French responded by introducing stricter prohibitive regulations in Lebanon. These included the establishment of uniform legislative regulations for dealing with narcotics, which now conformed more closely to the provisions of the League's 1925 Opium Convention; the creation of a Sûreté Générale antidrug squad with a regional mandate; and more vigorous efforts to destroy cannabis fields.[108] Apparently, these measures led to a temporary "diminution in Syrian [hashish] arrivals" in Egypt, for which the CNIB conveyed its "keenest satisfaction."[109] Ironically, however, this turned out to be a Pyrrhic victory of sorts. No sooner was the shortage in Syrian-Lebanese hashish supplies felt in Egypt than they were replaced by "stuff [hashish] bearing such marks as would seem to indicate Turkish provenance."[110] Indeed, by the late 1930s Turkish hashish had become a major illicit commodity in Egypt.[111]

Whatever the case may be, clientism and high-level structural corruption meant that stricter antihashish measures could not guarantee the "diminution," let alone cessation, of Lebanese-Syrian hashish supplies to Egypt for very long. This explains why in 1939 Russell found it expedient to file yet another complaint to the OAC concerning France's renewed failure to stand by its assurances that "all the cultivated areas [in Lebanon and Syria would be] torn up and large stocks of prepared hashish confiscated and destroyed."[112] The reason for the continued hashish flows to Egypt was not lost to Russell: "Many of the governing classes of the Lebanon had defied the Mandatory Authorities and planted vast areas of hashish cultivation, with the natural result that the smaller landowners had followed their example thinking that they could do so with impunity." According to Russell, this was nothing short of "a national revolt against authority."[113] Hashish supplies from Lebanon to Egypt continued throughout the remainder of the Mandatory period, demonstrating that the cultivation of and trade in the drug enjoyed the protection and patronage—if not the direct sponsorship and partnership—of the state's elites and institutions. As a result, "most hashish enforcement campaigns were of a theatrical nature, and primarily intended to appease foreign governments such as Egypt."[114] William Goustoun-Boswall, British envoy to Lebanon between 1947 and 1951, branded these circumstances "an open scandal."[115]

According to the drug historian Paul Gootenberg, a typical "global hot zone of drug production," whether remote from or close to its final markets, is "a zone of refuge, with a displaced, alienated, or ethnically segregated peasantry (for working drug plantations) and an especially weak state or ill-defined borders."[116] Gootenberg identifies Lebanon—or, to be precise, Lebanon's Bekaa Valley—as one such hot zone among the many that now exist (e.g., the Golden Crescent, the Golden Triangle, the northern Mexican Sierra Madre badlands of Sinaloa and Chihuahua).[117] As we have seen, the history of the Lebanese hot zone of hashish production, with Egypt its principal market, dates back to the early Mandatory period in the Levant.

CONCLUSION

Owing to the push and pull of supply and demand, restrictive measures against commodities in general—and, quite clearly, against border-crossing illicit commodities such as drugs—will only add to their appeal and increase their market value.[118] It is for this reason that what Arjun Appadurai describes as "enclaved commodities"—that is, "objects whose commodity potential is carefully hedged"—invariably tend to divert from their specified paths. "The politics of enclaving," Appadurai suggests, "far from being the guarantor of systemic stability, may constitute the Trojan horse of change."[119]

Hence, as the Greeks progressively submitted to demands from the British and Egyptian governments and the League of Nations to clamp down on its domestic cannabis industry—thus turning hashish into an "enclaved commodity" and inducing shortages in Egypt—Egyptians turned to Lebanese- and Syrian-grown cannabis to compensate for the loss of Greek supply. This diversion of supply origin inevitably led to a diversion of the supply routes to Egypt; from this point on, the routes had to pass through Palestine, whether by land, sea, or air. When Britain assumed the mandate over Palestine, the territory had already served as a critical link—a "transit route"—in the Levant hashish trade that extended at the time from Lebanon-Syria in the north to Egypt in the south. In 1939 a cannabis expert on the League of Nations Subcommittee on Cannabis, Dr. Joules Bouquet, thus declared: "Palestine seems at present to be the most important hashish depot in the Levant, [though] it must be remembered that Cannabis is not grown there."[120] This development was destined to have marked effects on the volume of hashish smuggling across and consumption of the drug in Palestine.

2

SMUGGLING IN MANDATORY PALESTINE

THE YEAR IS 1948; the place Al-Raml prison in Beirut. The convict Hanna al-Salman awaits the execution of his sentence, death by hanging, for the murder of two prostitutes. Hanna listens attentively to the tales of his two cellmates, Ahmad and Munir. He is fascinated by their stories about the exploits of "the boss" (*muʻallim*), Sami al-Khoury, "one of the most dangerous smugglers in the world of drugs." Hanna is particularly impressed by the story of the cabbages (*malfuf*), which illustrated the boss's ingenuity and "amazing ability to elude the police networks pursuing him":

> [The boss] instructed us [Munir and Ahmad] to sow cabbage. We thought that he lost his mind. He said: Obtain a plot of land and sow cabbage. . . . We said, Boss, we came here to eat bread, we're not farmers. He repeated: Sow the cabbage, and I'll take care of the rest. So we sowed. You know, when cabbage starts to grow, the leaves open. . . . We kept on watering the cabbage, looking around and not understanding. . . . We [were instructed] to see to it that the cabbages opened. One moonless night, the boss arrived with ten young men carrying Magnum revolvers, and ten trucks loaded with hashish. We took the hashish and planted it inside the open cabbages. We worked all night. The *Raʼis* Sami insisted on rolling up his sleeves. This wasn't a smuggling operation for him. It was a hobby. He placed the hashish between the cabbage leaves, as though he were a physician giving medicine to a patient. . . . After ten days, which felt like

a hundred years, the cabbage leaves had shut, covering the hashish and swallowing it up. I swear to Allah. After that, we collected [the cabbage], and sent it in cargo planes to Egypt, under the cover of a cabbage export deal.

This story, about the illustrious Lebanese drug kingpin Sami al-Khoury and his ingenious hashish-smuggling escapades, is told in the 1994 novella *Majma' al-Asrar* (*Bundle of Secrets*), by the celebrated Lebanese novelist, playwright, and critic Elias Khoury.[1] To be clear, the novella is primarily a work of fiction. However, it does echo a credible historical reality, and demonstrates the extent to which the creation of the Levant hashish trade, stretching from Lebanon to Egypt with Palestine in between, provided a bonanza for many hashish smugglers, Lebanese and others. The credibility of this tale is reinforced by the fact that al-Khoury was indeed a Lebanese drug trafficker, both during the interwar period and afterward. He is described as "the most powerful and notorious drug traffickers in Lebanon's young history."[2] At an early stage of his career he indeed may have run hashish trafficking operations from Lebanon to Egypt, along the lines recounted in *Bundle of Secrets*. As a matter of fact, in 1947 al-Khoury was imprisoned in Egypt for three years, after he attempted to smuggle 266 kilograms of hashish and 47 kilograms of opium aboard an airplane.[3]

In this chapter I zoom in to conduct a close examination of Mandatory Palestine's enmeshment in the Levant hashish trade. I reconstruct the "biographies" or "life histories" of the henceforth illicit commodity, traversing Palestinian territory on its journey from Lebanon-Syria in the north to Egypt in the south. To borrow from Appadurai, commodities acquire "very specific biographies as they move from place to place and hand to hand, just as the men who exchange them gain and lose reputation as they acquire, hold, and part with these valuables."[4] I am particularly interested in the human agents who were in charge of these flows, and the subterfuges (à la *malfuf*) they employed to transport their contraband safely from French to British Mandate zones, and from there to Egypt. Following Itty Abraham and Willem van Schendel, I veer away from questions of "Why move?" and instead ask *how* the movement of this illicit commodity took place, and what meanings were attributed to its movement—especially by those who did the moving.[5]

These meanings were, by and large, determined by the creation of the Mandate states in the Levant. The emergence of a post-Ottoman order turned the tables on the people behind the hashish trade of the period. Defined as "drug traffickers," these persons rarely considered the political borders of the new states as faits accomplis, and crisscrossed territories with total disregard for the states' sovereignty. In transporting their illicit merchandise, these borders "were all but invisible" to them.[6] This put the very legitimacy of these states into question, vis-à-vis their ability to supervise and their capacity to protect.[7]

All that said, these very borders did pose unprecedented difficulties for the traffickers, together with the new dispensation created by international conventions and local legislation, which explicitly criminalized their activities and further restricted their operations. Customs and police outposts erected along the borders of the states, together with internal antidrug enforcement activity within them, restricted the free movement of our traffickers; they could no longer assume that their illicit cargo would go undetected. These inauspicious circumstances prompted them to devise a range of ploys and deceptions in order to safely transport their illicit cargoes to their final destination.

For the most part, the hashish traffickers that traversed Mandatory Palestine were overwhelmingly successful in their illicit undertakings. The exceptionally creative smuggling stratagems they deployed certainly contributed strongly to this achievement. Another important cause was antihashish enforcement—or, to be precise, its lack—in Palestine, which allowed the southward movement of these flows to progress unimpeded. Running their mandate on a barely adequate budget, the British in Palestine lacked the infrastructural ability, the economic capacity, and the willpower to meticulously and effectively prevent hashish trafficking into and from the country.[8] In addition, the fight against hashish smuggling was accorded a low priority, against the competing imperatives of battling illegal Jewish immigration and contending with spiraling tensions between Arabs and Jews.[9] Combined, these perspectives underscored the perforated nature of the borders between the Mandate states, which in turn eroded the legitimacy of the colonial state.[10]

HASHISH SMUGGLERS: A PROFILE

Palestine remained on the margins of the Middle East hashish trade, not to mention that of the world, until the early twentieth century. But then, international drug control efforts gathered momentum alongside Egypt's demands for the abolition of cannabis cultivation in Greece. Consequently, Egypt's primary source of hashish relocated to Syria-Lebanon from Greece, where cannabis cultivation began to take root in the first decade of the twentieth century.

And so it was that by the interwar period and the creation of the Mandate state system in the Levant, Palestine, sandwiched between the grower-cum-producer countries in the north and the consumer country in the south, became the main theatre of smuggling operations between them. As Joseph Broadhurst, a former Palestine Police Criminal Investigation Department (CID) commander, explained in 1936, "Palestine . . . lies between Syria, where large quantities of hashish, a forbidden aromatic grass, are grown, and Egypt, which . . . was one of the world's largest customers for the drug."[11] This situation continued throughout the Mandatory period. A 1947 Palestine police report thus stated: "Hashish and opium are the main drugs illegally transported through Palestine for the onward passage to Egypt, in the majority of cases . . . hashish arriving from Syria and the Lebanon."[12]

Who were the human actors who controlled the movement of hashish across Palestinian territory? First and foremost, they were "ordinary" Palestinian Arabs—shopkeepers, peddlers, taxi drivers, garage owners, mechanics, tradesmen, railway workers, peasants, Bedouins—or otherwise Arabs from neighboring countries such as Egypt, Lebanon, Syria, and Iraq.[13] Russell Pasha described these smugglers as "a low class crowd with little toughness or discipline among them."[14] Douglas Duff, another contemporary observer, who had joined the Palestine Police Force in 1922 and served until 1926 as commander of the nascent Port Police (see below), alleged that they "had no masters in the world . . . [and] feared neither God nor man and would do anything for a few piasters."[15] Dr. Joules Bouquet, inspector of pharmacies in Tunis hospitals and a member of the League of Nations Subcommittee on Cannabis, also denounced these smugglers. They belonged, he said, to an "underworld adventurer class to whom regular work is repugnant and who hope to reap a sufficient profit by introducing and reselling hashish in Egypt."[16]

Next on the list of hashish traffickers across Palestine were those described as "international gangs" or "rings of dope smugglers,"[17] made up of criminals from many countries around the world (Egypt, Italy, Greece, Cyprus, and Bulgaria, to mention but a few). These groups cooperated with local and other Levantine smugglers to facilitate the transportation and delivery of their illicit commodity. While little or nothing is recorded about their general demeanor, we can safely assume that they were not particularly pleasant folk. Henry de Monfreid's amusing description of a gang member involved in smuggling hashish from Greece to Egypt earlier in the century could also apply to the international gang members running the Levant hashish trade:

He washed down his salad with great gulps of black wine out of a skin, and when he saw me coming he wiped his mouth with the back of his hand. He glowered sullenly, stuck his pipe insolently in his mouth, and sent forth a jet of saliva which nearly fell on my feet, just to show me how welcome I was. After several attempts on my part at conversation . . . this master of God deigned to send me to hell in a jargon which bore some faint resemblance to Italian.[18]

British military servicemen stationed in Egypt and Palestine were also not impervious to the rewards of smuggling hashish across Palestine to Egypt. Indeed, drugs and military life are familiar bedfellows. Soldiers consume drugs to allay the boredom and fatigue that are ever-present aspects of military life, or to "facilitate the transformation of man into warrior . . . [and arouse the] destructive instinct that impels men to war."[19] My sources have nothing to say about whether these British servicemen stationed in the Levant were prone to smoking hashish. However, it can be established that, as a Jewish informer of Harry J. Anslinger claimed, many were involved in drug running operations, having been "tempted by promises of big rewards or directly by high profits."[20]

Clearly, in comparison to the Levant hashish smugglers mentioned above, British troops benefited from one critical advantage which made them uniquely positioned to smuggle drugs across the Levant with impunity: they could not be searched by civilian police and customs officers at border crossing points. In addition, because many of the soldiers had access to several forms of transportation—automobiles, trains, boats—they were a reliable means for transporting contraband in relative safety. "The underworld soon realized the value of [this circumstance] for their illegal commodities, and they were not long in finding among the tens of thousands of servicemen those who could be tempted by women or money," suggested a contemporary British observer.[21] In fact, one of the greatest hashish hauls during the Mandatory period, completely accidental, involved British troops transporting hashish to Egypt. A truck carrying the props and equipment of the "Juke Box" entertainment road show—a revue that performed across many camps in Palestine—overturned north of Gaza. Three hundred kilograms of hashish (and a little under 250 kilograms of opium) were found inside the overturned vehicle. Following the discovery, which led to a public uproar, the British authorities declared that they were "on the trail of one of the biggest drug rings in the Middle East whose activities are spread into Syria and the Lebanon and possibly as far as Turkey, as well as Egypt and Palestine."[22]

Lastly, in very rare cases, Jewish soldiers serving in the British army in Egypt were also accused of smuggling hashish "from the countries of the Levant, via the Land of Israel to Egypt."[23] Occasionally, too, Jews not serving in the British military also participated in hashish trafficking operations to Egypt. This is ascertainable not from detailed expositions, but rather from a handful of terse press accounts of the arrests of "gang" members, both Jews and Arabs;[24] and from official British reports to the League of Nations, which now and then included distinctively Jewish names (e.g., Theodor Shamit, Alexander Rudintzki, David Shamai) in the lists of individuals arrested after aborted hashish smuggling operations.[25] It should be kept in mind, however, that there may very well have been more Jewish hashish smugglers than were indicated in press and official reports. It is not unlikely that the absence of Jewish names was due to the bias the Palestine Police Force tended to exhibit in favor of Jews over Arabs: "Arabs were more heavily policed, Jews were more likely to accuse an Arab than a Jew, the attorney general was more likely to prosecute an Arab than a Jew, and Arabs were also more likely to accuse an Arab."[26]

Three comments are in order here. First, the apparent dearth of *Jewish* hashish smugglers in Mandatory Palestine is a likely indication that Jews in Palestine, for reasons I will explore in chapter 4, generally shunned hashish-related activities (including hashish consumption), and did not cooperate with Palestinian Arabs in these matters.[27] Secondly, the few Jewish hashish smugglers who did operate in Palestine should not be confused with the eastern European Jews connected, to various degrees, with the interwar Jewish Viennese underworld; this group did extend their drug-dealing businesses, into which they were increasingly and disproportionately drawn during the interwar period, to the Levant.[28] Based mainly in Cairo, this group concentrated on the heroin trade to Egypt, Europe, and the United States, leaving for others the far less lucrative and more limited Levant hashish trade along the Lebanon-Palestine-Egypt axis. Still, a brief consideration of their criminal activities will shed light on yet another aspect of the region's entanglement in the global networks responsible for the flow of drugs.

I have already mentioned the extent to which the regulatory and prohibitive regimes enforced against heroin and cocaine by the League of Nations during the interwar period only served to push the production of these drugs more irrevocably into the hands of organized crime. What is more, because most restrictive legislation against these "white drugs" was directed only toward domestic consumption and not manufacturing and export, many manufacturers—especially in Switzerland, France, and Turkey—exported large quantities of the drugs to Egypt.[29] This export trade, also noted in the previous chapter, was controlled by crime networks in which eastern European Jews played a crucial role.[30] Some of these Jews relocated to Egypt and operated their businesses directly from there. Referring to a smuggling ring broken up by Egypt's Central Narcotics Intelligence Bureau (CNIB), Henry D'Erlanger, Russell Pasha's associate, thus remarked: "The names of the members of the gang . . . read like the cast of one of the offerings of the Yiddish theatre."[31]

Paul Knepper claims that this and other statements in D'Erlanger's book are anti-Semitic in nature.[32] This may very well be true. But it cannot be denied that Eastern European Jews in the Vienna underworld played an increasingly pivotal role in the illegal smuggling of heroin into Egypt over the course of the 1920s and the 1930s. Arthur Aigner, Nathan Altman, Elie Chaskes, Pinkas Engelart, Salomon Eskanazi, Joshua Friedman, Albert Gedalia, Jacob Goldenberg, Mechel Halpern, Berthold Klein, Simon Lamm, Trajan Schor, Menachem Sion, Gabriel Weinstein; these and other distinctively Jewish names all featured in a "black list of traffickers and persons implicated in the illicit traffic in heroin, cocaine morphine and allied drugs" prepared by the CNIB, as well as in League of Nations reports about members of drug-running rings "importing heroin into Egypt." They were all described as the natives of Eastern European countries now "domiciled" in Egypt, with ties to the Viennese Jewish underworld.[33]

Of the relatively few local Jewish traffickers instrumental in advancing the commodity chain to Egypt, it is safe to assume that they were motivated mainly by material considerations. However, and this brings me to my third comment, there were other Jews in Palestine—namely, members of the Zionist organizations engaged in a low-level conflict against the British, whose motivations for running hashish to Egypt may have been less materialistic or self-serving. Their goal was something else altogether: to raise funds for their armed struggle, or to exchange hashish for arms. A contemporary observer thus recalls, albeit without naming names, the "vicious . . . traffic in arms and ammunition that put weapons into the hands of illegal groups in Palestine," adding, "The trade was skillfully organized—drugs from the Levant smuggled into Egypt to pay for weapons to be run back to underground forces in Palestine."[34]

Anecdotal evidence from reports by Shai, the intelligence arm of the Haganah—the main paramilitary organization of the Jewish Yishuv between 1920 and 1948—strongly suggests that members of the revisionist Irgun movement, which operated independently of the Haganah, were active in the hashish smuggling trade for this very reason.[35] Whilst the Irgun was a breakaway faction of the Haganah, there is also strong evidence suggesting that at the very least, the Haganah also considered smuggling hashish from Lebanon to Egypt via Palestine. This clearly comes through testimony given in 1970 by Shimshon Mashbetz, a founding member of Shai.[36] Mashbetz described in detail how the idea initially came up. He recalled a meeting in a Haifa café, either in 1942 or 1943, where he and his associates in the Arab division of Shai discussed various options for reinvigorating the organization's "dwindling resources." Mashbetz credited his comrade Yehoshua (Josh) Palmon with the suggestion that they consider hashish smuggling as an appropriate solution. David Shaltiel, district commander of the Haganah in Jerusalem during the 1948 war, was particularly enthusiastic about the idea: "His eyes began to shine through his spectacles . . . and he uttered at once, 'Let's do it [Qadimah].'"

According to his testimony, Mashbetz was entrusted with the mission of exploring the issue further. Utilizing personal connections in Lebanon—after all, "some Yishuvi patterns echoed region-wide patterns, and the *Yishuv* was an integral part of region-wide structures"[37]—he traveled to Lebanon to assess the hashish market there. In Beirut, Mashbetz met "a quintessential Middle East smuggler" who lent him an automobile and a driver: "[We] drove through Lebanon's Beqaa Valley, [through] hashish plantations and opium plantations. . . . I studied the whole issue—how to cultivate [cannabis], how to market [it], how to tell the difference between [cannabis] brands, what's good and what's bad, and how to tell the difference between the two."[38]

Returning to Haifa, Mashbetz briefed the Haganah leadership on his journey's findings. Everyone present, he says, was "enthralled" by his presentation, and a plan was drawn up for smuggling hashish from Lebanon to Egypt via Palestine. Alas, Shaul Avigur, an instrumental figure in the foundation of Shai, objected vehemently to the idea: "He listened to [my] story quietly and, lowering his head, announced conclusively, in a quiet and confident tone but in a manner that made it impossible for us to disagree, 'Impure money shall not [be permitted to] desecrate the purity of our arms.' Clearly, after these words, the entire plan was shelved and we forgot about the issue."[39]

The Haganah may have engaged in hashish smuggling operations; but others, likely the more unruly and adventurous elements within the Zionist camp and its group of British sympathizers, made it their occasional business to raid hashish smuggling operations across Palestine and confiscate the lucrative illicit cargo. For instance, when "lacking a penny for fixing a campfire," the skipper

Aryeh Bayevski—a pioneer of "Jewish shipping" in Palestine—would, together with a friend named Isaac, "embark upon the adventures of 'pirates'":

> The two would . . . take to sea in a tiny sailing boat and await the arrival of Arab smugglers transporting "hashish" from Lebanon or Syria to the Land of Israel. The "bandits" would intercept boats of smugglers and quickly land on their decks armed with hatchets and knives. Isaac, fluent in Arabic, would demand—and receive—from the Arab skipper[s] a modest ransom [ma'ut] [in the form] of hashish [in return for allowing the ship to proceed]. Bayevski and Isaac would then return to shore with the booty at hand and spend all the money on wild campfire drinking.[40]

HASHISH JOURNEYS AND TRICKS OF THE TRADE

As indicated in a 1937 British report, to get hashish supplies through from Lebanon to Egypt via Palestine, "both land and sea routes are used by traffickers and latterly there has been some evidence that aircraft is being employed."[41] At the beginning of their journey southward, cannabis products were sold by Lebanese-Syrian cultivators to "wholesale exporters," to be packed in "small packages" and prepared for smuggling.[42] Automobiles, trucks, trains, and beasts of burden ferried the packages overland to the Lebanese or Syrian border. In Lebanon, smugglers traveled south by car on the Beirut-Haifa highway running parallel to the Mediterranean coastline, "outsmarting Gendarmerie patrols by using fake identity cards, hiding cars beside the road, driving off-road at points, deliberately turning off their lights at night, or using secondary roads."[43] Upon reaching the Naqura customs station on the Palestinian border (fig. 1), where sometimes the customs police, the gendarmerie, the Sûreté Générale, and the political Services Spéciaux would all be present—the smugglers attempted to pull the wool over the eyes of the authorities and smuggle their illicit cargo across the border.[44] Other smugglers chose to enter Palestine via Damascus, in which case they would pass through the customs station at Rosh Pina, in the upper Galilee.[45]

Transporting consignments of hashish from Lebanon into Palestine was a relatively easy task. This is because at the time, the border that should have divided Lebanon and Palestine was virtually nonexistent. One Marjayoun man, born in 1939, recalls, for example, that "there was no border. There was, each kilometer, a block, a stone, painted in white."[46] Once inside Palestinian territory, hashish traffickers could choose a route southward from several options. The first option, probably the safest and easiest, was to ferry their illicit merchandise

FIGURE 1. Naqoura border crossing, 1940. G. Eric and Edith Matson Photo Collection.

on trains. It was here that our smugglers took advantage of the convenience offered by the railway system installed and upgraded by the British during the Mandate era. It may be that trains were the preferred overland means of transportation because, even though the highway and road infrastructure had been significantly extended during the interwar years, contemporaries complained that "in Palestine, the Administration is unduly hampering legitimate road construction and maintenance in its effort to safeguard the interests of the Railways (which are state-owned)."[47]

Indeed, after the end of World War I, control of the country's railways was transferred to Palestine Railways, Telegraph and Telephone, a company run by the British government. The new management shut down many of the little-used lines built in the Ottoman period, but over the years it also constructed new lines and upgraded several existing lines to the standard gauge.[48] Until 1942 the railway's main line linked the Egyptian town of Qantara, to the west of the Suez Canal, with Haifa (fig. 2).[49] Hence, hashish smugglers, once inside Palestinian territory, would try to reach Haifa with a view to depositing hashish supplies on trains running from Haifa to Qantara, the latter connected to other rail destinations across Egypt.[50] That Palestine's railway authority was headquartered in Haifa, with Lebanese and Egyptians nationals working there too,[51] may have made smuggling from the north to the south of the Levant easier and more convenient.

In 1942 the British extended the Qantara-Haifa coastal line northward to Beirut and Tripoli in Lebanon, the latter recently captured by the British from Vichy France. This expansion not only brought about a huge increase in the number of trains in the company's service but, in 1946–47, also increased capacity to carry 1.9 million tons of freight and some 900,000 passengers.[52] For

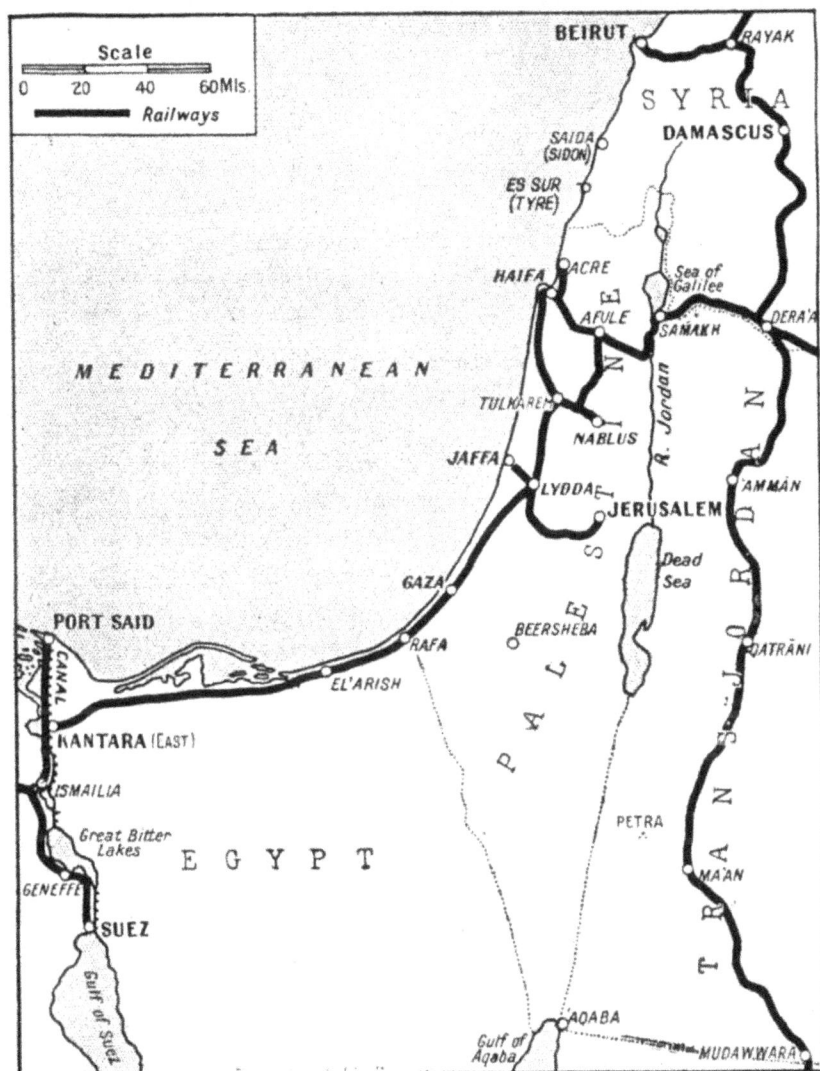

FIGURE 2. Map of Palestine Railways and associated lines in World War II. Railway Wonders of the World, UK. Reprinted with permission.

hashish smugglers en route to Egypt from Lebanon, this railway expansion would have been manna from heaven; from now on, they could—theoretically, at least—transport their illicit cargo by train, directly from the growing-cum-producing country in the north to the consumer country in the south.

It is noteworthy that Palestine Railways routes in Palestine determined, among other things, the locations of the main hashish waystations and hubs in the country, both for the onward journey to Egypt and for servicing the budding local hashish market. As can be seen in fig. 2, the line linking the Egyptian town of Qantara with Haifa (and, after 1942, with Beirut and Tripoli as well) passed through Lydda, centrally located next to the country's largest urban conglomeration, Jaffa/Tel Aviv, and connected to them by a train line.[53] Consequently, Lydda, Jaffa, and Haifa became Palestine's main hashish depots.[54]

That trains were the favored means of transportation for smugglers ferrying their illicit merchandise across borders and across Palestine is beyond doubt. All the pertinent sources point to this conclusion. A case in point is a 1929 incident, of some embarrassment to the British authorities, involving none other than the British High Commissioner to Egypt, Sir George Ambrose Lloyd. Following a visit to Damascus, the train carrying the dignitary back to Cairo was searched during a stopover at Lydda. Twenty-four slabs of hashish were found in his train car, the suspected culprits the accompanying "Egyptian guards and servants."[55] This was not an isolated event. A similar hashish seizure occurred a few days later at the Jerusalem train station, with hashish seized from the car of a Palestine Railways British official traveling from Syria; here too, the culprits were the "car workers," presumably Palestinians.[56] Palestinian railway workers, thoroughly familiar with the structure and layout of the train engines and train cars, tended to conceal hashish in less obvious locations, where they hoped it would not be discovered. What we do know concerns cases in which the hopes of smugglers were dashed by discovery. Hashish was hidden in the lighting fixtures of train carriages, in engines, in operating rooms, in train kitchens and saloons, and in the carriages' grease boxes.[57] Such cases demonstrated "the corrupting effect of the [hashish] traffic on small officials such as engine drivers, railway guards, etc."[58]

According to the historian Zachary Lockman, unlike virtually all the Arab- and Jewish-owned enterprises in the country, the Palestine Railways employed both Arabs and Jews; "it was . . . one of the few enterprises in which Arabs and Jews worked side by side, encountering similar conditions and being compelled to interact in the search for solutions to their problems."[59] However, the sources are silent about hashish smuggling by the *Jewish* employees of Palestine Railways, and by Jews generally. True, there were cases in which the latter group used trains to smuggle arms and ammunition from Egypt into Palestine for the Haganah.[60] Nevertheless, contemporary sources discussing hashish smuggling on the Palestine Railways only refer to Arab employees, either as smugglers or as the accomplices of smugglers.[61]

Other individuals and groups, not connected to Palestine Railways, also ran hashish on Egypt-bound trains. One example was a British military man who—in a manner typical of many in his position—wanted "to earn some money before he went home to England." He agreed to take a bag packed with hashish to Egypt via the Haifa-Qantara train, and then gave his operator away when the train reached its destination.[62] Another was a young man from Jaffa who planned to smuggle hashish to Egypt by train using a clever concealment technique; he came to the Jaffa train station

> asking for a special carriage so he could deliver a car to Qantara. Customs officials became suspicious of one of the [car's] wheels. Searching it, they found contraband [*homarim muvrahim*] hidden inside it. Police officers brought [to the place] an expert mechanic who disassembled the car, finding in it a great treasure of hashish and opium.[63]

Smugglers opting to traverse Palestine using nonrailway overland routes usually went to Deir al-Balah in the central Gaza region, where hashish consignments were reloaded "for delivery to Egypt . . . by camel caravan" through the Sinai desert.[64] As I will demonstrate below, the Gaza area in general and Deir al-Balah in particular were important points in the journey from Lebanon and Syria to Egypt, "the historic trade route now used by drug runners bringing hashish from Syria," known historically as the "King's Highway."[65] In the meantime, it should be kept in mind that reaching that area was not an easy task for hashish smugglers traversing Palestine. I have already mentioned the Rosh Pina customs station in northern Palestine, where searches for drugs and other contraband were conducted. Additional obstacles included routine police patrols and investigations into drug trafficking operations, the latter conducted on the basis of prior intelligence information. To avoid discovery, smugglers did their outmost to conceal their illicit cargo. Hence, we are told that smugglers concealed hashish in shoes with thick, hollow soles and heels; in hollow slabs of chocolate; in Turkish sweetmeats; in hollow sandwich loaves; in consignments of dried apricots, lemons, watermelons, and bananas; in sacks of potatoes; in egg cartons; in cases of olives; in tins of powdered glue; in barrels of tomato sauce, oil, and wine; in sacks of prunes; in hollowed crucifixes; in hollowed planks of timber; in book covers; in concrete slabs; in table legs; in tool boxes; in petrol tanks; in bags strapped to the thighs of the smugglers under their trousers; on the persons of men impersonating monks and priests; in spare wheels and in secret compartments built into automobiles, buses, and lorries; in sealed petrol tins; in garbage and coal trucks; in suitcase false bottoms; in cylinders inside cement slabs; in luncheon baskets; in musical instruments such as pianos and violins; in pails of dirty water; and so on and so forth.[66]

Overland routes aside, hashish traffickers also traversed Palestinian territorial waters to steer their cargoes across political borders and to Egypt. No doubt the British, like their French counterparts in Lebanon, were well aware that "certain ship crews were notorious smugglers."[67] The British also recognized that Palestine's ports, specifically Jaffa and Haifa, served as points of entrance and exit for drugs en route to Egypt from Lebanon, and that much of the smuggling was carried out by seamen who regularly sailed Palestine's territorial waters between the Syrian-Lebanese coasts and Alexandria. The latter usually employed inferior vessels, the quantities of drugs carried relatively small (four kilograms here, six kilograms there).[68]

Larger quantities of hashish were carried aboard passenger ships sailing the Mediterranean between eastern Europe and the ports of the Levant. In the early 1930s, for instance, several ships that had embarked from Constanţa, Romania, were suspected of picking up "large consignments" of opium and hashish amounting to several hundred kilograms during stopovers in Haifa and Jaffa. These consignments were intended for delivery to Alexandria, the ships' final destination.[69] At other times, large quantities of hashish and opium were creatively concealed on Alexandria-bound ships while they were docked in Palestinian ports, the smugglers themselves not actually accompanying the consignments. We know, for example, about a gang of Jerusalemite hashish smugglers that "brought suspicion on itself" because over several months it had purchased "every battered third or fourth-hand cars [sic], which nobody but an Oriental could possibly want to make use of," and shipped them by sea from Jaffa to Egypt. A search conducted on one shipment of these cars confirmed the suspicion: the wheels of the cars were "packed with hashish."[70]

In interwar Europe, the airplane revolutionized the character and methods of criminal activity; drug traffickers and "white slave" traders were singled out as using them in ways that "eliminated frontiers and the problems of Customs examinations."[71] As a matter of fact, in Europe airplanes raised the most alarming concerns about cross-border criminal activity, with some contemporaries viewing these "flying machines" as "dreadful weapons turned against the nervous constitution of the western races."[72] "Flying machines" in the service of the drug traffickers of the Levant were certainly not as common or as angst-arousing as in the Europe of the same period, though they were used from time to time.[73] After all, this means of transport was not available to most of the smugglers in the Levant; they lacked the resources necessary to purchase an airplane, not to mention the technical skills required to operate one.

However, airplanes were occasionally pressed into service, mainly by the international gang members who flocked to the Levant to cash in on the hashish trafficking bonanza. In 1937, for example, one such gang—made up of Palestinians, Greeks, Egyptians, and Italians—transported its illicit cargo all the way from Lebanon (where gang members procured the drug) via Jaffa (where the cargo was stored in preparation for its journey south) to Port Said in northeast Egypt by cars, train, and an airplane piloted by an Italian gang member. The intricate ploy was foiled due to the alertness of the undercover agents of Russell's CNIB.[74] Although smuggling hashish by airplane was not commonplace in interwar Palestine, in 1934 the British took care to state—following the crash of a smuggler's airplane in Cairo—that "the potentialities of aircraft as a means of smuggling narcotics are not . . . overlooked."[75] Particularly, the British had their eyes fixed on a civilian airfield in Haifa, constructed in 1935, specifically because it connected Haifa to both Cairo in the south and Beirut in the north.[76]

It can therefore be said that in their endeavors to direct hashish supplies to Egypt, drug traffickers took full advantage of "world-shrinking technologies": trains, cars, ships, and airplanes, all products of the long nineteenth century. In interwar Europe these speed technologies prompted angst "about an emerging generation of border-crossing criminals empowered by advances in transportation and communication."[77] In Palestine, however, our smugglers found it expedient to employ, in addition to these novel technologies, a more traditional means of transportation: the camel. As previously noted, the camel leg of smuggling operations usually began once the life histories of hashish supplies intersected with the Negev desert and Deir al-Balah in Gaza, where the consignments were handed over to local Bedouins. The latter not only "showed an ingenuity and adaptability that many [British] desert officers . . . did not anticipate"; they considered hashish smuggling a legitimate economic enterprise, and "treated the drug trade as a windfall . . . to be exploited while it lasted."[78] They reloaded the contraband onto camels, and marched them across the desert between the Palestine frontier and the Suez Canal and into Egypt.[79]

Russell Pasha—whose views on cannabis were quite progressive for the time—did not hold these Bedouin smugglers in contempt, as he did the other drug smugglers operating in the Levant at the time. On the contrary, he expressed sympathy for their penchant for hashish smuggling, noting that they had been "driven [to it] by hunger and lack of grazing."[80] While applauding their resourcefulness and audacity, he also viewed them as helpless marionettes, manipulated by powerful and avaricious puppeteers working from a great distance: "the fat-bellied notables of Beirut and the Lebanon." While the latter surely "rub[bed] their hands with pleasure at the profits they [made] on each consignment safely run into Egypt," Russell said, the former risked death and imprisonment for a "few pounds' commission."[81]

The Bedouin smuggler's most common method of concealment was to sew parcels of the drug into the upholstery of camel saddles, or to glue such parcels beneath the hair of the camel's hump.[82] The problem with this method was that it was used ad nauseam, up to the point when law enforcement officials began to make a mockery of it. As CID officer Broadhurst commented, referring to this very ploy, "These desperadoes have now played so many tricks on the Police and been found out so many times, that they can no longer invent any new ones, so that the game has become simplified for the authorities."[83]

But invent "new ones" they did, exemplifying the well-known and vicious dialectics of the fight against the drug trade: the greater the effort put into combating this illicit trade, the greater the efforts directed toward evasion and the continuation of that very trade, and vice versa.[84] Russell, the seasoned antidrug warrior that he was, appreciated this rule and thus always assumed that in the war against smugglers "[every] victory could only be looked upon as temporary."[85] He couldn't have been more accurate in his statement. In 1939, a highly sophisticated but outrageously sinister and cruel method of smuggling hashish to Egypt by camels was revealed. This new ploy caught the British in Palestine and Egypt completely off guard. Indeed, so flabbergasted were they by the audacity, originality, inventiveness, and cruelty of this ploy that the 1939 CNIB report to the League of Nations devoted no less than six pages to the affair (not including illustrations).[86]

The ploy was reportedly devised by "certain persons" in the southern Gaza region who were in the business of running hashish to Egypt through Sinai.

Realizing that the old smuggling method, the concealment of hashish *on* camels, had run its course, they devised a new system, smuggling hashish *inside* camels: "filling a number of tin cylinders with the drugs and forcing them down the throats of cheap butchers' camels, which once through the [Qantara] Quarantine and the Customs and safely into Egypt would be slaughtered at some quiet spot on the road and the valuable cargo recovered."[87] The authorities, for their part, seemed to be concerned less about the cruelty inflicted on the beasts than about the serious challenge the new ploy posed to law enforcement agents. The 1939 CNIB report spells out this challenge:

> As some 30,000 to 35,000 camels pass through the Customs and Quarantine Station of Qantara from the east every year, it can be readily imagined that finding the "offending" beast was rather like looking for a needle in a haystack.[88]

Per a recommendation originally put forth in the 1939 CNIB report, a technological solution to the problem had been devised and implemented by the early 1940s. By installing X-ray devices at the Qantara station, law enforcers and customs officers were thereafter able to select camels randomly to be screened by "searching beams," as a Shai report pointed out in reference to this specific smuggling method.[89] As will be seen in chapter 5, Bedouin smugglers persisted with this concealment ploy after 1948 by using hashish containers undetectable by X-ray.

Finally, whether employing modern or traditional means of transportation, most of our protagonists were in the hashish smuggling business for the money, as it were. Thus, it was very much in their own interest to cut down the number of hands involved in the commodity chain from origin to destination; the fewer the number of people engaged in facilitating the drug's onward journey, the greater the profit. In this sense, it was only a matter of time before our Palestinian smugglers decided to weed out these intermediaries by reducing the distance from one end of the journey to the other. This explains why, in the mid-1940s, Palestinian Arabs began to cultivate cannabis in small independent plots—three to four dunams, approximately one acre—across the country, but mainly in the Jenin and Tulkarm areas, and sometimes in the Haifa area as well. The aim was to export hashish to Egypt, and possibly also to meet the increasing local demand for the drug (see chapter 3). Internal CID correspondence and police reports began to warn about this turn of events after 1946.[90]

The police's management of some of these cases suggests a lack of oversight and a degree of negligence. This can be discerned from a letter written by a concerned Palestinian to the high commissioner, Sir Alan Cunningham, informing him of a certain Jenin resident who over the past two years had been planting cannabis on his land. The letter's author explained that he had taken the unusual step of writing directly to the highest colonial authority in the country because previous appeals to colonial officials of lower rank had been ignored: "I have personally noticed this [cannabis plantation] and drew the attention of the responsible officers to this action, but they neglected the matter."[91] As will be seen, indifference to or oversight with regard to drug offences was a typical response of the British authorities.

THE LIMITS OF ANTIHASHISH CONTROLS

> Stopping hashish smuggling is rather like an attempt to dam
> a stream with a clay barrier—directly you have plugged up
> one hole the water comes through in another place.

Thus Claude Scudamore Jarvis, the British governor of Sinai between 1923 and 1936, expressed his annoyance with the persistent failure of his forces to prevent the border-crossing flows of hashish from Palestine to Egypt.[92] In the previous section I suggested that hashish traffickers' ingenuity may have been a primary cause of this failure. In this section I examine the response of the enforcement forces, especially the Palestine Police, to these challenges posed by hashish traffickers. My argument here is that the former had no chance of emerging victorious in the fight against the hashish trade, due to lack of resources and multiple concerns that led to drug smuggling receiving a lower priority than other exigencies.

By the time that the British assumed the Mandate over Palestine and the smuggling routes to Egypt had shifted from Greece to the Levant, the ban on hashish in Egypt had already been in place for at least three decades. The first reference to the introduction of an antidrug—and antihashish—regime in Palestine was in 1919, when the British military government issued a warning to the public that henceforth it would be "an offence to cultivate, export, introduce, buy, sell, offer for sale or be in possession of hashish."[93] This proscription was confirmed by the 1925 Opium Convention, which introduced global control over cannabis products.[94]

The convention went into effect on September 25, 1928. In the meantime, the Mandatory authorities in Palestine promulgated the Dangerous Drugs

Ordinance of 1925.[95] This ordinance was based on British metropolitan legislation of the Dangerous Drugs Act of 1920 and 1925, which established controls over opiates and cannabis respectively.[96] In the ordinance, the British categorically outlawed "the manufacture, importation, exportation and possession of certain dangerous drugs" in Palestine: opiates, coca leaves, cocaine, and, significantly, "Indian hemp."[97]

This latter ruling made little difference. By 1926, the British authorities in Egypt, reflecting on the situation, had acknowledged that "narcotics continue[d] to come into the country in large quantities,"[98] mainly from the northern end of the Levant, via Palestine. The 1925 ordinance was amended a few times in the following years—in 1928, 1932, and 1936. Bearing the same title, "Dangerous Drugs Ordinance," they were all designed to incorporate recommendations spelled out by the OAC regarding drug consumption and drug trafficking, specifically "increasing the penalties to be imposed on illicit traffickers in dangerous drugs."[99] The 1936 ordinance also reiterated, more clearly than its predecessors, that "any person who conveys any dangerous drugs through Palestine in transit shall be guilty of an offence."[100] The very same ordinance also contained stricter limitations on hashish smokers in Palestine, as will be discussed in chapter 3.

On the whole, however, it must be stressed that these ordinances remained a dead letter; the British in Palestine had neither the infrastructural ability nor the economic capacity—nor the willpower—to enforce them efficiently. Clear indications of this can be seen not only in official reports prepared by the British and the League, but also in secondary literature on the Palestine Police Force, and in memoirs penned by the former policemen, mostly British, who served with that force. In going over this material, one is left with the distinct impression that drug control in Palestine was primarily an annoyance and a burden, an obligation the police fulfilled tepidly or unwillingly, lacking keen interest and genuine enthusiasm due to higher priorities and inherent incapacity to control the extensive and cross-border flow of hashish. It is also worth remembering that many of their servicemen "were demoralized, undisciplined, and suffered difficult conditions including low wages and the hostility of the societies they policed."[101] This seems to have damped their motivation to fight against hashish-related crimes.

A 1934 OAC memorandum concerning the global "problem of Indian Hemp" illustrates this clearly. With regard to the Asian countries "especially concerned" with cannabis, the memorandum notes that "the Palestine authorities [exerted] constant efforts to intercept consignments en route [from Syria to Egypt]." In this endeavor, however, the authorities were invariably on the losing end: "the lives of Police and Customs officers on this service [were] exposed to grave risk, for smugglers are usually armed and fire without hesitation to avoid falling into the hands of the police." Secondly, overland the police were at "a disadvantage," owing to "the long line of frontier" and "the ingenious methods of concealment employed [to] preclude complete and through searches." By sea, too, "seizures [were] few," because there were "many miles of coast" to police, and "the smugglers' intelligence service [was] good." As a result, smugglers "not infrequently succeed[ed] in introducing hashish into Palestine and dumping it in various hiding places close to the southern frontier, there to await suitable opportunity for transportation across the Sinai desert into Egypt."[102]

Three departments within the Palestine Police Force, established in 1920,) were charged with combating drug-related offenses: the CID, the Camel Corps, and the Port and Marine Section. It would seem that none of the three departments were really prepared for the task. That aside, with bigger fish to fry—investigations into political assassinations, weapons smuggling, robbery and extortion, illegal immigration, and bombs and sabotage[103]—these departments placed drug prevention at the lower end of their scale of priorities during the interwar years.

Founded in 1920, the CID Palestine branch, like other CID departments across the British empire, was charged with the investigation of crimes such as burglary, murder, and the smuggling of arms, illegal immigrants, and drugs. The department also took charge of forensics, political intelligence, surveillance of political and subversive activities, and the development of a criminal archive, which included fingerprints and photographs.[104] Given that at the height of its activities, in the 1930s and 1940s, the CID was a force of no more than fifty-two to fifty-six men, including clerical staff,[105] it is hard to imagine that it would have been able to attend to all these duties and activities, and at the same time provide an effective response to the tide of illicit hashish pouring into and across Palestine.

In his memoir, Joseph Broadhurst, Palestine CID commander between 1924 and 1930, bemoans "the immensity of the smuggling problem that faced the Palestine Police." In the process, he provides a telling testimony of the British authorities' dismal performance in combating the conduct of the Levant hashish trade on Palestinian territory. Describing, in anguished language, the kinds of smuggling operations taking place along this axis of Syria-Palestine-Egypt,

Broadhurst notes with exasperation the so numerous "smugglers of originality" who, by virtue of having been "born with great natural cunning," had "played so many tricks on the Police" and "gave us endless trouble." He goes on to say: "By every manner of trick hashish is smuggled over the Syrian-Palestinian frontier, through Palestine, across the burning Sinai Desert, over a lonely part of the Suez Canal and up to Cairo."[106] Broadhurst, it seems, was unable to bring himself to categorically admit the CID's utter failure in its battle against the flow of hashish in Palestine. Yet his account underscores his despair in waging a war against hashish smugglers, a war that could not be won.

Edward Horne, a former Palestine Police officer considered the Force's official historian, whose 1982 book on the subject remains the only book exclusively dedicated to it,[107] takes the formation of the Palestine CID as a sign of British imperial benevolence, a harbinger of progress in the East. "The Turks had nothing . . . comparable with the British system of using a professional Criminal Investigation Department within the police service to investigate crimes, detect and arrest criminals and prosecute them with vigor,"[108] he claims. The Camel Corps, also involved in acts of "good neighboring" with regard to Egypt's hashish problem, provides a different scenario altogether: its 1921 formation was not without precedent, given that it was probably modeled after the camel-riding corps of the Egyptian desert patrol, set up in the 1880s to maintain public security and track down drug smugglers in the Sinai Peninsula.[109] On the whole, the Palestine Camel Corps, manned by Bedouin forces, sought to impose order and security in the Southern District.[110] Equally, it was entrusted with the task of patrolling the southern Negev (al-Naqab) desert—"one of the most desolate areas in the Middle East . . . and notorious for hashish smugglers and other outlaws"[111]—to prevent the smuggling of drugs into Egypt.

Horne's account of the camelry's performance is not a tale of desert exoticism and imperial valor and chivalry, à la Lawrence of Arabia. Rather, it is the story of a comparatively small unit (160 men plus 120 camels in the 1940s), constantly contending with—and often overcome by—harsh desert conditions: intolerable heat and sandstorms ("sand devils"), and rain which would come "in such measures as to destroy everything," prompting the men "to curse in Arabic or English, according to natural inclinations."[112] Inadequate communication links and other mechanical problems also prevented the men from performing their duties promptly and efficiently. Hence, because wireless telegraphy and telephones were almost nonexistent, "a camel patrol would disappear for days, before emerging from the shimmering heat to report upon their work."[113] It was only late in the

Mandatory period, in 1945, that the Camel Corps acquired the radio communication equipment and modern vehicles that allowed it to "surprise smugglers."[114] If this was not bad enough, adverse political conditions frequently disrupted the Corps activities, sometimes halting their operations altogether. For instance, in the course of the 1936–39 Palestinian Arab Revolt, the force, having been targeted by rebels, was abandoned and "melted away into a virtual state of non-operation."[115] In fact, the camelry's antismuggling performance was so poor that sometimes patrols of the British Frontier Districts Administration in Egypt were granted permission to enter the Negev in pursuit of raiders and smugglers.[116]

As shown previously, hashish smuggling from Lebanon via sea routes to Egypt had also caused the British authorities in Palestine no end of trouble. To counteract this and other challenges, a coast guard service was established in 1923, operating from Ras al-Krum (located at the foot of Mount Carmel on the Mediterranean coast, today the location of the Haifa suburb of Bat Galim). However, its "efforts to maintain the law offshore," according to Horne, were "comparatively feeble and became the subject of much criticism."[117] Douglas Duff, commander of the nascent Port Police, provides telling accounts of the force's lack of initiative, sophistication, and technological prowess. Patrolling the sea from Ras al-Naqoura in the north to Jaffa in the south, he describes one case in which a schooner under his command pursued a vessel suspected of carrying hashish from Sidon in Lebanon, only to discover too late that "whilst we were chasing her they ran their cargo in another vessel and got it safely away."[118] Elsewhere, Duff complains about the poor quality of the equipment the force were expected to use to combat smugglers at sea. Recalling an attempt to start a schooner engine so as to chase a smugglers' vessel, he laments the fact that "not a sound came down the night-breeze," and the smuggler's vessel escaped into the darkness. This, and other futile and abortive episodes at sea, got Duff "mad with ourselves and the Government for the useless tools they gave us to discharge our duties."[119]

According to Horne, the incompetence of the Port Police throughout the 1920s and the early 1930s explained, in part, why "every conceivable offense relating to smuggling, illegal fishing and thefts of cargoes was committed [at sea]."[120] The 1935 creation of the Port and Marine Section, headquartered at the newly constructed Port of Haifa, supposedly changed this terribly poor record.[121] With a team of forty policemen and, by 1939, ten vessels—"which enabled the section to perform any task given to it"[122]—a few major successes came its way. Its most well known accomplishment occurred in February 1941, when the force intercepted a vessel carrying nearly one ton (approximately two thousand pounds) of opium and hashish combined. The seizure, estimated to be worth some fifty thousand Palestinian pounds, was declared "the largest ever made in Palestine."[123] It so happened that the vessel had received its illicit cargo from a Syrian boat offshore, "for delivery to smugglers operating camel caravans across the Sinai Desert to Egypt."[124]

Horne suggests that, due to the activities of the Port and Marine Section, "smuggling . . . became a very hazardous pastime and consequently dropped to almost insignificant proportions."[125] However, one suspects that these accolades are somewhat inflated. For one, I have not come across any corroborative reports confirming additional major hashish hauls by the section. Second, the fight against hashish smuggling was merely one of the force's several additional duties. It was also responsible for preventing illegal immigration, arms smuggling, and fishing offenses, as well as administrating of port rules.[126] With so many other things on the force's plate, it hardly seems plausible that it could direct its fullest energies to practically eradicating the illicit flow, at sea, of hashish from Lebanon to Egypt. Lastly, as Horne himself would recognize, the opening of the new harbor was destined to generate "new sorts of crimes as well as a massive increase in traditional marine crimes in Haifa by the local underworld."[127]

The surge in criminal activity in the port of Haifa during the Mandate was not unique to that city. The port in Singapore, for example, incubated criminal activity, including opium smuggling. This spread throughout the city, with local law enforcement authorities unable to figure out how to respond appropriately.[128] Infractions of the law also characterized the port and city of Beirut during the interwar period, making enforcement authorities there "somewhat blinded by the frenzy of [criminal] activity."[129] This may explain why, in 1935, the Port and Marine Section in Palestine was placed under the (nominal, at least) command of the CID.[130] The combined duties of these two police departments were consequently quite daunting:

> With a view to preventing the smuggling of narcotic drugs into Palestine by ocean-going steamers . . . members of the Port and Marine Police are posted on all ships calling at Jaffa and Haifa during their period of stay. Lighters, motor launches and fishing vessels are closely examined and [all ship crews] are carefully searched on coming ashore. The baggage of incoming passengers is examined by the Customs Authorities. Prompt advance information in regard to suspect ships or individuals coming to Palestine is passed to the Customs Authorities by the Criminal Investigation Dep.[131]

This move toward cooperation in drug control did not stop at the level of the Palestine Police Force. As it became evident that the problem of hashish smuggling was a border-crossing issue, involving most of the Levant states, 1927 saw the beginning of Egyptian-led international police cooperation in drug control involving also Palestine and Syria-Lebanon.[132] This coordination included the sharing of lists of known smugglers, and the preparation by the CNIB of a catalog of important drug traffickers.[133] Broadhurst, the Palestine Police CID chief, took credit for the initiative. Most of the hashish in Egypt, he wrote, "came from Syria via Palestine, and it occurred to me as odd . . . that no kind of liaison existed between the French Syrian, the Egyptian and Palestine Police Chiefs."[134]

This cooperation between the Levant police forces officially debuted in May 1929, with a conference on the drug traffic problem in Egypt, Palestine, and the French territories. It took place in Haifa, and was attended by the chief of the Cairo Police, the chief of the Palestine Police, and the inspector-general of the Police Forces of the Levant States under French Mandate.[135] The participants agreed to cooperate in the field of drug enforcement by sharing lists of smugglers operating in the four territories and reporting on their movements and activities. To this end, the authorities in Egypt agreed to provide "a sum of money" to each of the other three states, to be used in the campaign against smugglers.[136] From this time on, Egypt and Palestine spent a combined sum of five hundred thousand British pounds each year (approximately thirty million at today's value) to block the trafficking of hashish.[137] This quadrangular cooperation lasted until the very last days of the interwar period.[138]

Russell was beholden to the Palestine Police Force for the services it rendered Egypt in the fight against incoming hashish supplies, suggesting that its efforts derived not from self-interest but from pure solidarity with a sister state. "Drug consumption in Palestine is rare," he explained, and hashish supplies passing through the country "are entirely destined for Egypt."[139] As I will show in the next chapter, these claims about the paucity of hashish use in Palestine were not entirely correct. Nonetheless, Russell asserted that the assistance rendered by the Palestine Police to Egypt in the fight against drug smugglers was a genuine act of "*bon voisinage.*"[140]

My discussion thus far has shown that the collective efforts of the police forces of the respective Levant states scarcely deterred hashish traffickers from transporting their cargoes from Lebanon and Syria to Egypt via Palestine. Although the actual quantity of Lebanese-Syrian hashish supplies that entered Egypt via Palestine is difficult to ascertain, it is likely that the bulk of them completed their journey successfully. This can largely be gleaned from British administrative

TABLE 1.   Hashish Seizures in Mandatory Palestine.

YEAR	SEIZURES (IN KG)	YEAR	SEIZURES (IN KG)
1923–1924	400	1938	72 or 148*
1928	680	1939	155
1930	470	1940	676 or 840*
1931	502	1941	3,050 or 3,540*
1932	128	1942	4,415
1933	154	1943	2,647
1934	63	1944	1,051
1935	42	1945	830
1936	39 or 45*	1946	1,204
1937	75		

*Depending on the report type

and police reports from the Mandate period, which include details of hashish supplies seized by the police or customs authorities inside Palestine as a result of searches and routine patrols.[141] As table 1 clearly illustrates, with the exception of the early 1940s, a period when Lebanese hashish smuggling increased significantly due to World War II,[142] the paucity of annual hashish seizure rates during the Mandate years is indeed striking (though the fragmentary nature of the records makes it impossible to fully quantify the hashish trade running from Palestine to Egypt). In his memoirs Russell acknowledged as much, stating that the authorities only succeeded in seizing, at most, only 10 percent of the volume of drugs smuggled into Egypt via Palestine.[143] The Palestine-Egyptian border—which, though demarcated, was not fenced—may have contributed to the ease with which hashish traffickers successfully smuggled the lion's share of their hashish contraband into Egypt.[144]

CONCLUSION

Before the interwar period, hashish was a relatively negligible issue in the lives of Palestinians. This changed dramatically over the course of the British Mandate due to the emergence of a vigorous hashish trade in the Levant region, extending from Lebanon and Syria to Egypt. Consequently, many people—Levantines, other Middle Easterners, Europeans—took advantage of Palestine's

key geographical position to smuggle vast quantities of the drug across its territory on the journey to Egypt. Successful border-crossing enterprises of this
nature owed as much to the resourcefulness of the smugglers as to the lack of
preparedness and will on the part of the British to forcefully impose a ban on
hashish.

I conclude by dipping into Hebrew-language detective or crime fiction of the
interwar period, which neatly packages and illustrates some of the main arguments presented in this chapter. This genre debuted in Palestine in the 1930s
and 1940s, -a period known as the "Golden Age" of crime fiction, characterized
by the soaring popularity of detective fiction around the world.[145] Like that of
its counterparts elsewhere, the popularity of this genre with Palestine's Jews
was due at least in part to rising anxieties about the new forms of criminality
that had emerged in the wake of World War I.[146] As such, the genre provided
radical dramatizations of real criminal activities that had occurred in Palestine,
and which Zionist discourse and historiography tended to downplay. Thus,
to borrow from Pablo Piccato's fascinating study of crime, truth, and justice
in Mexico, reading crime fiction was a reliable way of enhancing "criminal
literacy" among Palestine's Jews.[147]

It is therefore no coincidence that fights against international and regional
rings of hashish traffickers traversing Palestine provide the storyline for two
separate detective series. The first, featuring the character of David Tidhar
(aka "the first Hebrew detective"), was published in 1931–32, and was the first
original crime fiction in any language published in Palestine.[148] The second,
featuring the character of Gad Magen (aka "the detective from the Land of
Israel"), was published in 1946–47.[149] Tidhar, it is worth mentioning, was a
real-life Palestine Police officer turned successful Tel Aviv private investigator
in the Mandatory period who lent his persona to the fictional protagonist of the
series. His portrait adorned the cover of every book in the series; some of the
plots were loosely inspired by his experiences as a police officer.[150] I will return to
the real-life Tidhar in the next chapter. In the meantime, it is important to note
that in one of the fictional Tidhar stories, the villains are all European members
of an "international organization" (*aguda beinleumit*) of hashish smugglers;[151]
and in one of the Gad Magen stories, published in a time when the prospects
of Jewish-Arab accommodation in Palestine were at their lowest ebb, the ring's
members were portrayed as cruel and cunning Palestinian and Egyptian Arabs,
their smuggling operations inspired as much by the desire to annihilate the
Zionist project as the wish to make lots of money.[152]

As can be expected, the sphere of operations for both smuggling rings was the entire Levant, in defiance of the boundaries separating the region's emergent nation-states. For instance, in the course of one investigation, Gad Magen discovers that "someplace across the northern border of the Land of Israel, there begins a network [*reshet*] which spreads out into three countries," Lebanon, Palestine, and Egypt;[153] that after production in Lebanon, hashish is transported to the Lebanon-Palestine border by local smugglers aided by corrupt Lebanese gendarmeries; that Palestinian Arabs receive the illicit produce on the Palestine side of the border and transfer it southward to Jaffa to be stored in temporary "warehouses";[154] that the illicit commodities are then transferred further south, to Deir al-Balah in the Gaza region, where Bedouins take control of the contraband and conceal it by forcing hashish-filled cylinders down camels' throats and into their stomachs;[155] and that once this is completed, the camels are escorted safely into Egypt via Qantara.[156] With these revelations in mind, Magen and his associates take steps to foil the plot:

> When the large camel caravan arrived [at Qantara] . . . all the camels were placed before strange devices which officials had brought from Cairo. Residents of Qantara didn't know that these devices were X-ray machines; and they were taken by surprise when a butcher was brought in to slaughter all the camels. When [the camels'] stomachs were opened up, six small round boxes filled with hashish were revealed in each and every one of them.[157]

All this should ring a bell—the hashish smuggling routes to, across, and from Palestine; the transit of contraband hashish within Palestine to a temporary depot in Jaffa; the Negev leg of the illicit commodity's journey to Egypt; and the smugglers' ruses, concealing hashish cylinders inside the camels' stomachs. But the Gad Magen plot leads us to yet another familiar theme: the directness of the Palestine Railway's north-south route along the coast, from Beirut to Qantara—the easiest, cheapest, and safest land route for smuggling hashish into the Egyptian frontier. When Magen boards this train in Jaffa, he glances casually at an Egyptian money changer who is making money off passengers who need Egyptian currency.[158] The man's frequent visits to the train's toilets raise our detective's suspicion. Magen inspects the toilets, where he discovers "multiple boxes of hashish, each one sewn inside a cloth bag," inside the water cistern.[159] This fictional account bears striking similarities to a 1944 CNIB report to the League of Nations. In that report appears an Egyptian man who, for a very long time, "used to travel forwards and backwards on the Cairo-Haifa train under the guise of a money changer," all the while smuggling "drugs for his gang."[160] In this spirit of authenticity, the same Gad Magen story also introduces us to "Levingston Pasha," "the greatest enemy of all drug dealers" and the commander of the Cairo-based "Central Bureau of the War against Intoxicating Drugs."[161] This is an obvious reference—and homage, perhaps?—to Russell Pasha and the CNIB.

In August 1928, Leopold Amery, secretary of state for the colonies, expressed alarm at the seizure of "large quantities of hashish" in Palestine in the previous year, mistakenly assuming that Palestine was the drug's "country of origin." Seeking to correct the error, E. Mills, acting chief secretary of the government of Palestine, wrote back to the imperial dignitary, clarifying "that for the most part Palestine is a country of transit and not a country of destination in so far as the traffic of hashish is concerned."[162] Mills was apparently trying to allay Amery's concerns about the state of hashish abuse in Palestine, intimating that there was no such problem in the country. If this was what Mills meant to say, he was—deliberately or not—conveying only a partial truth, as we will see.

3

THE UNDERWORLD OF USERS

*Further on they came upon a dilapidated shack which served as a coffee
house. Listless men sat or lay around on the ground as their wives tilled
the fields. Some played backgammon. The air was foul with the mixed
aroma of thick coffee, tobacco, hashish smoke and the vile odors of the
rest of the village.*

THIS DEPICTION OF THE FIRST ENCOUNTER between Zionist settlers and
Palestine is taken from Leon Uris's 1958 blockbuster "historical novel" *Exodus*.[1] Similar portrayals of such encounters appear in an equally popular 1983
novel by Uris, *The Haj*.[2] In both novels, as the journalist and scholar Jeremy
Salt pointedly observes, Uris presents Palestine to his readers as "a stagnant
land, groaning under the weight of Ottoman and Arab neglect. . . . The Palestinian people are portrayed as passive, uncaring and fatalistic. Their villages
are dirty, their men are stupefied by hashish."[3] These portrayals, Salt argues,
reduce Palestinian Arabs to "a series of ugly stereotypes," framing their culture as "rotten to the core."[4] Uris also seems to be consciously advancing one
of Zionism's main foundation myths: that Palestine was an empty land, "a
land without a people for a people with no land."

The literary merits of *Exodus* and *The Haj* are debatable; however, "bad histories they certainly are."[5] Indeed, Uris's description of early twentieth-century

Ottoman Palestine as an essential lack is unequivocally false; the related claim, that Palestine's Arabs were incurably stupefied by hashish intoxication, is equally untrue. Contrary to nineteenth- and twentieth-century Orientalist accounts like Uris's, and unlike some other societies the British had ruled beginning in the early modern era (especially India and Egypt), Palestinians were not known as a cannabis-oriented population. As Salt rightly contends, hashish "was certainly not used widely if at all in Palestine at the time of which Uris is writing."[6]

The general disinterest in hashish on the part of Palestine's inhabitants began to shift on the eve of the Mandatory period, due to circumstances far beyond their control: the creation of the Levant hashish trade connecting Lebanon-Syria and Egypt through Palestine, as detailed in the previous two chapters. As Palestine grew into a critical link in the hashish supply chain running from Lebanon and Syria to Egypt, in the process becoming the most important hashish depot in the Levant, hashish smoking by the country's urban working-class Arab population increased significantly. "The history of commodities," as Sebastian Conrad contends,

> traces particular items—most famously sugar (in the classic study by Sidney Mintz), but also cotton, soy, porcelain, and glass—across distant geographies and across time. These are studies of interconnectedness that link sites of production and consumption in different locations and show how these commodities impacted individual households as well as larger groups and social formations.[7]

In what follows, I demonstrate the extent to which the newly forged links between the sites of hashish production and consumption, Lebanon-Syria and Egypt respectively, affected the leisure culture practices of many a Palestinian Arab by prompting a dramatic spike in the recreational use of hashish.

In recent years, historians of drugs have begun to question the long-held convention that supply necessarily determines the demand for drugs. This convention, the perspective holds, is simplistic in that it ignores or denies the cultural and social factors that sustain drug consumption, and overlooks the agency of drug users and would-be drug users.[8] Through such erroneous understandings,

> inanimate substances are granted agency, while human beings become passive objects. . . . However, opium pipes and morphine needles do not have lives of their own: they are granted social lives by their users. . . . Historians and

sociologists no longer seriously consider all users to be "addicts" governed by physical dependence but see them rather as complex human beings whose social experience should be the main focus of attention if we are to understand substance-influenced behavior. . . . The intricate and diverse ways in which drugs interact, collude and even collaborate with human beings in a range of diverse social contexts give psychoactive substances their particular epistemological interest.[9]

Although supply may matter less than "the personal and cultural values that modulate demand and comportment,"[10] in this chapter I will nevertheless demonstrate that exposure to drugs is at times a critical precondition for an increase in drug use. As seen in the previous chapter, Palestine's evolution into a transit route for the passage of hashish to Egypt meant that vast quantities of the drug would cross its territory. With some hashish smugglers preferring to sell part of their forbidden goods to the domestic market, a steep increase in hashish consumption occurred among the country's urban working-class Arab population, thus confirming that proximity—and, consequently, familiarity and availability—do matter, at least to some extent. Even if hashish smoking in Palestine did not reach the magnitude of Egypt's concurrent hashish and "white drug" "epidemics" (successfully quelled by the 1930s),[11] the British authorities in Palestine, lacking the necessary resources and willpower, could not stamp out the habit.

HASHISH CONSUMPTION BEFORE THE 1930S

I have already commented on the rampant hashish problem of late Ottoman Egypt. Likewise, if one accepts at face value the accounts of the exiled Italian princess Cristina Trivulzio di Belgiojoso (chapter 1), we may conclude that "hashish orgies" were a common phenomenon in late Ottoman-era Damascus, especially in the city's coffeehouses. Yet I have not found any compelling evidence suggesting that hashish consumption in Palestine during the same period was at all comparable. It is likely that hashish was used in the Palestine of the time, albeit in moderation—in much the same way that opium was commonly used, in moderate quantities, in nineteenth-century England without any ensuing "loss of control."[12] If indeed there was hashish use to any degree, it was anything but remarkable, which would explain why it did not receive even the slightest attention in my sources.

If works of fiction are a reliable gauge of social realities, then Yitzhak Shami's 1927 novella *Vengeance of the Fathers* (*Nikmat ha-Avot*) should support the view that hashish smoking in Palestine prior to World War I was not a commonplace recreational practice.[13] Born in Hebron in 1888 to a Damascene silk merchant father and a Hebronite Sephardic mother, Shami is representative of the "forgotten milieu of those Mashriqi Jews who identified themselves with the rising Arab national movement and its emancipatory program, and who shared language and culture with their Muslim and Christian compatriots in greater Syria, Iraq, and Egypt, as early as the Ottoman administrative reforms of 1839."[14] Thus, even though he did eventually embrace Zionism, seeing in it a path to secular modernity, in his fiction Shami repeatedly strove to present an Arab voice and to portray the Arabs from the inside, as it were.[15] This empathy with the Arabs of Palestine might explain why, until very recently, Shami was absent from the pantheon of modern Hebrew prose, his works all but forgotten.[16] Fortunately, most of Shami's works (including *Vengeance of the Fathers*) have been rescued from oblivion in recent years, and have been republished in a single volume.[17] He is today acknowledged as a "great Jewish writer," his fictional works recognized as "a vanguard of the Mediterranean trend in Hebrew literature."[18] *Vengeance of the Fathers* is considered the most important of all his works of fiction—an "exemplary novella" and "one of the highest highpoints of modern Hebrew literature."[19]

The plot of the novella is based on a series of real events that occurred twenty-five years before its writing, as Shami himself confirms in a footnote.[20] Although he does not provide a specific historical time frame for the novella, the internal clues all point to the late Ottoman era, the eve of World War I.[21] The story begins with preparations for the annual spring festival of Nabi Musa, a major event in Palestinian Muslim life until the mid-1920s, when processions of pilgrims from all over Palestine converged at the presumed burial place of Moses, some twenty-five miles east of Jerusalem.[22] Three major groups travel from Jerusalem, Hebron and Nablus: each group has its own leader and flag bearer, drummers and musicians, lancers and fencing champions. They arrive on horseback and on foot: men, women, and children, with camels bearing enough provisions to sustain them for several days.

We meet the novella's hero, Nimr Abu al-Shawarib ("The Mustached One"), leader of the Nablus group, amidst the commotion and excitement of the festival. Tensions are developing between Abu al-Shawarib and Abu Faris, leader of the Hebron group. After being repeatedly insulted by Abu Faris, Abu al-Shawarib is finally provoked into killing him. Fearing blood vengeance, Abu al-Shawarib flees into the wilderness. He ends up in Cairo, a shadow of his former self. Shami's "descriptions of the [Cairo] setting, the misery of exile and the power of remorse are incandescent."[23] Indeed, during his Cairo sojourn Abu al-Shawarib unwisely spends the little money he has, suffers acute outbreaks of depression and—worst of all—becomes addicted to hashish. After experiencing distressing visions, he returns to Palestine to seek the pardon of the Hebronites and the prophets buried in Hebron. As Abu al-Shawarib climbs down into the prophets' burial cave, he is struck dead by the "vengeance of the Fathers."

Nearly all of Shami's stories are concerned with the gradual, tormented downfall of a single individual. "This process represents the condition of all human beings . . . in Palestine and beyond: men and women, young and old, Muslims and Christians, Jews, Ashkenazim and Sephardim, Arabs of different classes from all corners of the country, Bedouin, Turks and Bulgarians."[24] *Vengeance of the Fathers* depicts the gradual downfall of Abu al-Shawarib, a Nablusi notable. Yet what distinguishes this novella from Shami's other works is that hashish plays a crucial role in the protagonist's ultimate demise. As noted, Abu al-Shawarib sinks ever deeper in despair during his exile in Cairo, finding "refuge . . . in the arms of hashish":

> [He] would rush to shut himself up in his room and inhale the amazing and intoxicating smoke, gulp after gulp. Hashish—more than all the amulets and charms given to him by *hajji*s and saintly dervishes—seemed to him to be a sure and effective means of relieving his pains, dulling his afflictions and subduing the endless moments of fear to twilight and slumber. The more he took of this poisonous and malignant drug, the more impaired his health became, and the more his condition worsened.[25]

Shami devotes nearly half of the novella's latter section to portrayals of Abu al-Shawarib's hashish-induced physical and mental disintegration in Cairo's darkest alleys. Hashish makes him violent; he yells obscenities, wails, curses, gets himself involved in senseless brawls; his entire life becomes pointless and hopeless: "Nimr spent his life in idleness and waste, consumed by [hashish] intoxication, debauchery and forgetfulness. Each day seemed like the day before, and each night like the night before. Coffeehouses and music were his entire world, and hashish and card [games] his [only] joy and vision."[26] The pernicious effects of his hashish addiction are such that his vitality disappears, his stamina virtually that of a lifeless being:

> At nights his limbs and muscles were heavy as lead, but he could not shut his eyelids without multiplying his hashish dose. His friends . . . who often

inquired as to his health, would find him stretched out to his full length, motionless, on the mat, his legs spread wide open, his caftan askew and rolled up underneath him, his hairy chest naked, his bleary eyes focusing on a rusty tin oil lamp . . . gazing at it with no expression of life. His lower jaw was dangling and crooked, just like a dead man's.[27]

As observed earlier, Shami wrote about Arab life in Palestine from the viewpoint of an empathetic insider: "Even as he wrote Jewish-Hebrew prose that viewed Arabs as an enemy, a threat to the Zionist enterprise, Shami also seemed deeply committed to giving Arab culture a Hebrew voice."[28] In this sense Shami belonged to those pre-1948 Sephardi Jews in Palestine who came to endorse what Michal Haramati posited as an "alternative Zionist theory," namely "autochthonous Zionism."[29] This position in relation to the subject matter, coupled with a familiarity with the contemporary Arab and Jewish-Arab worlds that he developed while working as a journalist,[30] makes Shami's account of hashish use by Palestinian Arabs of the late Ottoman era highly credible. It is, I believe, no coincidence that Shami did not make Nablus or Hebron, or Jerusalem or Jaffa, the center of hashish use in his fiction. Nor was it sheer poetical choice that prompted Shami to send his protagonist to Cairo—"the promising and alluring city far away"[31]—in order for him to become a hashish addict. It is likely that these preferences derive from the fact that hashish use in Palestine at the turn of the twentieth century was, simply put, a very limited phenomenon.

Although the trans-Levant hashish trade was already up and running by the early 1920s, its effect on hashish consumption in Palestine was not yet seen as alarming. On this point, too, my evidence is circumstantial. It derives from the views of David Tidhar—not, however, the *fictional* "Hebrew detective" we met in the previous chapter, but the real Palestine Police inspector turned private detective, and—more pertinent to my discussion here—author of the first nonfiction book ever written on crime and criminality in interwar Palestine. Titled *Criminals and Crimes in the Land of Israel* (*Hot'im ve-hata'im be-eretz yisrael*), the book was published in 1924 in both Hebrew and English editions.[32]

Among the many criminal activities in Palestine that Tidhar refers to, he hardly mentions hashish use or hashish smuggling as things to be seriously reckoned with. Tidhar begins by enumerating the various ethnic groups (*'edot*) inhabiting Palestine, and each one's unique "penchant" for specific criminal activity. To say that his account is extremely Orientalist would be an understatement. He begins by asserting that the Jews (both those of Eastern European extraction and veteran Sephardim), together with the European inhabitants of Palestine ("the sons of England, France, Germany, Italy, Greece, Russia and so forth") are "the most advanced law-abiding people in the country"; they are "learned" (*yod'ei sefer*) and "cultured" (*ba'lei tarbut*), and "there are hardly any criminals among them."[33] In sharp contrast, Palestinians of most classes and denominations (urbanites and villagers, laborers and peasants, Christians and Muslims, Bedouin and Druze) are, to his mind, "ignorant," "idle," "negligent," "illiterate," "hot-blooded," "deceitful," "innocent of the necessities of culture," "prone to emotions and nervous disorders" (*za'azu'ei 'atsabim*), and "obedient to thugs and fist wielders." Hence, Tidhar claims, they are incorrigible criminals with a vast criminal repertoire: "theft, beating, stabbing and murder," "organ amputation," "arson," "robbery," "daughter kidnapping," and "perjury." Even Christian Arabs, he says, though often "thorough in education," are associated with such criminal activities as "intoxication, bickering, beating, stabbing, embezzlement, forgery, theft and sometimes murder as well."[34]

Tidhar mentions in passing the habit of "hashish smoking and cocaine sniffing" by the Egyptian "rabble" (*'erev*) in Palestine, presumably those who arrived in country in the wake of the British occupation in 1917.[35] Official British reports from the 1920s and early 1930s confirm this observation. Stressing that "the hashish habit" is not widespread in Palestine, these reports still maintain that that hashish (and sometimes cocaine) "may possibly be taken in very small quantities by a very few people and by occasional Egyptians of the laboring classes"; "the majority of addicts [in the country] are of Egyptian origin."[36] Yet, the fact that Tidhar ignores hashish in his lengthy list of illegal activities allegedly perpetrated by local Palestinian Arabs of all descriptions is revealing. It may indicate that in the early 1920s, Palestine's Arab population had not embraced the habit in large numbers, even though by this time the country had already begun to function as a corridor for the Levant hashish trade to Egypt. As will be seen in the next chapter, Mandatory Palestine's Jews, particularly the Zionists among them, were seldom shy of expressing their strong contempt for the habit of hashish smoking by the country's Arabs. They viewed it is a contemptible Oriental vice and—to borrow from David A. Guba in another context—a stereotypical marker of Oriental barbarism.[37] Hence, the fact that Tidhar, a Zionist, did not find cause to condemn hashish use by the territory's Arab population—though he was free and easy in attributing a long list of other illegal vices to them—suggests that in the early 1920s the magnitude of the habit was still limited.

"DISHONEST PLEASURES": HASHISH
CONSUMPTION SINCE THE EARLY 1930S

Nevertheless, hashish consumption increased significantly over the course of the 1930s. As Egyptian demand for Lebanese- and Syrian-grown cannabis multiplied, more and more Egypt-bound consignments of hashish traversed Palestine's territory, with some left behind to service the local market. In 1933 a forensic expert with the Palestine Police CID called attention to the fallout of Palestine's evolution into a critical link in the Levant hashish trade to Egypt, writing: "During its transit through Palestine, a certain amount of hashish is placed on the local markets for home consumption. It is sold [locally] in either pure or adulterated form."[38]

Indeed, it is evident that from the 1930s onward, the hashish-smoking habit gathered momentum, especially in Palestine's urban centers. As Edward Horne, the Palestine Police official historian, reminisced half a century later: "Many hashish addicts smoked the stuff in and around the biggest towns (very rarely so in the villages)."[39] Hence, one can find multiple press reports on the matter in Arabic, Hebrew, and English. Generally anecdotal and lacking in specifics, the reports call attention to increased hashish smoking by Palestinian Arabs and migrant workers from neighboring countries, in Jaffa, Haifa, Jerusalem, Acre, Nablus, and Tiberius.[40] For instance, in 1935 a concerned reader informed the editor of the *Palestine Post* that in Jerusalem there were "not one, but dozens of hashish addicts . . . to be found in the Old City,"[41] and press reports from 1936 estimated that in Jaffa alone, there were "more than 5,000 hashish smokers [indulging in the drug] in seven *special places* (*imkan khasah*), mostly in the Old City."[42] During the same period, men and women were regularly arrested for wandering the streets of these cities in a state of hashish-induced "delirium." For example, "an Arab youngster" riding a bicycle "ran into a wall and was injured. The police took him to the hospital where it was found that he was intoxicated from hashish smoking."[43] Minuscule quantities of hashish were often seized on the persons of individuals: 0.7 grams here, 1.5 grams there, quantities suited to individual use, not large-scale hashish trafficking.[44] On other occasions the drug was "confiscated while it was being smoked."[45]

Who were these hashish smokers, besides being local Palestinian and Arabs from neighboring countries, and what exactly is meant by the "special places" where they indulged in the forbidden drug? As in many other regions around the world, a decisive majority of hashish users in Palestine belonged to what the British described in their reports as "the lower classes" or "the working class."[46] Moreover, possibly in contrast to other British colonial possessions, where the middle classes eschewed and condemned cannabis use, in interwar Palestine at least a few of the burgeoning Arab urban middle classes—which on the eve of the 1936 revolt numbered fifty thousand, the great majority of them Christian[47]—were not adverse to this habit (and sometimes to cocaine-sniffing as well). The middle-class Jerusalemite composer, oud player, poet, and chronicler Wasif Jawhariyyeh and his associates are a case in point, as Salim Tamari explains:

> [Jawhariyyeh's] memoir introduces us to a rich social milieu of postwar Je-rusalem in the early 1920s that could be described as hedonistic. Wasif re-cords numerous occasions of public celebration in the streets of the Old City, marked by musical processions and open consumption of alcohol. . . . Nightly episodes of drinking, dance, and occasional hashish smoking recur during this period. . . . Wasif [would also participate in] . . . intimate parties. . . . Heavy drinking and cannabis enhanced the atmosphere of these evenings.[48]

Urban social venues for smoking hashish included makeshift "hashish dens," sometimes called "hashish-smoking clubs" (*klubim shel me'ashnei hashish*), located in rundown neighborhoods.[49] Aside from card-playing and the smoking of hookahs and cigarettes containing hashish mixed with tobacco,[50] we don't really know very much about what actually happened in these establishments. This is in stark contrast to graphic and fanciful accounts of what transpired in hashish dens in 1950s and 1960s Israel—as we will see in chapter 6.

Be that as it may, hashish dens were not the main venues of hashish smoking in interwar Palestine; like elsewhere in the Arab, Ottoman, and Iranian Middle East, the coffeehouse was the place for it. This is not surprising. A Middle East-ern invention, coffeehouses first appeared in the Ottoman Empire and Safavid Iran in the sixteenth and seventeenth centuries (more than a century before their inception in Europe), and soon emerged as urban venues for new kinds of sociability and new patterns of public conviviality.[51] One of the main reasons cited in explaining this development is that in the coffeehouse, patrons could socialize in a leisurely manner while enjoying various stimulants at the same time. Coffee and tobacco were the most natural pairing. As Jordan Goodman notes, "In contrast to the use of tobacco as a supplement to betel in India and south-east Asia, in the Near East tobacco was clearly associated with coffee and with the coffeehouse."[52] The following observation by Rudolph Matthee, about the intimate link between tobacco and coffee in Safavid Iran, could just as easily have been made about the Ottoman Empire:

> It is tempting to see a causal link between the quick acceptance of tobacco and the near simultaneous introduction of coffee in Iran. . . . To be sure, both became important accessories to life in Iran, each other's pendant, so to say, in that tobacco calms while coffee stimulates.[53]

Probably more than anything else, it was the water pipe (*huqqah, qalyan, nargileh*)—first popularized in India or Iran in the early seventeenth century, then rapidly transported westward to the Ottoman Middle East—that brought together coffee and tobacco in the coffeehouse: "Relatively bulky and time-consuming in its preparations, the water pipe was nonetheless perfect for the most relaxed venues, such as the coffeehouse or bathhouse, where patrons and their employees were always on hand to bring more tobacco and replenish burning coals."[54] Incidentally, the fact that in the Middle East these two stimulants (coffee and tobacco) were intimately linked and consumed together is reflected in the expression that one "drank" one's tobacco—a phrase used by Middle Easterners even today.[55]

Tobacco enabled intoxicants such as opium and cannabis, until then consumed mainly by ingestion, to be smoked as well.[56] This explains why the convergence of opium and the native Amerindian pipe is considered "one of the most evil cultural exchanges in history."[57] As elsewhere in the world, tobacco smoking in the Middle East turned drug taking from an individual and solitary concern performed in moderation into a sociable and communal affair in which opium and cannabis could be consumed in excess: "Throughout the Middle East, tobacco emboldened a growing leisure culture that, now armed with pipe and hookah, inadvertently liberated illicit drugs such as hashish, which made their own unwelcome debut in public."[58]

Rudi Matthee suggests that the rapid acceptance of tobacco and the concurrent development of the water pipe in the Middle East may have derived from "former habits of hallucinogenic drug-taking."[59] This may explain, in part, why hashish and opium smoking became one of the most practiced and cherished activities in Middle Eastern, Ottoman, and Iranian coffeehouses.[60] But at the same time, this very pastime dealt a serious blow to the reputation of these institutions.[61] That these same coffeehouses also came to be identified with a variety of other improper activities—including gambling, pederasty, prostitution, and frivolous sexuality in general—did not help their reputation much either.[62]

To be fair, such reservations regarding Middle Eastern coffeehouses were not always fair or reliable. Indeed, cafés in eighteenth- and nineteenth-century Istanbul, Cairo, Jaffa, or Aleppo were not necessarily wanton or disreputable spaces. Rather, they were "places of business and leisure, an extension of the street or market, a venue of entertainment, a space of courtship, an arena of communication, a place in which to read and a realm of distraction."[63] Yet it cannot be denied that since the sixteenth century, drug taking had been one of the most unseemly pleasures offered by the coffeehouses of the Ottoman Empire and Iran.[64] These circumstances, in turn, reinforced European presumptions about the "luxurious, effeminate, and corrupt nature of oriental societies."[65] With the transition to modernity, the association of these institutions with drug consumption also became the target for severe denunciation by the indigenous middle classes, who viewed them as the epitome of uncivility and retrogression. Hence, in late-nineteenth-century Egypt, for example, 'Ali Mubarak—quint-essential representative of the West-emulative Ottoman-Egyptian elite—de-scribed Egyptian cafés as "the source of numerous infections and diseases, and a refuge for the unemployed and the indolent, especially in those places noted for the consumption of hashish."[66]

To underscore the miserable state of the hashish-infested Egyptian cafés, Mubarak compared them to the cafés he had visited in France.[67] Indeed, coffee, much like cannabis, is a substance of "Oriental" origin with clear psychoactive properties.[68] However, and in contrast to cannabis, coffee drinking had been fully indigenized in Europe, despite the controversy and opposition it initially aroused there as it did everywhere else—so much so that by the eighteenth century coffee had been identified as "the great soberer,"[69] a beverage befitting bourgeoisie virtues of temperance, respectability, rationality and entrepreneur-ship—leading to the proliferation of coffeehouses as institutions enshrining these virtues.[70] In this way, coffee culture reinforced the bourgeois disasso-ciation from both the local working classes (getting drunk on alcohol) and colonial subjects (getting high on exotic drugs), while retaining the pleasures that otherwise would have been squandered by it:

> Coffee offered a new social beverage which could be drunk in public settings in a manner akin to alcoholic beverages like ales, beers, or wines, but it could be consumed without fear of consequent intoxication. Furthermore, it had the

added appeal of other exotic, mind-altering substances, but without the fear-ful associations with unreason and illicit sexuality that plagued many of the other foreign drugs that [European] travelers and virtuosi introduced to their countrymen. Coffee drinking ultimately came to be seen as associated with sober and civil conduct and as such it became a key part of an ethic of "re-spectable" behavior shared by both the middling and elite classes.[71]

The emergence of coffeehouse culture in late Ottoman Palestine, and its ex-pansion during the interwar period, has received at least exploratory scholarly attention.[72] It is my contention that this expansion of coffeehouse culture in the interwar period can be linked to the emergence of Palestine as a major depot of hashish commodities in the Levant, as discussed previously. Indeed, it may not have been a coincidence that the recreational activities that became a part of coffeehouse life in Palestine included—in addition to small-scale gambling (cards, dominoes), the performance of music, and prostitution—the sale and consumption of tobacco and hashish.[73] As elsewhere in the Levant, the "trans-gressive nature" of these coffeehouses was particularly conspicuous in port cities like Jaffa and Haifa as well as in other localities, albeit to a lesser extent.[74] The unscrupulous, even promiscuous disposition of these establishments can be clearly seen in a contemporary police report about Café Baghdadi, one of the many cafés that operated at the time in Jaffa's Manshiyyeh Quarter:

> Without a doubt this place is the main attraction of [the Quarter]. All hours of the day it is crowded with very shady characters who sit and gamble, play-ing all manner of card games and dominoes. . . . Many women, undoubtedly prostitutes, gather in the café and hang about, passing from table to table.[75]

That hashish was served to patrons in these cafés in the early 1930s is certain. Hence, we know about "certain low-class cafés" in Jaffa, Haifa, Jerusalem, Acre, and Nablus that offered their clients hashish for recreational use, either openly or stealthily; and that in 1939 even cafés in the heart of Tel Aviv were serving hashish to their *Jewish* clients,[76] though "drugs occupied the margins of [Jew-ish] society [in Palestine], and . . . were seen as rare phenomena . . . of [Jewish] urban life."[77]

Whatever the case, it is certain that hashish-serving cafés were a thorn in the side of the British authorities in Palestine. This likely explains why café patrons and café owners were regularly arrested for hashish smoking and/or possession;[78] and why, from the 1930s onward, the police conducted repeated, coordinated raids on cafés across several cities.[79] That these hashish-smoking venues concerned the British authorities can also be gleaned from the Dangerous Drugs Ordinance issued by the government of Palestine in 1936. Article 14 of the ordinance, which had not featured in the previous ordinances of 1925, 1928, and 1932, was intended to contend with a previously unknown situation, "offences in connection with premises used for sale or smoking of opium of hashish"; in other words, recreational hashish smoking in cafés and other spaces designated for this activity.[80] The new article outlawed the use of these "premises . . . for the purpose of the preparation of opium or hashish for smoking," and the possession of "any pipes or other utensils for use in connection with the smoking of opium or hashish."[81]

Hashish was also smoked during religious celebrations in Mandatory Palestine. The annual festival (*mawsim*) at the shrine (*maqam*) of Nabi (Prophet) Rubin (Reuben, son of the biblical patriarch Jacob)—located some nine miles south of Jaffa, and desecrated during and after 1948[82]—is a good example of this. This event was one of two major celebrations staged by Palestine's Arab Muslim population during the period, the other being the annual spring festival of Nabi Musa, discussed at the beginning of this chapter. Both celebrations date back to the twelfth century, when the Ayyubids sought to mobilize the rural and urban populations of central Palestine against the Crusaders.[83] Over the course of the nineteenth century, Nabi Rubin became a predominantly urban celebration, Jaffa and Jaffaites taking an increasingly leading role and transforming it into a secular happening no less than a religious one: "The popular traditional festival creatively adapted to the diktat of modernity, without either tradition or modernity prevailing over the other," Salim Tamari observes.[84]

It is not surprising, then, that with the onset of the Mandatory period, the Nabi Rubin celebration embraced a relaxed and uninhibited social milieu, and was as much a summer resort as a religious festival.[85] With the festival commencing with the August new moon,

most families would spend two to three weeks at Rubin, in elaborate tents. . . . Ringing the residential tents were makeshift markets, cafés, restaurants, bands of entertainers, theaters, and outdoor cinemas. During the day, horse and camel races . . . took place on the outer ring. At night, live entertainment competed with radios and phonographs. . . . A daily repertoire of plays, musical concerts, and motion pictures was presented. Performers were local musicians and singers, but their ranks also included singers and players from Egypt and Lebanon.[86]

The festivities were not without expressions of permissiveness, which is where hashish usually came into play. In 1933, for instance, the police forbade café owners at the festival from permitting gambling and the sale of alcoholic drinks and drugs on their premises.[87] One indication that café owners did not necessarily pay heed to these warnings—that the vices of some festival participants "did not take a holiday at Rubin"[88]—can be found in 'Iton Meyuhad, a right-leaning Jewish tabloid founded in 1933. A story carried in the paper during the 1934 festival alleged that

> one of the [festival's] tents is used as a café for spending time in honest pleasures [sha'shu'im ksherim], but those who wish to indulge in dishonest pleasures can do that as well. Not far from the tent of the police, who are responsible for the eradication of hashish in the country, a few young men were sitting in the café tent smoking hashish surreptitiously. Each would order a hookah, and offer it to his companions for a toke.[89]

'Iton Meyuhad, with its eye for the sensational, was never known for its credible reporting.[90] However, a reporter from Davar—the mouthpiece of mainstream Zionism's labor movement, and the most popular Hebrew-language newspaper in interwar Palestine—who attended the festival in the same year (1934), returned with similar impressions:

> Our host, a sailor with broad shoulders and a pleasant face, his eyes radiating the wisdom of the experienced, greets us with the customary calls of "Welcome." This coastal man, his livelihood dependent on the sea and the port, arrives in [Nabi] Rubin ahead of time. He sets up a quadrangular and spacious tent, bringing the necessary tools for a bayt qahwa [coffeehouse], from short stools . . . to long hookahs. . . . In a remote corner, hidden behind a screen, one can also find those intoxicating leaves which demand concealment. This is "the weed" (hashish); each and every painful drag on which precipitates heart palpitations [and] grants its owner one of the sixty heavenly rewards promised to "believers."[91]

My discussion thus far proposes that Palestine's transformation into a critical link in Egypt's hashish supply chain spawned a significant increase in hashish use by its Arab working-class population, among whom recreational consumption of this drug had previously not been commonplace. However, it can be suggested that even at the heights of this phenomenon in the 1930s and 1940s, the practice remained comparatively limited in scope despite its upward trajectory. This conclusion can be cautiously ascertained by taking note of two types of silence. With the first, it is telling that the upward trend in hashish smoking was not reflected in any of the official British reports. On the contrary, throughout the interwar period the British stated persistently, year after year in report after report using nearly identical phrasing, that drug abuse was not a serious problem in Palestine. In the 1920s ("There is little evidence of drug addiction in Palestine"),[92] the 1930s ("There are still no indications that Palestine is becoming a market for the consumption of narcotic drugs"),[93] and the 1940s ("The number of [hashish] consumers in the country is not great"),[94] the British repeatedly and consistently emphasized that the use of drugs of any kind was not a pressing issue in their mandated territory. Although they were not oblivious to the fact that "the most common of such drugs in this country is hashish" (and to a much lesser extent, opium as well), they invariably took care to qualify this assertion by stating that "hashish addicts are few" and that hashish is "smoked [only] by a few of the lower classes."[95] In his memoir, former Palestine Police CID commander Joseph Broadhurst put it most clearly and succinctly, stating that "Palestine herself has no dope problem."[96]

Why did the British remain silent about the surge in hashish smoking in interwar Palestine? It could be that the British were being deliberately disingenuous in these reports, since "to acknowledge [the] prevalence [of hashish smoking in Palestine] would have been tantamount to admitting British failure to control illegal drug trafficking."[97] But, as shown in the previous chapter, the British never did have a problem about admitting their failure in drug enforcement; they freely conceded that in general, they never succeeded in confiscating any more than 10 percent of the hashish consignments passing through the country into Egypt. Liat Kozma alludes to another possibility for this silence in her study of prostitution in the Middle East and North Africa: League of Nations reports issued by the authorities of the French and British Mandate states either ignored or denied the phenomenon of woman trafficking in their territories. Kozma suggests that this denial may be explained by a common assumption among colonial officials at the time: "that there was something unique about the sexuality of indigenous women in . . . the Levant that made them different and thus irrelevant from the perspective of international law."[98] This may apply to hashish smokers in Palestine as well, whom colonial officials—as will be seen in chapter 4—considered to be different and eccentric, and for whom hashish intoxication seemed to work differently (i.e., more perilously) than for Europeans.

Another plausible answer to the British silence may be connected to the issue of comparability. Simply put, compared to what the British had experienced in India and Egypt, the hashish problem in Palestine seemed minor. Although hashish consumption must have been bothersome to Palestine's law enforcement agencies, it rarely, if at all, matched the gravity of the drug situation attributed by the British to their Indian and Egyptian "subject races," known as cannabis-oriented peoples—the first since ancient times, the latter since the Middle Ages. My contention is that the effects of even the most excessive cases of hashish consumption in Palestine were seen by the British as negligible in comparison to what they were obliged to contend with in India and Egypt.[99] Moreover, it is certain that the problem of hashish consumption in Palestine was inconsequential not only in comparison to Egypt or India, Britain's other colonial possessions, but also in comparison to the problem of the border-crossing flows of hashish across Palestine's territory, as discussed in the previous chapter. "Much more [hashish] is conveyed from Syria and the Lebanon for the disposal in Egypt than is consumed in the country," as the British pointed out.[100]

That hashish use in interwar Palestine may very well have been comparatively limited in scope—even when taking into account an undoubted upward trajectory—can also be ascertained, albeit with caution, by the silences in Palestinian public discourse. In Egypt, "a growing indigenous bureaucracy, an emerging medical profession, educated in Egypt itself, and a growing middle class, the *effendiya*, produced its own debates on hashish prohibition." These were published in several sites, including the local press.[101] This is understandable, given that drug users practically everywhere have been "an object of elites' concerns in the political game of disciplining, modernization and public order."[102] In Palestine, however, there is no evidence to suggest an organized or systematic (Arab) middle-class preoccupation with the dangers of hashish abuse. As a matter of fact, though Palestine's Arabic-language press carried regular reports about seizures of cannabis consignments and the arrest and prosecution of hashish offenders, I have found just one editorial commenting on the phenomenon of drug consumption and its harmful effect on Palestinian society.[103] This resounding silence perhaps indicates that the representatives of the Palestinians and their middle-class spokespersons under the mandate—who, like their Egyptian counterparts, have been "characterized as bourgeois and educated, similarly to bourgeois classes that have developed in the West in the modern era"[104]—did not consider the smoking of hashish in Palestine as a serious problem. This difference may be linked to the fact that, whereas members of the middle classes in the interwar Middle East usually played central roles in national movements,[105] in Palestine, where middle-class members were predominantly Christian, they remained aloof from the national movement, fearing, among other things, the prospect of an independent Palestinian Arab state dominated by Muslims.[106] Tellingly, even a commentator for *Davar* reproached the Palestinian middle classes for remaining silent on the issue of hashish smoking by their country's brethren:

> The Arab intelligentsia should have been the vanguard of the fight against this vice. They pretend to be the brethren of their people, and they should have been doing what the Chinese intelligentsia have done. The latter realized long ago that China could not be saved as long as opium is not eradicated in the country. . . . But the Arab intelligentsia in Palestine have not lifted a finger against such intoxication [*shikhrut*]. Those who read [Palestine's] Arab press regularly tell us that they cannot recall even a single article against hashish and opium.[107]

The author concluded by complaining about what the British themselves have acknowledged, namely that "the Government of Palestine has not been very effective in the war against intoxicating drugs.[108]

CONCLUSION

This chapter began with a celebration of the Nabi Musa festival in the late Ottoman period, as recounted in Yitzhak Shami's 1927 novella *Vengeance of the Fathers*. It advanced toward its end with accounts of the Nabi Rubin festival in 1930s Palestine. The two accounts are indicative of the great transformation in the culture of recreational hashish smoking in Palestine, a transformation that occurred in the interval between the late Ottoman period and the 1930s. From the first, it is possible to conclude that hashish consumption in Palestine on the eve of World War I was marginal; the second suggests that by the 1930s, hashish smoking may have been a very common practice among the country's urban working-class Arab population. The source of this transformation, I argue, is the evolution of the trans-Levant hashish trade between Lebanon-Syria and Egypt, with Palestine serving as a critical link between the two territories.

Indeed, contrary to nineteenth- and twentieth-century Orientalist representations, the consumption of hashish in late-Ottoman-era Palestine was negligible. But this state changed dramatically over the course of the Mandatory period, due to the territory's emergence as a way station in the burgeoning hashish trade unfolding across the Lebanon-Palestine-Egypt axis. With some of the Egypt-bound supplies left behind to service the local market, access to and the availability of hashish led to a significant rise in hashish use, mainly by the territory's urban working-class Arab population. By the 1930s, hashish smoking had spread through Palestine's towns and cities, and venues for consumption—makeshift hashish dens, coffeehouses, brothels—proliferated.

Conspicuously missing from the sources, and probably from drug-smoking activities in Mandatory Palestine as well, were the country's Jews: veteran Sephardim and Ashkenazim, as well as Eastern European immigrants. To get to the bottom of this abstention, I now turn to explore the relationship between hashish drug culture and the country's Jews before 1948.

4

JEWS AND INTERWAR ORIENTAL FANTASIES

RECENT SCHOLARSHIP GIVES rich context and detail to the political, social, and cultural interactions between Jews and their Arab neighbors in Mandate-era Palestine. These interactions were, at the least, as commonly established as the level of conflict and friction that existed between them.[1] Veteran Sephardi Jews in particular shared the customs and traditions of their fellow Palestinian Arabs, and inhabited the very same "Semitic or Levantine surroundings and context."[2] This position enabled them to function as vital and constructive mediators between Arabs and Jews and transcend the national divide between the two communities—a position that Eastern European Jewish immigrants to Palestine, the *Moscobim*, generally lacked the predisposition to fulfill. As Hillel Cohen explains, in reference to Jewish-Arab relations in Jaffa and Tel Aviv during the 1920s:

> Relations between Jaffa's long-standing Jewish population and its Arabs were not ideal, but they were smooth enough because of the groups' shared cultural background. The immigrants from Russia disturbed that harmony. They did not observe local mores. In addition, their arrival aroused fears that the Jews were trying to take over the country and push out the Arabs.[3]

It would seem, however, that in matters concerning hashish use and smuggling, the Jewish population, old-timers and new immigrants alike, seldom interacted with Palestine's Arab population. This chapter starts off by asking why this was the case. By exploring the public discourse of Palestine's burgeoning Jewish community, I demonstrate that the underlying reason for this nearly universal Jewish abstention was the fear of accommodating an "alien" Oriental artifact—hashish—in much the same way that the white middle classes in the United States of the time were wary of marijuana, because of its association with "alien" Mexicans and blacks.[4] In other words, during the first decades of Zionism, Jews largely refrained from hashish smoking—partly due to its awful reputation as an "Arab" vice, and partly due to the idea that hashish use would put the Zionist project in danger of submerging in the Levantine environment.

I then move on to show the extent to which colonial presuppositions—framed as empirical knowledge—about cannabis were instrumental in confirming these Jewish concerns. This knowledge was introduced to Palestine from three main sites: India and Egypt, where the British had long contended with cannabis-oriented cultures; and the Geneva-based League of Nations, where colonial experts produced, debated, and exchanged knowledge about cannabis throughout the interwar period. Coupled with Orientalist fantasies of various kinds (such as the myth of the medieval Assassins or *hashishiyyin*), this knowledge molded hashish into a distinctively racialized Oriental drug, capable of animating the supposed pathologies inherent in the mentality of Oriental peoples—including inordinate and excessive (homo)sexuality, irrationality, insanity, indolence, and manipulability. To demonstrate this, I will focus on proceedings of the League of Nations Subcommittee on Cannabis between 1934 and 1939, which had been commissioned to undertake an extensive study of several issues related to the drug and its intoxicating qualities. It was through this knowledge, alongside other considerations, that Palestine's Jews made sense of cannabis products, and thus viewed them as an epitome of Oriental savagery.

ZIONIST PUBLIC DISCOURSE ON HASHISH

> *In agonies of delight*
> *I hover 'twixt death and resurrection*
> *Waves of resonating brass*
> *Cascading from the chapel's summit*
> *My spirit ebbs, my body's strength all spent*
> *My mind sinks, sleep no-sleep*
> *The peal of bells*

Like a thundering sentence in my ear.
Untouched, a silver fire burns
and into the arms of a formless nymph
a dream of naked shame pulls
me to the cradle of torment
and, in the intoxicating madness,
bids me: "Come"—and I make haste

The above poem, titled simply "Hashish," was penned by none other than Ze'ev Jabotinsky (aka Vladimir Yevgenyevich), the renowned Russian Jewish Revisionist Zionist leader, author, poet, orator, soldier—and founder of several militant Jewish organizations in Palestine.[5] Jabotinsky probably wrote this poem in 1901, when he was a law student at the Sapienza University of Rome. As can be gleaned from the text, in the poem he recreates a personal mind-altering experience resulting from taking hashish, a vice he was probably conversant with as a young man in the Europe of the time.

Admittedly, Jabotinsky's hashish poem may not be the most appropriate starting point for a discussion of hashish and Jews in Mandatory Palestine, and may even be misleading. Jabotinsky's experimentation with hashish would have taken place in early-twentieth-century Europe, at a time when Jews in Palestine (and elsewhere too), as well as Europeans in general, shunned the drug altogether, because of its Oriental connotations and alleged links to violent frenzy and insanity (see below).[6] That is to say, Jabotinsky's hashish adventures were not in keeping with the leisure habits of either his European contemporaries or his Jewish compatriots in Palestine and beyond.

At the time when Jabotinsky had supposedly ingested or smoked the drug, Ottoman Palestine was in the throes of the "Second Aliyah," the immigration of about 35,000 Jews, most from the Russian Empire. They were followed by more immigrants from Eastern and Western Europe during the period of British rule in Palestine, such that the Jewish population of Palestine ballooned from 56,000 people in the wake of World War I to 650,000 by the end of the Mandate period in 1948. On the eve of the 1948 War, the number of non-Jews residing in Palestine was approximately 1,267,000.

On the whole, I argue, the Jewish population stayed clear of hashish. First of all, there were Zionist values to be considered. Intoxication by drugs did not sit well with a movement that valorized the virtues of abstemious frontier pioneering and Hebrew labor; "It was working the land, and hence reworking one's presumably weak diasporic body and soul, that formed the material and symbolic crux of 'practical' Zionism," Cyrus Schayegh maintains.[7] The "new Jews" were supposed to take responsibility for the nation's destiny. If they succumbed to the rich repertoire of diversions available in the Palestine of the time, there was a risk that they would neglect their national duties and drift into hedonism and licentiousness—clearly antithetical to the puritanical objectives of the Zionist endeavor.[8]

Augmenting Jewish aversion to hashish was the fear of overassimilation into the Orient. I emphasize *over*assimilation, because Zionist attitudes toward the Orient were laced with tensions and contradictions. Despite their rejection of the Orient per se, some of its tropes held a certain attraction for pre-1948 Zionists. For instance, they were fascinated with the image of the Bedouins as noble warriors and sought to emulate them, and they contemplated the life of the *fellahin* as a window onto biblical times. In short, before 1948, many Zionists viewed the Orient not simply as enemy territory, but also as a utopian space of possibility for Jewish renewal.[9]

What is more the tendency to keep away from anything "Oriental" conflicted with the habits and traditions of the Sephardi members of the "old Jewish settlement," as well as those among them who embraced Zionism early on: "The effect of Arab culture on the recreational patterns of [Jewish] women and men . . . was seen in Sephardi communal parties in the singing and dancing, but also in additional aspects, such as the way of sitting, the food and drink that was served, and in hookah smoking."[10] The same attitudes manifested in mundane issues as culinary preferences. Dafna Hirsch argues that Jews discovered hummus—the popular Levantine dip and spread—in the late Mandate period; they introduced it into their cuisine because they considered it part of a repertoire of Arab food purportedly capable of consolidating "an authentic tie to the land." Moreover, beginning in the late 1950s, hummus was gradually "nationalized," its Arab identity suppressed, with Jewish immigrants from Middle Eastern countries acting as intermediaries.[11]

For the Jews of Palestine, however, the social life of hashish was perceived in a totally different light. The use of hashish amounted to an extreme act of border-crossing between Jews and Arabs, one that would take them too far down the road of Orientalization and expose them to the social danger of turning into Arabs. The historian Ofri Ilany recently demonstrated how, during the Mandatory period, the "'contraction' of sodomy by Jews, and particularly by European Zionists, [was] described as an especially severe symptom of ideological laxity and the 'harming effect' of the Arab environment."[12] Like sodomy, hashish smoking manifested as "a form of backwardness linked to living among Arabs in the Middle East,"[13] to borrow Ilany's formulation; it was a vice that would expose Jewish bodies most perilously to the temptations of an alien space.[14] Besides, during the same period, both drug users and observers in Europe and the United States conceptualized drug taking as something "feminine"; this too might have threatened the masculine perception of the "new Jew" in Palestine.[15] As will be seen immediately, that is why hashish dens, coffeehouses, and brothels, where Arabs and Jews could comingle and assimilate while sharing a hashish-filled cigarette or a hookah, were construed as a national-political threat. That these venues were also signaled out as disreputable places of (homo) sexual conduct is not coincidental.[16]

Examples of this can be gleaned from Hebrew-language detective or crime fiction set in interwar Palestine. As I showed in chapter 2, this genre—in Palestine as elsewhere—provided radicalized or dramatized versions of real criminal activities in Palestine, activities which Zionist historiography tends to downplay or ignore. Given that this body of Hebrew-language detective fiction was published during the formative phase of the Jewish colonization of Palestine and escalating conflict with the Palestinians, it also embodied the Zionist nationalist ethos in its most pristine form.[17] Hence, this literary genre prescribed the kinds of behavior that would be acceptable from a Jewish nationalist point of view, and the kinds of behavior which would not. In Hebrew crime fiction, hashish smoking was definitely not considered an acceptable pastime.

To exemplify this, let us return to the fictional figure of David Tidhar, "the first Hebrew detective," and to his pursuit of a 1930s Levant-based European hashish smuggling gang, already examined in chapter 2. Tidhar's investigation leads him to a "hashish den" in an Arab quarter of Haifa's lower city. He is escorted there by an interlocutor of sorts, who guides him through an intricate maze of narrow, winding, seemingly orderless, "Arab" alleys.[18] Tidhar's fictional journey through these streets brings to mind Gustave Flaubert's sense of disorientation while touring the streets of Cairo in 1850, as described by Timothy Mitchell: "The disorienting experience of a Cairo street . . . with its arguments in unknown languages, strangers who brush past in strange clothes, unusual colors and unfamiliar sounds and smells, is expressed [by Flaubert] as an absence of pictorial order."[19]

Arriving at the entrance to a hashish den, the escort knocks on the door with a secret tap; it opens, "swallowing Tidhar into its open mouth." Once inside, he spies "an old Arab man with a black beard, who scrutinized him with a penetrating gaze under the dark glow of a lamp" (p. 26). The interior was unclean and unwelcoming: Tidhar "walked through a narrow and foul-smelling corridor and entered a wide-open room. The room was dim and he could not make out anything" (ibid.). As Tidhar's eyes adjust to the darkness, he makes out the pitiable condition of the den's Arab clientele:

> Various people were either sitting down or lying down; others were smoking hookahs, and the rest were lying motionlessly as if dead. Their lips mumbled meaningless broken words and syllables, their faces glowing with silly smiles.... Within two hours all the guests were fast asleep. The only sounds were fleeting words and unintelligible roars coming out of the sleeping men's mouths (ibid.).

A fictional account this may be, but it does bear the air of verisimilitude. By the same token, it shares characteristics present in observational portrayals of the Turkish hashish dens of the period, which suggests the existence of a shared Eastern Mediterranean hashish culture. Note the resemblance between these excerpts from the Tidhar story and the following description of an Istanbul hashish den, provided by a League of Nations cannabis expert in the late 1930s:

> The addict gives a password on coming in, greets the company and sits down. While coffee is being served, the hashish cigarettes, pipe . . . or nargileh, are prepared. . . . The pipe passes from . . . mouth to mouth, and as he puffs, each smoker sinks deep into his dreams and illusions; there is no conversation and not a word is heard except an occasional courteous request to the owner of the premises for some small service. An hour or two is spent in this way. . . . The smoker's eyes remain open, but he is wholly absorbed in dreams and visions which seem to come to life in an oneiric delirium or hallucination.[20]

Returning to the subject at hand, to further dissuade Jews from becoming hashish users "like the Arabs," Zionist public discourse drew on contemporary (i.e,. interwar-period) colonial knowledge about cannabis. Interspersed with Oriental fantasies, this knowledge branded cannabis as a specifically Oriental substance, its unique intoxicant qualities *racially* compatible with the ascribed pathological mentality of Arabs, and theirs only. I will explore this issue of co-lonial knowledge about cannabis in more detail in the next section. But for the sake of momentarily putting the cart before the horse, take for example Dr. Jules Bouquet, inspector of pharmacies in Tunis Hospitals, and a leading member of the League's Subcommittee on Cannabis (about which I will also elaborate in the next section). Bouquet "confirmed" that cannabis use by Orientals aroused their (homo)sexual potency, driving them to violent frenzy, but at the same time purportedly explained their indolence and manipulability.[21] This is yet another example of interwar colonialism's presumption that "colonized men could be . . . docile and effeminate or alternatively . . . barbaric and violent—and thus incapable of self-rule."[22]

Interwar Zionist discourse reproduced these ideas, at the same time adapting them to local circumstances. A 1938 editorial in the Hebrew-language daily *Davar* exemplified this point.[23] Like others of its kind, the commentary was published at the height of the 1936–39 Palestinian Arab Revolt, commonly considered "the most significant anticolonial insurgency in the Arab East during the interwar period."[24] This revolt had three underlying causes: the Arab peasantry's economic hardships and distress caused by the Great Depression of the 1930s, their disillusionment with the Palestinian leadership, and continued Jewish immigration into Palestine.[25] The commentary writer's primary objective, however, was to deride the revolt, and to reduce its myriad causes and motivations into one overarching cause: "Oriental intoxication or poisoning, intergenerational and on a massive scale, by means of Oriental drugs [*samim mizrahiyim*]," hashish and opium.[26] To develop his case, the writer enumerated the putative effects of the hashish "venom" on Oriental peoples. First, he claimed, hashish "begets powerful erotic feelings and, generally speaking, it increases sexual drives and sexual activity." Then he added:

> The Oriental woman was invariably compelled to fight to have a share in her husband-master [*ba'lah-adonah*], so she could engage in sexual intercourse with him and bring him gratification. [This is why she served him] "love elixirs" and "love herbs" that were essentially erotic stimulants [made of cannabis]. . . . These women can testify to the many diabolic acts done to them [under the influence of these drugs]. . . . Because of this effect, hashish is very common in Egypt; and the gates of heaven would open up forever and without limits for the man who takes pleasure in this effect.[27]

Second, the commentary continued, hashish induced violent insanity; it begat "angry behavior which can easily reach brutal and fearless aggression." The hashish user was "easily given to boiling rage or homicide, with remarkable cold-heartedness." This was because hashish "stuns [his] mind," "weakens or destroys his recognition of reality," and neutralized the "natural and social inhibitions" without which there could be no civilized and rational life to speak of.[28] And third, hashish "increases suggestibility"; the "chronic" hashish smoker "becoming a man stripped of all willpower," "a blind tool in the service of anyone seeking to manipulate him." The writer concluded: "Logic dictates that the man [who takes hashish] will follow whoever wants to lead him, and will accept whatever he is being told and demanded."[29]

Note that excessive sexuality, irrational frenzy, and manipulability were among the character traits assigned to Muslim and Arab peoples by classic Orientalist discourse, irrespective of hashish use. This may be why the writer made sure to add: "In and of itself, Oriental intoxication on a massive scale cannot produce visions or historical events from scratch. It can only magnify that which already exists or is in the process of coming into being."[30] In other words, the effects of hashish were conflated with the blinkered manner in which Jews already viewed Arab Palestinians.

At this point, the author of the commentary paused in order to recount the history-cum-myth of the Shiite Nizaris, the so-called Assassins. Beginning in the 1090s, they waged active struggle against Sunni enemies—mainly the Seljuk sultanate, but occasionally the Crusaders as well. Known for their acts of spectacular violence—"the most terrifying ever seen" until that time[31]—they were referred to as *fida'yyin* ("devotees" or "'those who sacrifice themselves"). Their story was picked up locally in the Levant by the Crusaders and their European observers. The story of the Assassins was first popularized in Europe by Marco Polo's fourteenth-century travelogue, *Livre des merveilles du monde*, amplified by a chain of European transmitters; later still, it was definitively anchored as canon by the spate of scholarly treatises on the sect published during the seventeenth and eighteenth centuries across Europe, particularly in France.[32]

In 1809, Silvestre de Sacy, the most prominent French philologist and Orientalist of his time, established an etymological connection between the word "assassins" and the Arabic designation of *hashishiyyin* ("hashish eaters") for the Nizaris. Hence, he was able to identify an unspecified "intoxicating potion" mentioned by Marco Polo as hashish, and argued decisively that the sect's leaders had given their disciples hashish so as to indoctrinate them into committing savage acts of murder. In the process, de Sacy embraced Marco Polo's account, but added his own original contribution to it in the form of a "'secret garden of paradise," where bodily pleasures were supposedly procured for the would-be *fida'yyin* by their mischievous and beguiling leader, the Old Man, with the aid of hashish, as part of their indoctrination and training.[33] It is hard to overemphasize the impact of de Sacy's theory: as a result of his prominent, indeed dominant, academic stature,[34] his conclusions about the medieval Nizaris and their etymological connection to and devious use of hashish "offered France's and [the international] scholarly community certified 'facts' about the Orient *and* hashish that . . . scholars, scientists, and policymakers absorbed, echoed, and built upon for centuries."[35]

It may now be easier to appreciate the purposes for which the *Davar* commentary incorporated the Assassins myth in general, and Marco Polo's account of it in particular. For one, it tied together in one neat package the *Davar* writer's reminder to his Jewish compatriots that hashish use was an age-old *Oriental* vice, one that induced raging madness, manipulability, and unbridled sexuality. Consider the following passage from the commentary, which seems to have been lifted directly from Marco Polo's account:

> Not far from the order's fortress, in a beautiful valley, a fine castle was built, in which [the Old Man] set up a traditional Muslim paradise. [He would] drug those who wished to join the order's army, until they were rendered unconscious. [The Old Man would then] bring [the would-be assassins] into the fortress. There, they would spend a few days with young female virgins [*huri-yot*]. Intoxicating them once again to utter unconsciousness, [the Old Man] would return them to the filthy world [of reality], where [once awakened] they would sing the praises of all the pleasures that were made accessible to them. . . . At an opportune time, they would be told that in order to return to paradise indefinitely, they would have to fulfill one mission for "The Man of the Mountains."[36]

Secondly, it enabled the contemporary Jewish writer to draw a direct line of irrationality between the *hashishiyyin* of old and the insurgents of the 1936–39 Arab Revolt, thus relegating the ongoing Palestinian insurgency to the domain of hashish-induced frenzy (i.e., one lacking rational or realistic justification):

> The bloody clashes of 1936 and their persistence provide faithful evidence of the intimate link between [the Arab gangs] and hashish in the country. . . . After all we have said about the "hashishiyyin," there is no doubt in my mind [of this link]. . . . While half of the gangs in the country come from the outside

[Transjordan, Syria, Egypt, and Iraq], the remaining half are the people of hashish and similar intoxicating drugs.[37]

Another *Davar* commentary, published in 1937, makes more explicit this claimed link between the Palestinian rebels and the Assassins legend. Titled "The Causes of the Clashes' Resumption," it identified rampant hashish use among Palestinian Arabs as one such cause. In particular, the writer referred to the "terrorist gang[s] inspired by 'Izz al-Din al-Qassam," the Syrian political refugee and one of the first leaders of armed resistance in the history of modern Palestine, who was killed by the British in 1935 in the events leading up to the Palestinian Arab Revolt of 1936–39.[38] According to the commentary, like the Old Man's disciples, would-be Palestinian rebels were initiated to their "gangs" by means of a special "ritual" that prepared them for "acts of murder and other crimes." This ritual, as the commentary noted, was designed to make the initiate foresee the "sublime bliss which is expected to him in paradise, once he will have fulfilled his sacred duty. Oftentimes intoxicating methods are used to this end."[39]

The only problem with de Sacy's direct association of the Shiite Nizaris with hashish taking is that it was utterly false. It was based on prejudiced contemporary *Sunni* polemics against the Shiites, which de Sacy mistook for facts, and on the fantasies of medieval Europeans fueled by an "imaginative ignorance" of Islam.[40] At a time when medieval Muslim societies were witnessing the rapid spread of hashish in their midst, *hashishiyyin* as a term tells us more about their fears and contempt toward the drug and its users than it does about what actually drove the Nizaris to commit frenzied public murders. *Hashishiyyin* was by no means a literal description of the sect's drug-consuming habits. Rather, it was a deeply offensive term, which the Nizaris' Sunni detractors employed in an abusive, figurative sense to emphasize the low social status of hashish users—"low class rabble"[41]—and, by extension, the sect's immorality, profanity, and enmity to Islam. As Franz Rosenthal suggests in his classic study of hashish in medieval Muslim society, "the reason for the choice of *Hashishiyah* might have been in the first place the low and disreputable character attributed to hashish eaters [in the medieval Middle East], rather than the sectarians' devotion to the drug."[42]

However, at a time when Western fascination with—but also, in the main, fear of—cannabis was interfacing with colonialism, Orientalism, and burgeoning international drug-control regimes, the Assassins narrative went virtually unchallenged in Palestine and elsewhere around the globe. "A text of virtually mythic status and power,"[43] which was "continually reinterpreted and translated into the language and symbols congruent with the specific historical stage of culture,"[44] this narrative was adapted to different socio-political contexts, and was introduced in many localities as an authoritative historical statement of cannabis-induced madness and acts of violence.[45] In interwar Palestine this narrative may have helped steer Jews clear of hash-ish, given that it epitomized in vivid fashion the claim that the drug was the exclusive domain of Arab societies and a major cause of these societies' misfortunes and pathologies. In this, I argue, Palestine's Jews would have been particularly receptive to the colonial knowledge about cannabis transmitted from the League of Nations in Geneva. In what follows, then, it may be well to digress from Palestine for a while, and to explore the kinds of knowledge about cannabis that were reproduced and disseminated by that interwar international institution.

THE DUBIOUS LEGACY OF THE LEAGUE'S SUBCOMMITTEE ON CANNABIS

A handful of recent studies have explored the debates about cannabis that took place in 1924–25 during the League of Nation's Second Opium Conference in Geneva, which led to the introduction of limited controls over the drug.[46] Liat Kozma, in particular, offers an in-depth analysis of the expert knowledge about cannabis produced in the League's Subcommittee on Cannabis, which was set up in the 1930s to investigate the "cannabis problem" worldwide.[47]

While I benefited tremendously from these scholarly interventions, in what follows I revisit the ideas and views about cannabis produced in the League's forums, particularly the Subcommittee on Cannabis, which operated between 1934 and 1939. My aim is to demonstrate the extent to which these views, which were constitutive of the "investigative modalities"[48] of the League's *colonial* project of collecting facts, may have been crucial in shaping Jewish attitudes toward hashish during the interwar period.

The League of Nations produced significant knowledge about cannabis, which ultimately proved an integral part of interwar colonialism. The League's honest universalism and its genuine social concerns aside, it was mainly committed to a distinctly Western vision of modernity and progress.[49] In fact, "one of the greatest and unintended achievements of the League's social work was the production of knowledge about the lives, views and agency of people who refused to conform to the norms and dictates of upper- and middle-class authorities, reformers or experts."[50] The League denied access to colonized populations and stifled their voices, even when discussion and debate were concerned with the destinies of the latter. "Colonial power relations," writes Kozma, "were reproduced in the League itself—colonized societies were analyzed without taking part in debates that would determine their future."[51] Knowledge about the colonies, instead, was mediated through colonial authorities and colonial experts.[52] In this and in other ways, the League of Nations can be seen as "a League of Empires,"[53] in which shared notions of civility, respectability, Europeanness, and otherness were produced and reproduced. Put differently, the League was based from its very inception on the presumed superiority of the great powers, and "was designed to serve as an instrument for a global civilizing mission."[54]

It should not come as a surprise, then, that the knowledge about cannabis that was produced in the League was rife with contradictions and errors, products of a priori thinking, and that at times it stood in contrast to the specific realities of cannabis-consuming people in the metropoles and colonies. As will be seen below, the League's Opium Advisory Committee (OAC) came to realize this in mid-1930s, and thus launched the Subcommittee on Cannabis—a group of international experts drawn from various fields, tasked with conducting an unprecedented investigation into various aspects of the drug. My contention is that, even though these experts did try to revise and add to previous knowledge about cannabis, a thick ceiling of taken-for-granted ideas and conventional wisdoms ensured that the new knowledge they sought would not—could not—catch up with the changing realities. In the final analysis, these experts did very little in the way of adding valuable knowledge about cannabis, and may have even ensured that false notions of the drug would be preserved for generations to come.

The mindset of certain policy makers in the League helps explain the fateful decision to include cannabis in the 1925 Opium Convention. In the first place, it was the product of ignorance at best, and imperialist or Orientalist racism at worst. For example, most of the delegates who supported the 1925 Egyptian demand that global controls be imposed on cannabis "raised their hands without knowing what cannabis actually was, and openly admitted this to be the case."[55] Similarly, the bulk of the *scientific* knowledge about cannabis produced by the League afterward was riddled with Orientalist fantasies and misconceptions, as will be explored below.[56]

Second, I argue, the decision stemmed from the presumed moral and social havoc that the drug had wreaked on Europe's colonies, and not from its effects on the various metropoles, where the drug was little known at the time and was not used for pleasure-seeking.[57] Dr. Muhammad El Guindy, head of the Egyptian delegation to the 1924–25 Second Opium Conference and the driving force behind Egypt's demand to include cannabis in the 1925 Opium Convention, expressed this understanding most vividly. In a bid to convince the conference's members to agree to a universal ban on cannabis, he declared: "For I know the mentality of Oriental peoples and I am afraid that it will be said that the question was not dealt with because it did not affect the safety of Europeans."[58]

To convince delegates to support the Egyptian proposition, El Guindy came to the conference equipped with a report prepared by Dr. John Warnock, the longtime medical director of Cairo's hospital for the insane.[59] Warnock, it must be stressed, was not known for his empathy toward Egypt and the Egyptians. Despite a twenty-eight-year sojourn in the country (1895–1923), his knowledge of Arabic was rudimentary (he boasted as much himself), and he had no patience for Egypt's demand for self-determination.[60] It may not come as a surprise, then, that Warnock's descriptions of the effects of hashish on colonial subjects in Egypt echoed Marco Polo and Silvestre de Sacy's accounts of the Assassins myth, as elaborated above. The report proposed that "Oriental devotees" of hashish attained "erotic illusions," enjoying both "euphoric and aphrodisiac effects" and "visions" of "temporary paradise." The report also viewed hashish as racially consistent with the Oriental temperament, claiming that its intoxicating effects were not found to be "so marked in Englishmen." And above all, the report made a direct link between cannabis use and insanity:

> Hashish cases are usually violent, exalted and quarrelsome. . . . Many have . . . delusions of an exalted kind, social or religious, and also persecutory ideas. . . . Later on they become so morally degraded, lazy and reckless in behavior that they are no longer responsible. The delusions may remain permanently. Hashishin [hashish users] commit a good many crimes of violence and thefts, and many of them become vagrants.[61]

For Warnock, as for so many other European psychiatrists practicing in the colonial world, hashish-engendered "Oriental madness" served as a convenient screen, allowing him to couch a civilizing mission project in the imperative of medical language. In French North Africa, too, "it suggested the capacity of psychiatric science to blaze a pathway of enlightenment through a landscape of sickness in order to conquer the tyranny of madness and injustice in a space . . . imagined as having rejected modernity centuries earlier."[62] Warnock's approach to "hashish insanity" in Egypt possibly drew from the same pool of a priori–graded civilizational conceptions.[63]

Arguably, then, the inclusion of cannabis by the 1925 Opium Convention, within a limited regime of international control, was strictly an attempt by the League of Nations to save "Oriental peoples" from themselves. Europeans were not expected to be the beneficiaries of this ban, because they were—ostensibly, at least—constitutionally immune to the effects of cannabis, and because the drug had not yet established a strong presence on their continent. In this sense, the 1925 ban on cannabis should be viewed as an integral part of interwar colonialism's civilizing mission.

Following the 1925 Geneva conference, the issue of cannabis did not attract very much attention for about a decade. One reason behind this was that the drug ostensibly remained an exclusively Oriental problem. Thus, in 1932 the OAC was still able to comment that "the contraband traffic in hashish does not seem to have an international character except between certain Asiatic countries bordering on the Mediterranean and Egypt. Considerable quantities are seized in some parts of the East, but these seizures are mostly of an internal character."[64]

But then, in the run-up to the OAC's nineteenth session in 1934, things became, as it were, more tricky. A report prepared by the League's secretariat estimated that there were no less than 200 million cannabis users worldwide.[65] This meant, in effect, that the problem of cannabis could no longer be considered as being limited to a well-bounded geographical and mental space; it had in fact evolved into a problem of global proportions, due to the proliferation of the drug into purportedly uncharted territories, essentially Europe and North America.[66] The moral panic against marijuana in the United States in the 1930s and 1940s, fueled by Harry J. Anslinger, director of the Federal Bureau of Narcotics, was part of the story.[67] Put another way, cannabis was increasingly viewed as a global problem in ways that were reminiscent of late-nineteenth-century continental anxieties of reverse colonialism, which spoke of an insidious invasion of Orientals and Oriental drugs disrupting metropolitan life by debilitating and immobilizing its citizens.[68] The image of the "Oriental" hashish smoker became a metaphor for drug addiction in general, and was eventually conceptualized in terms of a *foreign threat* to Western civilization:

What made the illicit drug trade so threatening was not the specter of a superior foreign power posed to overwhelm. Rather, it was the possibility that drug trafficking would enable an otherwise inferior people to turn the tables on the imperial rulers. And, given past exploitation, these peoples were motivated to seek revenge. Thus, the response to drugs was tinged by emotions of hatred and revulsion, but also guilt and fear.[69]

With the 1925 cannabis ban proven to be unsatisfactory, a Subcommittee on Cannabis was convened in 1934 by the League, to develop "a well-informed and comprehensive position on all scientific, medical, social and legal aspects of cannabis use."[70] The members of the subcommittee were all experts in their various fields: clinical medicine, tropical medicine, psychiatry, neuropsychiatry, biological chemistry, toxicology, public health, and so on. The majority of them held, either at the time or slightly earlier, official posts with British or French colonial administrations in territories in the Middle East and North Africa (Egypt, Morocco, Syria, Tunisia, Turkey);[71] the colonized themselves were not represented.[72] The subcommittee members defined the problem they were authorized to explore as follows: "While a taste for Indian hemp products appears to be prevalent mainly among the Asiatic and African peoples, it is not by any means confined to them." Their report continued:

> The problem is no longer simply to combat a practice which is deep-rooted in ancient populations, but rather to cope with a vice that is extending to circles hitherto uncontaminated.... Not only must the evil be combated in the countries where it has already been prevalent for a long time past, but the development of a fresh menace of drug addiction must be checked in countries in which this vice is beginning to gain ground.[73]

The subcommittee mulled over the problem of cannabis "going global" for five long years. Its operations eventually came to an abrupt end in 1939, following the outbreak of World War II. All in all, however, it could not formulate a clear-cut position on cannabis, nor could it provide compelling explanations for its diffusion in the world or make useable recommendations for the OAC to pursue.[74] The subcommittee thus concluded that more studies were needed of the precise content of cannabis, the causes of addiction, and its connection with dementia and crime.[75]

The various reports and debates on cannabis produced by the subcommittee usefully provide clues about the group's failure. The subcommittee experts were unable to resolve a fundamental paradox that underpinned the issue itself: cannabis, a so-called quintessential Oriental drug, represented an essential dichotomy at the heart of the Orient-Occident divide, yet it was making headway among "circles hitherto uncontaminated," especially Euro-American devotees whose entire constitution should have been antithetical to that of Orientals.

The subcommittee's reports and discussions reflected enduring misconceptions. First of all, cannabis was still viewed as a quintessential Oriental drug, one that Oriental people were particularly attracted to due to their innate immorality, irrationality, backwardness, and mental incapacity. Subcommittee member Dr. Antoine Porot, of the Algiers School of Psychiatry, stated it thus:

> The North African native has a peculiar propensity toward drug addiction. It has been said that he is a born drug addict. . . . It must be recognized that his essentially passive temperament leaves him without defense against temptation. He lives from day to day, at the mercy of his instincts and desires. He has no idea of making provision for his future, and abandons himself to the satisfaction of his immediate needs.[76]

Dr. Joules Bouquet, inspector of pharmacies in Tunis hospitals, concurred. Declaring that the natural propensity of Orientals to cannabis was incurable, he stated: "Repeated prohibitions from the imams, edicts and penalties from the emirs and sultans, all were in vain. Hashish triumphed and triumphs still, for it is precisely owing to their special mentality that Muslims became and remained devotees of the drug."[77]

In general terms, the experts sitting on the subcommittee viewed "Oriental addicts" as contemptible people of low social standing, steeped in indolence and unproductivity, and incapable by their very nature of paying even basic attention to personal hygiene issues. These views were congruent with those of the European and indigenous middle classes in the colonies, who saw cannabis as a low-class "native" drug that undercut modernity and what Nile Green described in the Indian context as the "capitalist ethic of the nobility of work."[78] Mazhar Osman Uzman, subcommittee member and director and chief medical officer at the neuropsychiatric home in Istanbul, suggested that "the upper classes never use hashish, which they consider degrading, and the middle classes loathe drugs and avoid them like the plague."[79] In the opinion of these experts, hashish users belonged to the "lowest classes" and were "idlers, parasites and degenerates." Lacking "the elementary rules of cleanliness," "their appearance is disorderly and dirty," "they are content with a filthy hovel as a lodging," "they are . . . beset with diseases, outcome of their vice," and "they do not shrink from the most unprincipled and degrading acts to procure funds." They were, in short, "an unproductive burden on society."[80]

Subcommittee experts also reaffirmed the hashish and insanity theory, applying it exclusively to the Orient. Bouquet, for example, claimed that nine-tenths of the lunatics in Tunisia were hashish addicts, pointing to statistics prepared in the 1910s by Dr. Warnock at Egypt's Abbasiyya Mental Asylum to demonstrate the prevalence of the problem in the region.[81] Porot, for his part, agreed with Bouquet; he claimed that Orientals were more prone to hashish-provoked insanity than other "races." The native's "entirely instinctive way of life, the fact that his behavior is dictated solely by immediate reactions, and his fundamentally impulsive nature, soon give to his crises of intoxication a violent and tragic character," Porot asserted.[82]

Affirming the causal link between cannabis and raging madness, Mazhar Osman Uzman provided what can only be described as an updated version of Marco Polo's myth of the Old Man of the Mountain:

> It is well-known throughout the East that the Sheikhs of the "Tekkes" [Sufi Orders] secured machine-like obedience from hashish addicts and made them act as they pleased; a mere word from the Sheikh was enough to cause ad-dicts to throw themselves over a precipice, the sooner to achieve their dream of paradise. . . . Only a fraction of those [Sufis] on whom addiction has laid so firm a hold can be brought back to a normal state. Even they retain a more or less marked streak of abnormality in their character.[83]

The subcommittee's endorsement of the Oriental-hashish-and-insanity theory was accompanied by a second viewpoint: that cannabis use was an agent of uncontrollable (homo)sexuality among Muslims. Indeed, the subcommittee deliberations on hashish reveal an obsession with Arab sexuality, much the same as that of their nineteenth-century Orientalist predecessors.[84] Bouquet explained that an underlying cause of hashish use among Orientals was to reinvigorate their depleted sexual drives: "These people, weakened from their youth by sexual excesses of all kinds . . . cannot resign themselves to the sexual consequences of advancing age. Weakened as they are, not by their labor, [for, lest we forget, they are inherently lazy and indolent,] but by sexual excesses, they early turn to aphrodisiacs [such as cannabis]."[85] On another occasion, Bouquet turned to Egypt and held that the natives take drugs in the hope that they will enable them to increase, maintain, or regenerate, their sexual powers. . . . In Egypt it can be said that ninety percent of addicts have been intentional addicts but that the reason that these thousands of people took to drugs was that they believed them to be a potent sex-stimulant.[86]

Clearly, the subcommittee's expert opinion on cannabis drew on earlier colonial understandings of cannabis and cannabis intoxication, and were also in line with Zionist views on the substance, as explored in the previous section. However, these understandings could no longer be deemed sufficient. After all, the underlying proposition—that Oriental peoples were exclusively predisposed to cannabis because cannabis fit their mentality like a glove— did not sit well with the dawning realization that "a large proportion of the population in the various continents is in fact addicted to hemp," especially in the United States and Canada, where marijuana had had "terrible effects . . . on criminality."[87]

Resolving this obvious contradiction proved a difficult if not impossible task for the subcommittee members. Bouquet, for one, found it hard to abandon the racial-cum-racist explanation that Oriental peoples had embraced cannabis since time immemorial, that their indolence and thirst for carnal pleasure drew them to cannabis in the same way that insects are drawn to light. But, to make allowances for the fact that cannabis had found a path into the minds and hearts of non-Orientals as well, Bouquet was prepared to readjust this explanation. "It has been established beyond dispute," he reaffirmed, "that the use of Cannabis to induce a special form of intoxication is of Asiatic origin."[88] Note that the emphasis here is on a *special form* of intoxication. The understanding was that, while non-Orientals and even North Americans had been found to be attracted to the forbidden drug, their intoxication would likely be more benign and more manageable than that of Orientals. Indeed, there were many Europeans in Tunisia, Bouquet observed: French, Spaniards, Italians, Maltese, and Greeks. Yet, those among them "who have had a fancy to try hemp do not appear to have been driven to commit violent anti-social acts while under the influence of the drug." He explained, "The effect of cannabis [on these Europeans] is different from that generally found among Oriental addicts." In short, cannabis intoxication, he concluded, was "a question of racial susceptibility" or "of race receptiveness."[89] On another occasion he mused: "The question arises whether the effects differ according to race."[90]

But the problem presented to Bouquet and his fellow subcommittee experts did not end here. Because, if, as Bouquet claimed, non-Orientals could be considered immune to the *special form* of cannabis madness, how then could one explain, as the OAC cautioned at the time, the "increasing use of Indian hemp (chiefly in the form of marijuana cigarettes) throughout the territory of the U.S., and the terrible effects of this form of drug addiction on criminality"?[91] The experts' answer to this conundrum was an attempt to achieve two mutually exclusive objectives at the same time: they tried to revise knowledge about cannabis while retaining the dichotomies at the heart of the Oriental-Occidental divide. Uncritically accepting the racial and class-related marijuana moral panic orchestrated by Anslinger and the Federal Bureau of Narcotics in in the 1930s, these experts concluded that it was not white Americans of *European* blood who were falling prey to the "killer weed," but the country's despised and disenfranchised minority groups—especially, but not exclusively, Mexicans and blacks:

> Public opinion and the authorities [in the United States] have become alarmed at the spread of this form of [marijuana] addiction . . . [which] increased enormously [in recent years] . . . and spread especially among the younger generations of the Latin American population, Mexican, Turkish, [and] Philippine immigrant circles, and negroes. . . . It has been found that among the[se] contaminated elements of the population the abuse of the drug produces an unfortunate propensity to violence, and even crime.[92]

That the new proposals put forward by the subcommittee of experts still rested on tenuous foundations can be gleaned from heated exchanges in 1938 between Russell Pasha and Bouquet, with which I will conclude this section. Russell was not part of the subcommittee, and for the most part was not involved in its deliberations. Yet, widely considered a knowledgeable expert on the subject of cannabis, and with an international reputation thanks to the successful drug war he had waged in Egypt, Russell was invited to participate in the subcommittee's discussions during the fifteenth meeting of the OAC in June 1938.[93]

As mentioned in chapter 1, Russell was quite progressive for the time with regard to matters concerning cannabis and the drug's intoxication. He spent nearly forty-five years in Egypt (1902–46) in various colonial capacities—first as inspector of the interior, a position that enabled him to serve in virtually every province in Egypt; then as assistant commandant of the Alexandria Police;

and finally as head of the Cairo Police and as head of the CNIB.[94] His long-standing experience in Egyptian affairs earned him, in addition to the esteem of local politicians, a deep knowledge of the country and its people, including their hashish use habits—which, as he concluded, were relatively innocuous as compared to their abuse of "white drugs," opiates and cocaine.[95] It is also reasonable to assume that, like other British officials in Egypt at the time, he was well aware of the cannabis debate in the British Raj, where prohibition was ruled out due to the understanding that such entrenched practices in the country could not possibly be stamped out.

Consequently, Russell refused to tolerate Bouquet's propositions during subcommittee proceedings, especially those that connected Orientals to cannabis in terms of irresistible and excessive indolence, (homo)sexuality, and violent disposition. Russell strongly opposed such notions and made this clear to the subcommittee experts. In language quite atypical for a refined English gentleman of the time, he meticulously and methodically demolished the empirical, historical, and conceptual premises of Bouquet's arguments. First and foremost, he called him to order on the issue of temporality. Hashish addiction among Oriental Arabs, he said—Egyptians, whom Russell spoke for, but also Tunisians, for whom Bouquet had spoken—was not an ancient and perennial issue, but a purely *modern* phenomenon, and a fairly recent one at that. It had nothing to do with fixed pathological mentalities, but had to do rather with the crucial task of placing the problem in a proper historical context.

In Egypt, Russell explained, large-scale hashish addiction was traceable to the development of modern irrigation and cultivation systems in the Nile Valley, not to the ancient past. Thousands of square miles of the valley had gradually been converted to perennial irrigation, he said; with the land watered and cultivated all the year round instead of once a year, it had become a breeding ground for parasitic diseases such as bilharzia, ancylostomiasis, and malaria. The effect of these diseases, especially the first two, had been a great diminution in the strength and working efficiency of the population: His "physical and sexual powers being sapped," the *fellah*, "in his ignorance . . . has looked around for some stimulant to replace his lost energies which form his code of honor," Russell suggested. This accounted for why hashish smoking spread.[96]

In retrospect, Russell's explanation of the modern Egyptians' allure to hashish may be questionable, yet his attempt to place the phenomenon in concrete historical context—as opposed to attributing it to their radical alterity and to fixed racial, cultural, and mental attributes—was admirable. The desire of the *fellahin* to hash-ish was, he claimed, not a self-perpetuating force of nature. Nor was it a product of changeless racial and cultural attributes. It was a provisional and potentially short-term problem, one that would be resolved once their bodies stopped host-ing debilitating diseases. Indeed, like many others within and outside the League of Nations, including the subcommittee experts, Russell was an avid advocate of modern science. Optimism, he thought, was not naiveté on his part; rather, it was a realistic assessment supported by recent history. "Thirty-five years ago," he said, "drug addiction in the villages was practically unknown . . . and the *fellah* . . . did his twelve hours day without thinking of or needing a stimulant."[97]

Russell was also blunt with respect to Bouquet's broad generalizations about "Arabs." Egyptians and Tunisians were not one and the same people, he insisted. On the contrary, they were "of totally different characters and habits." Bouquet contended that lower-class Tunisians got high because they were irredeemably indolent—"laziness [being] the basic element in the character of Muslims," and added: "They love doing nothing and musing the hours away." Russell strongly opposed this view, saying that it did not apply to Egyptian peasants. "In point of fact, the *fellahin* of Egypt were a sober race, who did not touch alcohol. . . . The Egyptian *fellah* was on the whole an industrious person, did not drink alcohol, seldom nowadays had more than one wife and was fond of his children."[98]

CONCLUSION

The Bouquet-Russell debate may have been a big fuss over a trifle. As Kozma suggests, neither man questioned "the idea that gross generalizations can be made about inherent pathologies of entire populations. . . . Outside of history, outside of time and context, what Russell and Bouquet [were] actually debating was whether or not 'the Arab' was inherently lazy, or whether hashish made him one."[99] This may very well be true. Yet, the Russell-Bouquet debate can be interpreted in a different light if viewed from the perspective of "diagnostic events," à la anthropologist Sally Falk Moore, who deployed that concept to de-scribe moments when established explanations and collective mythologies can no longer function smoothly.[100] Practices undertaken to alter these established rules and understandings are thus "events that reveal ongoing contests, compe-titions, conflicts, and the effort to prevent, suppress, and repress these."[101]

The exchange between Bouquet and Russell, and perhaps the deliberations of the 1934–39 Subcommittee on Cannabis in general, can likewise be read in this light. Confronted with knowledge about cannabis that seemed neither reliable nor useful to understand contemporary realities, the OAC appointed a subcommittee of experts to generate new data and an enhanced knowledge base. But despite their strenuous efforts to revise and update this knowledge, they constantly kept running up against earlier collective perceptions and understandings of cannabis, and eventually succumbed to them. Moments such as the Bouquet-Russell polemic showcased the powerful contradictions and tensions underlying their reconfigured knowledge, as well as the effort to conceal certain facts and truths. Immediately after the Bouquet-Russell debate, the subcommittee chairman suggested that Bouquet, in consultation with Russell, "might be willing to redraft his text in such a way as to present factual data without hurting the susceptibilities in either country."[102] As far as I know, neither Russell nor Bouquet followed through. In other words, no attempts were made to discover alternative, let alone indigenous, forms of knowledge about cannabis that could refute dominant forms of knowledge grounded in Western modernity or interwar colonialism. Hence, it appears that the subcommittee's legacy was the global entrenchment of fanciful and misleading concepts about cannabis throughout much of the twentieth century.

As we have seen, the Jews of Palestine were particularly receptive to these latter forms of knowledge about cannabis. Consequently, they avoided hashish smoking almost entirely, viewing it as the exclusive domain of Oriental society and the source of many of its afflictions—and as a threat to the Zionist project in Palestine. A similar logic applies to other places around the word at the same time—Mexico, European countries, and the United States, for example.

In the midst of the 1948 Arab-Israeli War in Palestine, following reports suggesting the spread of hashish consumption in Tel Aviv, a *Davar* commentator issued the following warning: "Until now we had only card clubs, bridge and roulette. . . . That much we knew . . . but hashish . . . in Tel Aviv? Of that we had never dreamed . . . and all this [takes place] during a war when the community is fighting for its survival. What other surprises are in store for us?"[103] It is to these post-1948 "surprises" that I turn in the next two chapters.

5

HASHISH TRAFFICKING IN ISRAEL

Previously, the Land of Israel was . . . a major passageway for [the flow of]
dangerous drugs. . . . The vast majority of the smugglers and the majority
of the consumers were Arab. Because of the cessation of relations with the
neighboring countries, Israel is no longer a market for dangerous drugs.

This observation, made by the Israel Police in its 1948 report to the minister of
police,[1] was reiterated more confidently in its report the following year:

> This year [1949], too, the country was disconnected from the main producer
> country (Syria) and from the main consumer country (Egypt), and the transit
> trade in intoxicating drugs conducted via [our] territory prior to the establish-
> ment of the State of Israel is now virtually nonexistent.[2]

These two appraisals place the establishment of the State of Israel, in 1948, as
an abrupt epochal break point, creating a clean slate in the local history of
drugs. In hindsight this was perhaps a logical conclusion at the time, given
that the State of Israel was practically "a new political entity whose existence
erased Palestine off the map."[3] Furthermore, the era put an end to the diverse
and intricate regional integration. Hence, "Bilad al-Sham's nations-states were

[henceforth] directly involved, country by country, rather than in a mediated regional form."[4] Yet this overly optimistic view of the "end of (drug) history" in the post-1948 Levant, or at least in post-1948 Israel, did not last long. As the demand pull (in Egypt) and the supply push (in Lebanon) persisted after the establishment of the State of Israel, border-crossing hashish smuggling across the latter's territory to the destination country continued as well. This provides yet another example that in drug history one cannot speak of a succession of coherent and distinct epochs.

This comes out clearly in a 1950 Israel Police report to the Commission on Narcotic Drugs (CND), the central drug policymaking body of the United Nations and successor to the League of Nation's Opium Advisory Committee (OAC). Referring to hashish seizures on Israel's northern border and in the southern Negev desert, the report informed the CND that "as of late the drug trade has been revived, even though our country still has no relations with the neighboring countries. It is clear that the calmness prevailing at the state's borders is easing commerce across them."[5] Put differently, due to its geographic location, the territory under Israeli rule reemerged after 1948 as a critical link—and thereby a major depot—in the hashish trade between Lebanon to the north and Egypt to the south. As a 1962 Israel Police report to the CND pointed out,

> Israel is a natural junction for the smuggling of drugs from the producer countries in the north, Lebanon and Syria, to consumer countries, especially Egypt. Smuggling from Lebanon to Egypt takes place via [land routes], but also via the sea close to Israel's territorial waters along the coast.[6]

In what follows, I explore the changing patterns of hashish commodity chains and antihashish controls that evolved following the transition from British Palestine to independent Jewish statehood. The first section traces patterns of continuity and change in the drug's passage from Lebanon to Egypt via Israel, against the backdrop of post-1948 demographic transformations and border adjustments. The second section then explores the challenges that hashish smugglers posed to the Israeli authorities, contrasting these with the challenges posed by their pre-1948 predecessors to the British in Palestine.

The third section, with which this chapter ends, explores a most sensitive topic: the alleged involvement—significant, at that—of the Israeli military in hashish trafficking operations from Lebanon to Egypt from the late 1950s to as recently as the mid-1980s. The attributed objective of this long-standing enterprise was an attempt to immerse and immobilize the Egyptian population generally—and the Egyptian armed forces specifically—with hashish. Thus far, the Israeli authorities have zealously protected all the details of this long-lasting operation under a thick veil of secrecy, justified in the name of "security" and the need to protect the fragile relations with Egypt. This chapter brings to light the story of this secret enterprise by drawing on Arab League reports to the CND, Israeli archival documents, and more recent investigations conducted by the international press.

HASHISH SMUGGLING AND THE PASSAGE
TO THE STATE OF ISRAEL

In terms of hashish trafficking and its routes to Egypt, the passage from the pre-1948 to the post-1948 periods was characterized by both structural continuities and structural changes. The first obvious trend, carried over from the interwar period, was the overwhelming demand for hashish in comparison to that for the region's other habit-forming substances. Hashish was the most dominant of the drugs whose journeys commenced in Lebanon, and which at some point either passed through Israeli territory en route to Egypt or were redirected for local consumption.[7] This statistic can be confirmed from the two types of reports about hashish and opium seizures prepared by Israeli Police between 1948 and 1967, the one submitted to the Israel Police Ministry and the other to the CND. According to these reports, the accumulative quantity of hashish seized inside Israeli territory during this period amounted to 4,815 kilograms (a little over 10,615 pounds). This figure is three times larger than the total quantity of opium seized inside Israel in the same period, which amounted to 1,292 kilograms (a little less than 2,848 pounds).[8]

Smuggling routes to, across, and from Israel were also carried over from the Mandatory period. But significant breaks from the past also came into play. For one thing, land routes had to be adjusted to reflect the 1949 general armistice agreements between Israel and its Arab neighbors—Egypt, Lebanon, Syria, and Jordan. These agreements officially ended the first Arab-Israeli war. They established the armistice lines, including the so-called Green Line, as Israel's de facto borders until the 1967 Arab-Israeli war.[9] Secondly, Israel's military government, imposed between 1948 and 1966 over districts of the country that continued to be home to significant Palestinian populations, made it difficult for Palestinians to engage in drug trafficking. Including a "regime of checkpoints, travel permits, and other restrictions on Palestinian freedom of movement," the military government "impeded the ability of its Arab citizens to mount direct challenges to the state."[10]

Nevertheless, hashish traffickers—Arabs as well as Jews—continued to defy state borders as before, using more or less the same routes. However, the new geophysical conditions largely complicated matters for the Israeli authorities. It should be borne in mind that Israel gained control of approximately 60 percent of the territory allotted to the Palestinian Arab state by the original UN partition plan. Hence, Israel's southern border with Egypt and Egyptian-controlled Gaza consisted of approximately 160 miles of the southern Negev region, commanding large tracts of uninhabited desert. Hashish smugglers—particularly local Bedouins who, as a 1963 police report maintained, had "engaged in smuggling for generations and look[ed] upon it as a way of life rather than a criminal pursuit"[11]—were intimately familiar with the terrain, and exploited this knowledge to their advantage in the southward movement of hashish supplies toward Egypt.[12] This was, as another police report suggested, "an ideal area for smugglers. In fact, the largest [hashish] seizures are made when the drugs are en route here from one Arab country to another."[13] In this way the Negev region presented Israeli antidrug authorities with a far more serious challenge that it had given their British predecessors.[14] Also, in exchange for control over the Negev, Israel had consented to an Egyptian military presence in the Gaza Strip.[15] This made the fight to prevent hashish smuggling to Egypt via the land and sea routes even more difficult, as Gaza became the destination for many Egypt-bound hashish consignments.[16]

In the post-1948 arrangements, the Hashemite Kingdom of Jordan became a new actor in the Levant hashish trade, joining the veteran Arab states of Lebanon, Syria, and Egypt. Jordan acquired that position due to its acquisition, in the aftermath of the 1948 war, of what became known as the West Bank, territory it subsequently annexed in 1950. Previously an integral part of Mandatory Palestine, the smuggling routes running through this territory were policed by the British with the Emirate of Transjordan, and after 1946 by the Hashemite Kingdom of Jordan.[17] This active hashish land route, which now ran through Jordan, spilled over into the Negev desert. The fact that these borders were long, poorly patrolled, easily crossed, and often poorly demarcated,[18] made the smuggling of drugs into the Negev a relatively easy task. The Arab League Permanent Anti-Narcotics Bureau (*Maktab da'im li-shu'un mukhaddirat*, or PANB), established in 1950 to combine and coordinate efforts by the Arab nations to combat the narcotics trade in all its iterations, noted this state of affairs in a 1952 report to the CND.[19] Drugs, the PANB report stated, were "smuggled through Jordan into the Palestinian territory under its Administration, thence to the Israelite territory for re-smuggling across the Egyptian frontiers by land and sea."[20] A UN narcotics survey mission, dispatched to the Middle East in 1959 to study the drug problem in the region, also referred to "large-scale traffic flowing from the North through Jordan, over the Israeli border, across the Negev desert, then over the Israeli-Egyptian border on to a market in Egypt."[21]

Further north, the former Jordanian-Israeli armistice line—the Green Line—separating the West Bank from Israel proper further complicated Israel's dealings with the hashish supplies spilling over into its territory. The border between Israel and Jordan along the West Bank, spanning about four hundred miles, was "the most problematic and unnatural border. . . . The complete absence of natural obstacles and the rough, rocky, tree- and scrub-clad terrain made it easy for civilian and military raiders to cross the lines."[22] According to a 1963 Israel Police report, this border was

> an example of how not to demarcate frontiers. The border . . . runs only a few meters away from vital transportation lines, it separates . . . farmers who live on one side [from] the lands they have tilled for generations . . . on the other side. . . . And, the most important thing, it divides . . . Arab villages linked by ties of family and, even worse, on occasion cuts in half whole villages.[23]

The absence of a viable border between Jordan and Israel—it remained unmarked or poorly marked for years—naturally made smugglers' efforts to enter Israeli territory with their illicit cargoes much simpler, and sometimes safer too.[24]

Jordan's 1949 transfer to the State of Israel (out of a fear of renewed hostilities) of a strip of land in the northwestern part of the Green Line made the task of drug control even more difficult for Israel. This strip extended from Wadi 'Ara southwards to the west of Tulkarm and Qalqilya, then down to Kfar Qassim. These areas, which hosted a concatenation of Palestinian towns and villages, were collectively called "the Triangle" (Ha-meshulash in Hebrew; Al-muthallath in Arabic), named after the British designation of the territory as the "triangle of terror," due to its residents' habit of firing on police and soldiers during the 1936–39 Palestinian Arab Revolt.[25] They "included tracts of arable land belonging to several dozen villages on the eastern—i.e., Jordanian—side of the line. Thousands of West Bank villagers thus lost much of the cultivated land—and a greater or lesser part of their livelihood."[26] Artificially disconnected from their neighbors, relatives, friends, and business associates, inhabitants on both sides of the border continued to nurture links and networks, some of these illicit, beneath the radar of the Israeli and Jordanian authorities.[27] It can be safely assumed that the transfer of hashish and other contraband across the border constituted the backbone of some of these links. It was in this context that Umm al-Fahm—the social, cultural economic center of Wadi ʿAra and the Triangle region—was named by a 1958 Ministry of Health report as one of Israel's "centers of commerce in narcotics."[28]

Who were these hashish smugglers operating across the Jordanian-Israeli borders? In the main, they were Palestinian Arabs scattered across the poorly patrolled and easily traversed 1949 armistice lines. Most of them were refugees, former inhabitants of the Arab villages and towns in the areas that had become part of the Jewish state. Described in official and public parlance as "infiltrators" (*mistanenim*), their reasons for crossing the borders were manifold: searching for relatives, returning to their homes, recovering material possessions, tending and harvesting their fields, and—occasionally—exacting revenge. "Some of the infiltrators were thieves and smugglers; some were involved in the hashish convoys."[29] Contrary to the official Israeli discourse, most of the refugees-cum-infiltrators who made their way into Israel were not violent. Nevertheless, their presence frightened Jewish civilians living in the frontier regions.[30] In fact, economics was the principal motivation for most of these refugee smugglers operating along Israel's borders; hashish was only one of many items—including coffee, tea, sugar, rice, clothes, cigarettes, watches, fountain pens, sunglasses, nylon stockings, and sheep—that they ferried across the border and into Israel.[31] This was a bidirectional shadow economy: it was characterized, on the one hand, by the movement of hashish to Egypt via Sinai, and on the other, by the movement of household commodities and foods to Israel, where goods were made scarce due to the government policy of *tzena* (austerity).[32]

Let us move on to Israel's northernmost region and briefly consider the formation of Israel's border with Lebanon—the source country of most if not all of the hashish supplies that entered, remained in, or left Israel. In stark contrast to other regions taken over by Israel, where the Palestinian populations either fled or were expelled, the rural population of the lower and upper Galilee who survived the initial "northern border-clearing operation,"[33] numbering tens of thousands of Palestinians, was allowed to remain in the new state.[34] The reasons for this unusual concession are yet to be properly researched, but the fact that a relatively large Palestinian population remained in close proximity to the Lebanese border after 1948 played a significant role in facilitating the hashish commodity chain across the border separating the two countries.

Indeed, because hashish flows, by their very nature, "defy the norms and rules of formal political authority," and "systematically contest or bypass state controls,"[35] there was no reason to assume that hashish traffickers would accept the Lebanese-Israeli border as impenetrable. On the contrary: even if the Israeli-Lebanese border had become a more formidable obstacle than the pre-1948 Mandate border, these traffickers maintained illicit commerce networks on both sides of it, drawing on previous links and networks and cultivating new ones. These networks ensured that "the merchandise [was] smuggled across the border, deposited in Israel territory in a safe hiding place or with a local accomplice and subsequently marketed inland" or redirected to Egypt, as a 1958 Israel Police report suggested.[36] Most of the smuggling across the Lebanese border to Israel in the late 1940s and 1950s was carried out by Arab refugees working with Israeli Arabs in the Galilee, though military rule severely curtailed their free movement—but also sometimes with the collaboration of Israeli Jews, mostly immigrants from the Middle East and North Africa (Mizrahim).[37]

Police testimony given in 1956 by a resident of the village of Mi'ilya in the western Upper Galilee, some 4.6 miles from the Israel-Lebanon border, gives us an idea of the nature of Arab-Jewish border-crossing networks and the extent to which they extended into Israel's centers of hashish vice, and beyond them as well. Interrogated in connection with his involvement in "transactions concerning arms, ammunition and dangerous drugs"—to which he readily confessed—the man, a Christian Arab farmer, related his multifaceted career as a middleman in the illicit trade conducted between Lebanon and Israel from 1949 to 1956. To protect the man's identity, I will refer to him by the alias Isa.[38]

According to Isa's confession, in 1949 he joined a group of local associates (whose identities he provides) to transfer cattle across the Lebanese border; he then sold the cattle to fellow Mi'ilya residents and Jews in nearby "agricultural settlements." Later, in 1950, he claimed, an acquaintance proposed a shared venture "in hashish smuggling, which is easier than trading [in cattle] and more profitable." Isa then proposed the sale of hashish to a Jewish hog farmer from a transit camp (ma'abarah) near Nahariya, today the northernmost coastal town in Israel. The prospective purchaser's name clearly indicated his Mizrahi origins. Isa's testimony proceeded as follows:

> Three days later we [Isa and an associate] went down to a *wadi* [nearby] . . . and met [with another Arab associate] who brought us two okkas [about 2.6 kilograms, or 5.8 pounds] in eight [hashish] loaves, for which we paid 80 Israeli pounds [IP], 10 pounds for each loaf. The next day, I took a sample of [this] hashish . . . to the hog farm[er for him to try]. He smoked the little piece and liked it. . . . He then asked me to bring him the [eight hashish loaves] . . . for which he paid me . . . 130 IP. After that, I brought him 4–5 okkas of hashish each week . . . and he paid me 65 IP for each okka. . . . Me and [my associate] would split the profit in half.

Asked by the interrogating officer about the origin of the hashish he acquired at the *wadi*, Isa replied that he didn't know "for sure, but I . . . think that it was brought from Lebanon."

As time passed, the hog farmer's demands for Isa's hashish supplies multiplied. Consequently, Isa made more frequent business trips to the *wadi*, transferring six okkas of hashish to his Jewish costumer on a weekly basis for a higher price of 145 IP per okka. At the same time, he no longer needed to take personal responsibility for delivering the contraband to the hog farmer. With his increased income he could now afford to employ a driver—also bearing a Jewish name of Middle Eastern origins—who delivered the supplies by car. The driver would "conceal [the hashish] in his car's spare wheel, and deliver it to [the hog farmer]." Asked by the interrogator if he had any knowledge of what the hog farmer did with the hashish supplies, Isa answered that he "transferred the hashish to Jaffa, but I don't know to whom." As will be discussed in chapter 6, Jaffa at the time was a major market for local hashish consumption.

After a failed attempt to diversify into smuggling Lebanese silk—indeed, "between 1843 and 1914, 'Syrian' silk became an internationally traded cash crop of paramount importance in the economy of the [Lebanese] mountain"[39]— in 1954 Isa returned to his previous area of expertise, trading in hashish smuggled across the Lebanese border. Renewing his regular visits to the *wadi* to purchase his merchandise, he now cultivated business links with a Jew of Turkish provenance who lived in Haifa, another pre- and post-1948 hashish depot. Isa delivered hashish supplies to him by means of a motorcycle ridden by another Israeli Jew. He now charged 220 IP for each okka of hashish. This was a 340 percent increase from the original 65 IP he had received for the same amount of hashish at the beginning of his venture, back in 1950. However, these profits were sometimes offset by corrupted hashish supplies he was sometimes duped into purchasing—e.g., "hashish mixed with cocoa"—which he was obviously unable to sell.

Isa's testimony brings to light the workings of an Arab-Jewish illicit hashish trade network which extended from Lebanon to the Galilee, and from there to Haifa and Jaffa. It is the most detailed account I have found of such a network. However, it was by no means the only Jewish-Arab hashish network that was active in Israel over the course of the 1950s and 1960s. In 1950, for example, a police report laconically recorded the arrest of "two Arab-Israeli farmers" who, together with an Israeli Jew, had been in possession of approximately 10.5 kilograms of hashish. "In their interrogation," the report said, "they confessed that they purchased the drug from Lebanese merchants who crossed the border illegally."[40] Likewise, a 1955 Ministry of Foreign Affairs dispatch reported that in 1953–54 alone, two "Jewish-Arab gangs," specializing in purchasing hashish supplies from Lebanon and then smuggling them "to the south," had been arrested in northern Israel.[41] In the south of Israel, too, Bedouin and Jewish hashish traffickers teamed up to transfer hashish to Egypt via the Negev desert.[42] Interpol, the International Police Organization—with whom the Israel Police collaborated in transborder crime prevention matters, including drug trafficking—also commented on the increasing cooperation between Arab and Jewish hashish traffickers in Israel.[43] The notoriety of Jewish-Arab entrepreneurial cooperation in the realm of transnational hashish smuggling was such that in 1960 a keen observer wryly remarked, "It's not an amusing fact that the narcotics traffickers are just about the only people who have been successful in circumventing the Arab economic boycott of Israel."[44]

How did the Israeli authorities, and particularly the Israel Police, respond to this and the other challenges posed by transregional hashish traffickers and local hashish dealers? The short answer is that they responded poorly. The longer answer to this question is provided in the next section.

ANTIHASHISH ENFORCEMENT AND ITS CONSTRAINTS

An internal police report on dangerous drugs submitted to the head of the Israel Police Criminal Investigation Division (CID) in early 1953 included the following disclaimer:

> I must emphasize that with the exception of a few cases, the police has not
> engaged in discovering drug smuggling. . . . One of the main reasons for this

is the lack of manpower and other priorities. [Hence,] most of the [drug] seizures occurred at random. In a similar vein, the use of informers has been
minuscule.[45]

At about the same time, in early 1953, the commander of Israel Police's Tiberius
District, in the north of the country, communicated a message in the same
spirit, writing: "We are not taking enough action in this field [of dangerous
drugs], even though . . . the experience of other districts makes it hard to assume that this affliction has not appeared here as well."[46]

The Israel State Archives granted me only limited access to police files from
the 1950s. Thus I cannot confirm that additional police complaints of this nature
were made at the time. However, it is not unreasonable to assume, in the light
of evidence from other sources, that in the first decade after 1948, and perhaps
even after that as well, the Israel Police Force was unprepared to respond to the
resumption of hashish flows across the country.

In the first place, the exceptional circumstances that informed the establishment of Israel Police—in the midst of the 1948 Arab-Israeli War, following the
abrupt withdrawal of the British authorities—should be taken into account.
These factors created lasting structural problems, as well as labor force, equipment, and infrastructure shortages. As Bryan K. Roby suggests, "the transition
from a colonial to a nationalized police force was far from easy, and in terms of
equipment the Israel Police had to start from scratch."[47] This made it difficult
for the young police force to organize itself, in the manner required to achieve
its goals, for years to come.[48]

Indeed, during the Mandate period, the police's entire administrative ma-
chinery was in the hands of the British; Jewish and Arab policemen were only
employed in lower-level investigative capacities, and there were no Jews or Arabs
in senior command posts.[49] When the British departed, the task of establishing
a new police force was entrusted to relatively inexperienced Jewish personnel.[50]
The latter were required to work under circumstances that were inauspicious, to
say the very least. The following text, composed for the twentieth anniversary
of the Israel Police, conveys the gist of these circumstances, even if it is littered
with overstatements intended to embellish the force's accomplishments:

> The birth of Israel Police preceded the establishment of the State of Israel, and
> was marked by the bloody events of the last period of Mandatory rule and the
> storm of the War of Independence. The Mandatory Police did not transfer . . .

power in an orderly manner, and with its termination it bequeathed us chaos: police stations that were nearly emptied of manpower, and a severe lack of weapons and vehicles, which had been taken away. The equipment of different laboratories, the tools and instruments of workshops, the lion's share of records and documents—some of these invaluable from a criminologist and criminalist point of view—were removed or abandoned for plunder and disrepair.[51]

Following the establishment of the police force, and in addition to everything else, the most troubling and chronic problem that beset it throughout the time span of this chapter was the quantity and the quality of its labor force.[52] This formed the subject matter of lengthy discussions conducted throughout the 1950s in the Knesset Internal Affairs Committee, which repeatedly invited the police commissioner and the minister of police for questioning. In testimony to the committee in 1956, Police Commissioner Yehezkel Sahar took pains to argue that "our most fundamental problem is manpower," alleging that the force under his command was 50 percent short of its budgeted workforce. To illustrate his case, the commissioner added:

> You can wander around Tel Aviv at night or at day and hardly see a policeman in the streets. A large city like Tel Aviv has 1,000 policemen but needs at least 2,000 of them. In every large city in the world you will find at least one policeman present in the neighborhoods at all hours of the day and the night . . . preventing crime. . . . [And] there are regions in the country where there are no police at all.[53]

In the 1950s and much of the 1960s, the top brass of the Israel Police Force did not derive any pride from the professionalism of their work force, either. The harshest words uttered and written were reserved for the poor quality of new recruits, primarily of Middle Eastern and North African descent, who by the late 1950s constituted the ethnic majority of the police department.[54] Police Minister Bechor-Shalom Sheetrit, for instance, bemoaned the fact that more than half of the police force originated from "failing and primitive [read: Middle Eastern] countries," and consequently lacked the "enlightenment" (ne'orut) and "necessary cultural and social background" for proper police work.[55] On other occasions, Sheetrit, who himself hailed from a Sephardi family—albeit of the "Old Yishuv"—said of these policemen that they "lack the necessary ambition and initiative for any police activity."[56] Upon recruitment, he added, they appeared to be so ignorant and unfit for the job that they needed to be taught "to put on their shoes."[57] Indeed, throughout the period under study, senior police officials and spokespersons repeatedly expressed frustration with the "compromises" that had been made in employment procedures, due to the scarcity of suitable candidates for recruitment.[58] In testimony to the Knesset Internal Affairs Committee in 1956, Commissioner Sahar expressed this grievance most succinctly, saying: "I have given up on the hope that educated people will join the police. We therefore admit those who are totally uneducated, those who have completed only two or three years of elementary school or a religious primary school [heder]."[59] Significantly, in 1953, more than four thousand officers (67 percent) were unable to speak Hebrew at a fifth-grade level.[60]

Police unpreparedness notwithstanding, the renewed occurrence of drug-related offenses within and across Israeli territory could not remain unattended. Hence, during the first decade after 1948, the CID Economic Department took charge of fighting "smuggling by land, sea and air."[61] It is noteworthy that border-crossing drugs were merely one of several goods—cars, watches, groceries, foreign currency, even porcelain—whose smuggling the department was tasked with preventing.[62] In 1958 the specific task of foiling drug smuggling was transferred to the newly established Criminal Department, which also reported to the CID.[63] Additionally, a Coasts and Borders Division was established in 1949 to combat the smuggling of various goods, including drugs, at all entry and exit points to the country. In 1953 this division was replaced by a coast guard force. Headquartered at the Port of Haifa and under the supervision of the Port Police, the force was charged with patrolling Israel's coasts with the aim of, among other things, preventing drug smuggling by sea.[64]

That the Economic Department was tasked with overseeing the prevention of drug smuggling—even though, as the police themselves admitted, "this activity was not a typical economic crime"[65]—is instructive. It demonstrates that the prevention of drug smuggling *across* Israel was prioritized over the prevention of drug use *within* Israel. It is also instructive that drugs were but one category of several other smuggled goods the department was responsible for addressing.[66] Put differently, hashish was not singled out from other smuggled goods such as food and foreign currency. This must be understood within the context of Israel's austerity regime (*tzena*) through most of the 1950s, ensuing from the economic constraints created by massive immigration and the exigencies of nation building. These severe austerity measures led to a black market in goods like food and foreign currency, illegal quantities sold for a premium.[67] The Economic Department, which was part of the Investigation Department, "launched a largely ineffective 'war on the black market' that persisted throughout the 1950s."[68]

It should therefore come as no surprise that the Israel Police Force was singularly ineffective in the battle against hashish smuggling across the country's territory. In 1956, the antiestablishment magazine *Ha-'Olam Ha-Zeh* could claim with justification that "the police department . . . was unable to create the mechanisms of war [against drugs] at the same speed as drug traffickers could."[69] To be sure, in various international forums such as Interpol conferences and CND sessions, Israeli representatives praised the police's efforts to counter hashish trafficking operations across the country's territory. Take for example Michael Comay, Israel's ambassador to the United Nations between 1960 and 1967, who spoke at the January 1961 UN Plenipotentiary Conference for the adoption of a Single Convention on Narcotic Drugs, intended to replace the multiple treaties that had been promulgated since the early twentieth century:

> Israel's most urgent concern with narcotics is . . . due to her geographic position between countries where there is substantial production and countries where consumption is very large and addiction widespread. A constant flow of illegal traffic from the former to the latter passes through Israel territory. . . . The Israel police force has vigorously responded to this challenge, and hundreds of kilograms of opium and hashish are seized year after year.[70]

Such self-congratulation should not be taken at face value, however. In reality, the Israel Police's record of preventing drug trafficking operations across the country was much less laudatory than Israel's representatives in the UN and other international forums would have us believe. I will now take a closer look at this discrepancy.

Israel Police officials expressed their frustration with the never-ending tug-of-war with hashish smugglers in terms that recalled the exasperation of their British colonial predecessors in the pre-1948 period. As Israel Police Criminal Department Officer Yehuda Kaufman complained, in 1953:

> The possibilities [of hashish smuggling] are nearly endless and each time the police reveals one smuggling method, the smugglers come up with new [smuggling] methods . . . forms and . . . ruses. . . . Of all smugglers, drug smugglers . . .

are the most stubborn and most risk-oriented. Their operations are meticulous and organized, and they are cautious and cunning.[71]

On another occasion, Kaufman joined a chemistry professor from Haifa's Israel Institute of Technology (Technion) to file a complaint about drug traffickers across Israel:

> Drug smugglers never recoil at the severe and drastic measures which are taken against them, and they are never taken aback by the confiscation of drugs. As long as they succeed in transmitting their [illicit] consignments, or just a part of them, they are not even alarmed by fines, imprisonment, and infliction of bodily harm.[72]

Tricks of the smuggling trade after 1948 seemed to have been drawn from the very same textbook used by their pre-1948 forerunners. Even so, the authorities were caught as unawares as Mandatory officials had been before them. Hence, as the head of the Police Research and Statistics Department claimed, "smugglers do not hesitate to conceal drugs . . . on their own body, in intimate parts of it, [and] in orifices [*nikvei guf*]."[73] The same writer went on to list additional smuggling ruses, such as hiding hashish in

> cars' double compartments; in suitcases with double sides; in hollow soles and heels of shoes . . . in sofa upholstery; in bird cages; in framed pictures; . . . in pots used to cook soup; in prayer books; in old shoes; in doghouses; . . . in wine casks; . . . in pill boxes; in old newspapers; in cuckoo clocks; in baby clothes, etc. To these we may add pitchers, vases, flowerpots, and other home utensils.[74]

In practical terms, though, it was in the Negev region where, as mentioned earlier, the authorities found the task of anticipating, revealing, and foiling smuggling subterfuges, particularly those devised by Bedouins, the most difficult and unrewarding of undertakings. The war against drug trafficking in northern Israel improved substantially after 1948, due to stricter border patrols and the stronger police presence there. This can be seen clearly in a police report prepared for the Ministry of Foreign Affairs, enumerating "the most serious [drug] seizures" that occurred within Israel's borders in the years 1952 to 1959.[75] But this was not the case in the south of the country, particularly the Negev desert, where hashish smugglers were able to exploit their knowledge of the uninhibited terrain to successfully complete the journey to Egypt.[76] A reporter for the Israeli daily *Ma'ariv* formulated this advantage of Bedouin smugglers in poetic and ironic terms:

> It seems that only Allah himself knows the invisible and cunning ways of hashish smugglers. . . . But even Allah, the most compassionate and merciful, the guardian of the way of the believers, could not anticipate the various deceptions and methods which the experienced sons of the desert would come up with in order to deceive the guardians of the law.[77]

As the reader would recall, during the interwar period these very "sons of the desert" successfully deceived British colonial officials in Palestine and Egypt with an extremely sophisticated and unpleasant ruse for smuggling hashish: concealing packages of the drug inside the stomachs of camels, and—after making it safely across the border into Egypt—cutting the unfortunate beasts open to retrieve the treasure. In due course, the authorities came up with an equally imaginative method for dealing with this subterfuge. Because the concealed hashish was forced down the beasts' throats in tin containers, X-ray machines and mine detectors were deployed to the Palestinian-Egyptian border to inspect the insides of camels. Yet, as the head of Police Research and Statistics Department acknowledged in 1957, "as the means of defense [against drug smugglers] improve, the means of attack improve as well"; "as the efficiency of the police organization increases, so does the sophistication of the smugglers' ruses."[78] And so it was that after 1948 the Negev Bedouin hashish smugglers updated their tactics: "They started using cylinders made of plastic, rubber or leather which X-rays were incapable of detecting."[79] This ruse achieved an international notoriety of sorts, which is why the *New York Herald Tribune* elaborated on it in a 1960 story about "the Mid-East drug traffic":

> There's a good chance that any peaceful, romantically old-fashioned camel caravan plodding slowly across the Sinai Desert is carrying hashish and opium from Lebanon via Israel and by camel back to the Nile Delta. Or, more likely, by camel stomach. One of the common methods of transport is to put hashish powder and opium into undigestible plastic bags, which the camel is made to swallow. When the destination is reached, the camel's stomach is cut open and the dope is retrieved.[80]

It is clear, then, that the Israeli law enforcement authorities were unable to take effective action against hashish smuggling in the south of the country due to the difficult terrain and climate conditions, *and* the inventive machinations of the crafty smugglers. Endemic manpower shortages which militated against a significant police presence in the region didn't help either. During a 1956 meeting of the Knesset Internal Affairs Committee, Police Commissioner Sahar thus bemoaned the absence of a police presence in "the Negev area ... which is nearly half of the country's entire territory."[81] In testimony to the same committee three weeks later, Police Minister Sheetrit spoke about this same disadvantage, saying that the police Southern District, which covered Beersheba and the Negev desert, "is clearly larger than the Galilee District ... but doesn't have a police force that will meet [the district's] demands."[82] Consequently, police successes in preventing the flow of hashish from Jordan to the Negev, and from the Negev to Egypt, were extremely small. This explains why files prepared by individual police stations in the Southern District scarcely credit the police with seizures of large quantities of hashish; rather, the files refer to the comparatively large hashish and opium hauls by Israeli army patrols in the Negev, which occurred from time to time on a serendipitous basis after random and unplanned encounters with hashish-smuggling caravans. Indeed, many hashish seizures within Israeli territory, mainly those in the southern Negev region, were the outcome of unintended encounters of this kind.[83]

In sum, seizures of drugs (mainly hashish) in the 1948–67 period are evocative of the interwar period, as discussed in chapter 2. In both periods, the capture of trafficked drugs was coincidental or random; in both cases, the quantities seized probably represented merely a tiny fraction of the supplies of hashish that entered Palestinian-Israeli territory, either en route to Egypt or to remain in the former territory for local use. In 1958, during which a total of one thousand kilograms of hashish was captured by the authorities inside Israeli territory, a police official confessed that the quantity amounted to no more than "ten or fifteen percent of the entire hashish smuggled [into the country]."[84] The reader would recall that in the interwar period the British failed to apprehend any more than an estimated 10 percent of the hashish being smuggled through Palestine, and that they acknowledged as much. Thus, in terms of preventing hashish trafficking into and from Israel, not much changed in the transition from the interwar period to the State of Israel.

In the wake of 1948, then, hashish arrived in Israel—whether en route to Egypt or for distribution in the local market—either directly from Lebanon or via Jordan. A third route was "the sea route along the Mediterranean coast, [mainly] to Egypt."[85] Most of the smuggled hashish that traversed Israel's territorial waters left Lebanon in sailboats, fishing boats, or dinghies. Some hashish consignments were disembarked in Acre in the northern coastal plain region, from whence they were distributed across the country. Most of the contraband, however, was carried in these vessels along Israel's shore, in the open sea to the south; their destination, for the most part, was the Gaza Strip, which was under Egyptian rule.[86]

As indicated, the task of fighting and intercepting hashish smugglers at sea was invested in the Israel Police coast guard force. To be sure, this was a daunting task, certainly more daunting than that of the Mandate-era Port and Marine Section. It was especially so because the extension of Jewish sovereignty over Palestine, with the ensuing enhancement of border controls and greater police presence inside the country (in principle, although not always in practice), meant that more smuggling operations from Lebanon were diverted to the Mediterranean Sea.[87] With 254 kilometers—about 158 miles—of sea frontier to patrol, what can be said about the record of the coast guard force in apprehending hashish smugglers operating at sea? It is safe to assume that it was rather poor. Indeed, I did not find in the sources even one instance of a significant, *proactive* hashish haul made at sea. This silence may also be related to the smugglers' mastery of the art of concealment. From the late 1950s onward, for instance, the police and the press repeatedly reported one specific ruse that made it virtually impossible for the coast guard to apprehend the smugglers and their contraband red-handed, as it were. An Israeli reporter described this maneuver as follows:

> Hashish . . . is now smuggled in fishing boats sailing in the open sea. Tires containing hashish consignments wrapped in plastic bags are tied to the [exterior] sides of the vessels. In times of danger the crew cuts the ropes that secure the cargo to the boat; the tires sink into the water and are no longer discoverable. Once the danger has passed, the tires are salvaged [from the water] and are once again secured to the sides [of the vessel].[88]

This method was neither perfect nor safe, because the smugglers ran the risk of losing their cargo in the deep waters. Consequently, Israeli boats fishing off the southern Israeli coast sometimes drew in their nets tires containing large quantities of hashish.[89] Also, hashish-filled tires occasionally washed up on beaches in Israel's southern coastal plain, to be retrieved by beachgoers and hikers.[90]

DID ISRAEL REALLY TRY TO MAKE THE
EGYPTIAN ARMY GO TO POT?

That the Israeli military may have assisted in undermining the fight against smuggling operations across Israeli territory to Egypt, and indeed may have been heavily invested in these operations themselves, is a conjecture that cannot be ruled out. Building on untapped archival material and information drawn from the foreign press, in this section I explore the possibility that the Israeli Army undertook such smuggling operation, to disable Egyptians in general and debilitate the Egyptian army, Israel's main enemy at the time, in particular. This possibility shouldn't surprise. To be sure, it is common knowledge that armies, militias, and espionage organizations resorted, and still do resort, to drug trafficking—a means of waging war by other means, and of bolstering budgets restricted by other considerations. Allegations of CIA drug trafficking during the Cold War and afterward (in the Golden Triangle, for instance) are classic examples of such line of action.[91] But at the same time, allegations both true and fabricated of drug trafficking by foreign enemies, as a means of afflicting young lives and turning society's natural defenders into criminal menaces, are also abundant. Harry Anslinger, for instance, accused Japan of promoting drug traffic in the 1930s and 1940s to develop new revenue streams, but mainly to corrupt the morals of Western nations, and to enslave the peoples of the lands they had either invaded or had earmarked for invasion. Anslinger made similar allegations against communist China during the Cold War. Even the Islamic Republic of Iran repeatedly claimed in the 1980s, in the words of a contemporary Iranian daily, that drugs, particularly heroin, were "part of a long-term program by the enemies of the revolution . . . aim[ing] at making young people addicted."[92]

To begin my discussion, it is crucial to stress that throughout the 1950s and 1960s, Israeli public discourse was very keen on discussing Egypt's alleged "hashish affliction." This was probably informed by the domestic objective of political instruction: to denounce an enemy as a hopelessly evil and savage national threat, and to construct an insurmountable gulf between the self-styled progressive and modern Jewish state and a decadent, deviant, and autocratic Egyptian state. The following observation, made in 1966, is emblematic of mainstream Israeli discourse on Egypt's hashish problem across the time span of this chapter: "Hashish affliction is deeply rooted in Egyptian society, no less than the bilharzia virus incubating in the Nile."[93] Other observers drew comparisons between the pernicious consequences of opium addiction in nineteenth-century in China, and Egypt's "*hashishiyyin* living in the grip of addiction," describing the land of the Nile as "the China of the Mediterranean seashore."[94] Hashish, it was claimed, could be procured virtually anywhere in Egypt—"from wandering sellers, in cafés, and in haberdashery shops."[95] Hashish was smoked, the allegation went, by one-third of the population—eight million in the mid-1950s, nine million in the mid-1960s.[96] It was said that these many millions of "addicts" were drawn from all strata of Egyptian society: "the multitudes of Egyptian laborers," "the wretched and pitiable masses," "Egyptian high-society men and women," and culminating in the "whinny donkey and hashish smoker" Gamal 'Abd al-Nasser himself.[97] Egyptian men, it was further claimed, smoked excessive quantities of hashish in order to "intensify their sexual potency";[98] but it was more commonly smoked by people from both sexes to "forget their troubles by reaching a delirium of hashish-made paradise [*gan 'eden hashish*]."[99] In the process, hashish "destabilizes [the Egyptians'] health and sows inertia and stupor in their midst," ultimately "draining the strength of the Egyptian nation."[100]

These statements and observations are clearly hyperbolic. However, the likelihood that the State of Israel actually took an active and official role in engulfing Egypt in "a delirium of hashish-made paradise"—an obvious allusion to Charles Baudelaire's *Artificial Paradises* (*Les Paradis artificiels*, first published in 1860)—should not be dismissed as complete fiction. In fact, the Arab League's PANB filed repeated complaints with the United Nations about such actualities, beginning in the mid-1950s. It began with Israel's UN mission in New York receiving "confidential" information from "reliable" sources that the Arab League was preparing to submit a report to the tenth session of the CND in 1955, which was expected to allege that Israel was deeply complicit in the Levant drug trade in Egypt.[101] Zena Herman, member of the Israeli mission, immediately wrote to her superiors in Jerusalem, warning that "the Arab League is planning to publish a memo on the situation of dangerous drugs in the Middle East. [It] alleges that we're disseminating intoxicating drugs . . . with the intention of reducing the Arabs' strength. . . . We need to prepare for this.[102]

The anticipated report, drafted and signed by the PANB director, Egyptian Army Brigadier Abdel Aziz Safwat, was received by the CND just in time for its tenth annual meeting in May 1955. As expected, the report was scathingly damning of Israel, accusing it of two interrelated methods of "drug poisoning" the Arabs in general and the Egyptians in particular, as well as Europeans and Americans. The first alleged method was ambitious and expensive, required unusual infrastructure and expertise, but was also highly cunning in nature; the second was simpler and more economical. Safwat described the first method as follows:

> It seems certain that there are small factories in Israel for manufacturing co-caine, heroin, and synthetic drugs, and that it has been arranged to smuggle these drugs to certain countries in the Middle East and to certain European countries, using false labels bearing names of respectable firms. It has also ar-ranged to smuggle "white" drugs to the United States of America by sea via Cy-prus, Genoa and Marseille and by air by means usually arriving from Israel.[103]

Safwat's account of Israel's second and more modest method of disseminat-ing drugs among Arab publics focused specifically on hashish. This method merely required Israel to recycle hashish supplies smuggled into the country from Lebanon or Jordan and then seized for resmuggling to Egypt. The reports claimed: "The enquiries made by me have revealed that Israel is not intended to cultivate . . . Indian hemp within the country, [and] is considering [it] sufficient to deal with quantities of . . . prepared hashish smuggled into it from Lebanon and Jordan."[104] The same report was also quick to capitalize on the furor that erupted in Israel in 1954, following the revelation that Jewish immigrants from the Middle East and North Africa had cultivated cannabis plots in transit camps (this will be discussed in the next chapter). In his report, Safwat alleged that this cultivation had institutional backing, the objective being to direct the yield to Egypt. By 1955, Safwat went on to argue, cultivation had ceased because by that time "Israel was satisfied by the cannabis smuggled into its territory from [Lebanon], [which it seized] for subsequent re-smuggling into Egypt."[105]

Similar accusations reappeared in PANB reports to the CND throughout the second half of the 1950s and the early 1960s.[106] They were given further resonance by the Arab press. Hence, in the wake of the 1956 Suez Crisis, the Egyptian daily Al-Ahram reported that "hashish smugglers"—apparently Negev Bedouins—captured by the Egyptian military in the Sinai Desert disclosed that Israeli servicemen, whom they encountered during the Negev leg of their journey, had given them permission to proceed with their contraband towards Egypt. According to the report, "the Jews used military vehicles to transfer [hashish] to the desert during the period of [Sinai's] occupation [in 1956]."[107]

In the same year, the daily *Filastin* reported that Israel had been disseminating "large quantities" of "poisoned cigarettes" in unspecified "Arab countries," damaging the health of many a smoker.[108]

Needless to say, representatives and spokespersons of Israel's Foreign Ministry did not sit by idly as passive recipients of these allegations; they actively fought back. In the first instance, they categorically denied claims that Israel was producing "white drugs" for distribution in the Arab world and elsewhere: "Pharmaceutical factories in Israel operate under Government license and supervision. No incident involving the illicit manufacture of white drugs has come to light." At the same time, they denied that Israel was cultivating cannabis for similar purposes: "Cannabis was cultivated in Israel in negligible quantities [in 1954]. It was established beyond doubt that this hashish was earmarked for personal home consumption only. . . . No cannabis grown in Israel was ever smuggled abroad."[109]

To make the point that Israel was by no means a willing actor in the Middle East's "white drugs" and "black drugs" trades, Foreign Ministry representatives were quick to observe that the Arab League's allegations were, in effect, a projection of their own complicity in the region's drug trade. Because Arab rulers and Arab military and political elites were, they claimed, oblivious to the interests of their populations, they were prepared to sacrifice the health, vigor, and development of their citizens on the altar of the drug trade for a quick profit. To authenticate this charge, the Foreign Ministry regularly supplied its UN missions in New York and Geneva with intelligence reports and stories from the Arab press concerning the involvement of Arab rulers and other personalities in the Middle East—particularly the Levant—drug trade. Mission delegates were asked to pass on this information to their peers at the UN, and to leak it to the international press.

Understandably, Egypt and Lebanon were the two main countries Israel pointed the finger at. On the eve of the twelfth CND session in 1957, the Foreign Ministry sent the Israeli mission in New York a "confidential" twenty-one-page military intelligence report, asking it to disclose its contents.[110] The report allegedly contained information collected during the Israeli occupation of the Gaza Strip in 1956; it detailed the involvement of several Egyptian military and administrative personnel serving in Gaza in hashish trafficking. Actors reportedly included Major Mustafa Hafiz, the commander of Egyptian military intelligence in the Strip, who had done so, as the report claimed, "under the protection of the Egyptian military."[111] The report linked these Egyptians to Lebanese and Syrian hashish and opium smugglers, claiming that the latter were offered "bribes" in return for information about the location of Israeli military ambushes across the border. The report also included testimonies of Egyptian customs officials, police officers, soldiers, and attorneys. They claimed that armed Egyptian military units accompanied hashish traffickers across the Sinai desert, and that senior military officers personally escorted hashish supplies into Cairo and Alexandria.[112] The report was probably disseminated for propagandist ends, for it seems that the Egyptian authorities went to great pains to control such drug smuggling in Gaza. Yet there was "also evidence to suggest that some [Egyptian] officials were themselves involved in smuggling," though the scope of such undertakings remains an open question.[113]

To disassociate Israel from the Levant drug trade, it was not enough to implicate the Egyptian state in hashish smuggling. After all, Egypt was a victim of this trade and not an offender. What was needed more crucially was to draw attention to Lebanon as the center of the cultivation, distribution, and smuggling of drugs in the region. From the Foreign Ministry files made available to me, it can be easily established that the ministry's research department worked overtime to supply Israel's UN missions in New York and Geneva with accusatory material relating to these issues. Specifically, the research department provided these missions with Hebrew translations of numerous stories published in the Arab press, highlighting Lebanon's structural inability and unwillingness to prevent the cultivation of and trade in Egypt-bound hashish. Translated stories from newspapers like *Al-Ahram*, *Roz al-Yusuf*, *Al-Hayat*, and *Al-Difaʿ* were intended to enable Israeli UN representatives to name specific Lebanese politicians as complicit in the hashish trade, and to demonstrate the failure of Lebanon's political and law enforcement authorities to uproot hashish cultivation and hashish smuggling. At the same time, these stories allowed Israel to point at Egypt's own mistrust of Lebanon's declared commitment to eradicating such activities.[114]

Clearly, at least some of the Arab League's allegations against Israel were questionable, to say the least. For one thing, it is unlikely that the Israeli state was engaged in the production of cocaine, heroin, and synthetic drugs for distribution in the Arab world and beyond. I believe that such a complex and costly undertaking would have been impossible in the 1950s, when the young state was wrestling with the severe economic consequences of mass immigration and the exigencies of nation-building. Indeed, the Arab League's motivation for leveling such a charge may have been to transfer Lebanon's own culpability, as the opiates pipeline to Western Europe and the United States, to Israel. Arguably, by the 1950s it was already quite clear to the Federal Bureau of Narcotics, the Interpol, and the CND "just how pivotal Lebanon was to the world heroin market"—a market that subsequently became known as the French Connection.[115] Consecutive CND resolutions called Lebanon's observer to order due to this involvement. A UN survey mission dispatched to the Middle East to study the problem of illicit drug traffic in the region concluded in its final report that "opium was converted into crude morphine to facilitate its transport via Syria, Lebanon or Turkey to European countries such as France and Italy for refining, whence it is directed towards North America."[116]

Yet, despite Israel's repeated forceful denials, the Arab League's charge that Israel had *willfully* engaged in the clandestine smuggling of Lebanese hashish to Egypt is more credible than the allegation concerning the production of opiates and cocaine. In fact, similar claims about Israel's involvement in the hashish trade to Egypt have been elaborated in two separate investigative reports in the international press: the first in 1996 by *The Times* (London), and the second in 2010 by the French magazine *Revue*.[117] As will be seen shortly, these reports—coupled with vague and inconclusive references to the affair in the Israeli press—seem to confirm at least some of the claims made by the Arab League to the UN during the 1950s and 1960s.[118]

It should be stressed that, to this very day, this story still remains largely unknown to most Israelis. This is not by chance. Even though Israeli journalists and observers have progressively gleaned more information about this story over the years, the Israeli political, legal, and security authorities have put their entire weight and force behind concealing the affair. In the last half century or so, Israeli military censors, supreme court judges, cabinet members, defense and prime ministers, high-ranking military officers (including chiefs of staff), other powerful figures, and the courts have all ensured that information about the Israeli military's alleged hashish smuggling operations will not be leaked to the public.[119] Yossi Melman, *Ha-Aretz* national security correspondent, who for many years tried to unveil the smuggling operation, claims that it was

> one of the darkest and ugliest episodes of Israeli intelligence, and all information about it is still sealed. Because of the gag orders, I will code name it "Addictive Candy." . . . It involved systematic illegal activity by the state over many years, and publication of its details could bring disgrace to many former intelligence officials and give Israel a bad name. . . . [Throughout the years] I

have attempted time and again to report [this] tale. . . . I failed. The stubborn insistence by intelligence bodies to conceal and bury the story brought me to the conclusion that it stemmed from shame, and not from real concern for national security. The security authorities and the courts blocked every attempt of mine by means of secrecy ordinances, gag orders and sweeping censorship.[120]

Unsurprisingly, the reason cited for this comprehensive cover-up is "national security," mainly concerns regarding the impact of the story's exposure on Egyptian-Israeli relations.[121]

The idea of smuggling Lebanese hashish to Egypt by the Israeli military can allegedly be traced back to 1959, eleven years after Israel's independence and three years after the Israeli victory over Egypt in the 1956 Suez war. The alleged progenitor of the idea was Chaim Herzog, Israel's sixth president (1983–93), at the time the head of military intelligence.[122] As explored above, in these early years the State of Israel was compelled to fight the illicit hashish trade that ran into, across, and from the country. And so, instead of launching a futile and hopeless battle against hashish trafficking, Herzog and his close associates soon realized that "they could run the drug shipments themselves, flooding Egypt with cut-price narcotics and weakening the Egyptian army."[123]

Reportedly, the Israeli military's smuggling operation along the Lebanon-Israel-Egypt axis continued unabated for more than twenty-five years—from 1959 to the mid-1980s, long after Israel and Egypt established full diplomatic relations. Initially code-named "Toto," after the national soccer betting pool—and later "Lahav" (Blade), and "Tidhar" (a tree mentioned in the Book of Isaiah)—the operation was approved by successive Israeli governments, thus ensuring that the Egyptian military would be flooded with hashish for decades. No one dared question the idea, specifically its morality or its military value. Neither was the underlying logic of the operation questioned: no one asked how a handful of traffickers could paralyze an entire army by means of smuggled hashish. And worse: "That Egypt did not lack hashish is an understatement; hence the operation was like selling tea to Ceylon, or coal to Newcastle, or ice to Eskimos."[124]

The enduring and highly covert operation was entrusted to an elite military intelligence team, Unit 504, whose specialty was the recruitment and "running" of agents in neighboring countries (i.e., Syria, Lebanon, Jordan, and Egypt). Unit 504 played a crucial role in Israel's victory in the 1967 War by gathering valuable information about the Egyptian military.[125] However, its reputation has been badly marred in recent years by revelations about the unit's resort to torture, rape, and in at least one case "sodomizing [of a suspect] with a rod."[126]

Yossi Melman contends that the unit "was aware of the drug trade for decades, followed the route of the drugs—mostly hashish and opium—across the Middle East and also turned them to its own advantage."[127] To facilitate hashish smuggling to Egypt, the unit's agents allegedly recruited Lebanese drug traffickers and offered local Lebanese growers monetary incentives in exchange for cannabis and poppy products. According to the 2010 investigative report, "A lot of money passed from hand to hand. Wine bottles [also] facilitated the traffic. An Israeli who participated in [the] operation . . . [who was] dressed like an Arab and trained to speak Arabic in Lebanese dialect, recalls how he had travelled to the Bekaa Valley to deliver more than one million dollars in cash to a Lebanese grower."[128]

The routes chosen for the traffic were elaborate and diverse. Firstly, certain cargoes were transferred overland in trucks from Lebanon to Syria, and from there to Jordan. From Jordan, the drugs were then redirected to Israel via the smuggling routes described in the first section of this chapter. Additional supplies were transferred directly from Jordan to Egypt by boat along the Gulf of Aqaba. Other supplies were transferred by sea from the Lebanese coastal town of Tyre to Achziv, an old Arab village (known in Arabic as al-Zeeb) on the Mediterranean coast of northern Israel, turned into a haven for hippies, loafers, and "bohemians" in the 1960s and 1970s.[129] Finally, Israeli navy combat boats escorted Lebanese drug boats to the northern town of Nahariya.[130]

The 2010 report further revealed that, once on Israeli soil, Unit 504 officers dressed in civilian clothes accompanied the hashish consignments to a warehouse in Ha-Kirya—a military base in the heart of Tel Aviv, and the headquarters of Israel's Ministry of Defense—for storage. Approximately once a month, Unit 504 officers escorted military trucks from this warehouse to precise meeting points in the Sinai on the Israeli-Egyptian border, where they would transfer the cargos to Egyptian traffickers, or distribute the drug among Egyptian soldiers stationed in the area between the Sinai Peninsula and Cairo.

CONCLUSION

[My] country [finds] itself in a difficult position [with respect to] the suppression of illicit traffic in narcotics as a result of its situation at the very center of the Middle East area, and because it had no less than

> 951 kilometers of land frontier and 254 kilometers of sea frontier to
> guard. . . . [The] Israeli authorities [are] constantly engaged in vigorous
> and reasonably effective preventive action against the illicit traffic.

These are the words of Menachem Kahany, head of the Israel mission to the Geneva-based European Office of the UN, at the eleventh CND meeting in May 1956, attempting to portray Israel's challenges with respect to hashish pouring into and from the country.[131] A 1954 report issued by the Foreign Ministry Research Department spelled out this challenge more precisely. The report specified that Israel is situated between Lebanon, "the only country, with the exception of Turkey, that grows hashish," and Egypt, which is "the main consumer of intoxicating drugs in general and hashish in particular in this part of the world."[132] With necessary modifications, the hashish routes of the Levant hashish trade thus survived the transition to the State of Israel in the post-1948 era, the territory now ruled by that state continuing to serve as the crucial link with Egypt. The same can be said about the artful subterfuges of hashish traffickers, which made the task of combating them extremely difficult both before and after 1948.

As discussed in chapter 2, there is strong albeit unsubstantiated cause to believe that military and paramilitary Zionist organizations in pre-1948 Palestine had themselves engaged in hashish smuggling from Lebanon to Egypt, in exchange for arms and to replenish their budgets. The alleged promotion of the hashish trade in the region by the Israeli military after 1948, as examined in this chapter, may be seen as the survival of yet another trend of hashish smuggling, with one major difference. The alleged aim of the Israeli military was not to finance an anticolonial struggle, but to stoke the disaffection of Middle Eastern masses "by encouraging drug addiction and thus promoting political apathy."[133] Turning to the last chapter, I will now consider trends of continuity and change with respect to the issue of hashish consumption in the State of Israel during the first two decades of its existence.

6

MIZRAHIM AND THE "PERILS"
OF HASHISH SMOKING

[An] important factor in the categorization of substances such as opium and cannabis was their association with specific ethnic groups when increased population mobility in the nineteenth and twentieth centuries led to direct cultural contact with the customs of immigrant populations. These circumstances led to their stereotyping and an ethnocentric reaction against "alien drugs" and their predominantly working-class users.

WITH THE APPROPRIATE ADJUSTMENTS for time and place, these words by the late renowned archaeologist and world prehistorian Andrew Sherratt would correspond to the histories and discourses of drug consumption in many countries around the world—including Israel of the 1950s and 1960s.[1] Leaving aside for the moment the issue of Palestinian dispossession, Israel was a successful settler colonial project emerging from the British mandate, in that the settlers were "indigenized" and ceased to be seen as immigrants-cum-settlers.[2] Yet some of these former settlers—mainly Central and East European Jews and their offspring—were indigenized more thoroughly, as it were, than were Jews who hailed from the Middle East and North Africa and their descendants, collectively known as Mizrahim. The latter were particularly feared because the state perceived them as primitive, backward, and in need of a radical civilizatory transformation. Members of the state's ruling political party, Mapai, "simply took the arsenal of [Orientalist] images and symbols that [formerly] had been used to exclude [them in Europe] and applied them . . . to the Mizrahim. They thus presented themselves as the westerners that they had, up until that point, never been."[3]

It may be recalled (see chapter 4), that British Palestine's Jews largely kept at arm's length from hashish; as primary recipients of colonial knowledge and Orientalist fantasies about cannabis, they perceived the drug as a major cause of the pathologies supposedly inhering in "Oriental" Arab cultures. In this chapter I demonstrate that new demographic and political realities after 1948—the depopulation of the Arab population of Palestine in the Nakba, and the country's massive repopulation by Mizrahim—turned hashish into a Jewish "problem" where formerly it was considered an Arab one. Some of these Jews had used hashish in their countries of origin, and brought the habit with them to Israel. Other first- and second-generation immigrants from Muslim countries were not hashish smokers, but had picked up on the habit in Israel owing to their socioeconomic and ethnic-cum-racial marginalization.[4]

I begin this chapter by briefly exploring how the Israel Police handled the culture of hashish use inside Israel and the fight against the local hashish market. In the first two decades of the Jewish state, the police force was utterly unprepared for contending with such issues due to a variety of reasons, as I examined in the previous chapter: lack of appropriate labor force and expert know-how, as well as more important priorities linked to the exigencies of nation-building in the first decades of the state. Anti-Mizrahi ethnic-cum-racial biases were also in play, as these sometimes kept police enforcers away from centers of substance abuse.

In section 2 of this chapter I move away from the history of antihashish enforcement to examine the public discourse regarding hashish consumption in the formative years of the State of Israel. I will demonstrate that dominant perceptions of hashish smoking in the Jewish state represented an adaptation of earlier, pre-1948 Jewish understandings of this habit as an Oriental vice, now transferred from Arabs to Mizrahim. Although the number of hashish smokers during the 1950s and much of the 1960s probably did not exceed a few thousand, the habit reinforced and dramatized the Ashkenazi dominant classes' preexisting anxieties about over-Levantinization of Israel—the "possibility that if Orientals . . . had [their way], the state would be assimilated into an Arab domain."[5] At the same time, it exacerbated the marginalization and criminalization of Mizrahim in Israeli society. Hence, hashish prohibition targeted those categories that were at odds with the Jewish state's view of what Israeli society should look like.[6]

OF INFORMANTS, DOGS, AND "NEGROES": THE
FIGHT AGAINST THE LOCAL HASHISH MARKET

The massive influx of Jews from the Middle East and North Africa to the State of Israel after 1948, which came on the heels of the Palestinians' exodus and expulsion from the country, gained momentum during the 1950s.[7] Many of these immigrants were settled in transit camps (ma'abarot) that sprang up across the country, some on the ruins of previous Arab towns and villages, with some transformed into "development towns" by the 1960s. They remained unemployed or were diverted to blue-collar industries or physical labor. As their name implies, these camps were originally perceived as temporary dwelling places; yet many Jews remained there for much longer periods, some for as long as seven years. They were forced to contend with poor sanitary and hygiene conditions, poverty, and neglect, as well as ill treatment and discrimination by the state.[8] "Varying efforts, which unfortunately included all imaginable atrocities, were made by the state apparatuses to 'save' these 'underdeveloped' children from their fates."[9] Beset by these adversities, these places soon evolved into centers of drug dealing and substance abuse. Three Israeli experts described the immigrants' predicament:

> Many of these immigrants . . . experienced cultural shock as well as serious social and economic problems as a result of relocation. The result was the emergence of distressed neighborhoods in urban centers and rapidly established development towns. These neighborhoods, characterized by economic stagnation and social ills typically associated with anomie and disintegration, became centers of high rates of school dropouts and juvenile delinquency, unemployment, criminality, and an emerging culture of substance abuse.[10]

In the previous chapter I examined the issue of hashish smuggling from Lebanon to Egypt via Israel, and the Israeli authorities' response to the challenge. It must be remembered, though, that this was only one aspect of the state's concern with the hashish trade. A related part—more instructive in terms of notions of public health, national well-being, social inequalities, and ethnic-racial politics within Israel—was the fight against the hashish trade for home consumption, which fed on and owed its existence to the transregional border-crossing Levant trade. In 1965 an Israeli reporter summed up this dependence of the home market on the Levant hashish trade:

> Israel's position in the world of drugs is . . . unique. It is located in a region in which the use of drugs is widespread. . . . Due to its special geographical location [Israel] has been . . . a transit country for drug supplies running from [the countries] of production . . . to these drug's main site of consumption, Egypt. . . . A tiny portion [*heleq za'ir*] of the smuggled commodities remains in the country where it is distributed for the local market.[11]

A Ministry of Health report designated the cities of Lod, Ramla, Jaffa (allocated in the UN partition plan of 1947 to the Arab state), and Haifa (allocated in the same plan to the Jewish state) as centers of hashish commerce and use *inside* Israel.[12] As we have seen in chapters 2 and 3, this represented a salient continuity with the pre-1948 period, except that in this instance Jewish hashish dealers and hashish consumers either replaced Arabs who had fled or been expelled from the country, or joined the ones who were able to remain in Israel. To these "drug centers" we should add the area of Beersheba. This can be explained by the town's location in the Negev region, which served as a hub for Egypt-bound hashish supplies.[13] After the establishment of the State of Israel, as before, some of these supplies were redirected by smugglers to the local hashish market.[14]

The sources say very little about post-1948 drug dealers—Jews and, to a lesser extent, Arabs. The little information available about them is terse and nondescript. Hence, internal police reports from the 1950s identify the dealers simply as "new immigrants" (apparently from the Middle East and North Africa). Nor do the sources reveal much information about the measures taken against them. We learn that generally the police engaged in "intelligence-gathering, ambushes . . . and surveillance . . . inside Israeli territory." The police also engaged "in constant battle against local merchants who are . . . making use of [Egypt-bound] smuggling caravans as supply sources [for local use]."[15]

We also learn that in order to deal more effectively with the problem of drug dealers and their clients, a canine unit was established in 1953, trained to track down hashish by smell. Although this was in line with British tradition of "forensic dog tracking" in the colonies since the late nineteenth century,[16] Israel was apparently the first country ever to make use of sniffing dogs to discover drugs.[17] During its first years of existence, the police "Animal Section" owned one dog—predictably and unimaginably named Lassie. By 1960 an additional dog had been trained for the task; both dogs were deployed in sites around the country, especially in Israel's "drug capitals."[18] An enthusiast journalist reported in 1953 that "the wiles of [hashish] dealers are almost limitless," but "Lassie . . . is beginning to give them serious concern, because the particular smell of hashish is unavoidable."[19] The periodical that served as a police mouthpiece for reaching out to the public, 999, was of similar mind, eagerly reporting Lassie's exploits to its readers. Participating in a house search in Jaffa, Lassie led the police officers to a chicken coop in the backyard, where she discovered 1.5 kilograms of hashish hidden under a heap. Likewise, in Haifa, "the same dog discovered various quantities of hashish hidden inside a desk drawer and inside a wardrobe belonging to a resident of the city."[20] Despite the praise heaped on Lassie, she was not always successful in her missions. For instance, in 1953 she was dispatched to search for drugs in the houses of two suspected hashish dealers in the "Arab area" of Lod, but no drugs were discovered. On the same occasion she was employed in "three Arab coffeehouses . . . suspected of [dealing in] hashish, but no hashish was found in them."[21]

Whether or not the canine unit did cause hashish dealers to "tremble in their boots" remains an open question;[22] the unit was clearly not enough to compensate for the police's inherent deficiencies in contending with this vice. Accordingly, the police came up with another tactic: offering various incentives to people who were prepared to report on hashish dealers, including "large monetary rewards" (*prasei kesef gdolim*) reaching up to 15 percent of the captured drugs' value.[23] To encourage informants of this kind, the police held periodic ceremonies to honor children who, by assisting in identifying drug dealers and uncovering hidden hashish supplies, "had shown initiative and good citizenship." These ceremonies, in which "gifts of appreciation" were awarded, were held in the presence of the children's families and senior police officers.[24] "It is a pleasure for the police . . . to host children who have carried out good deeds and helped in exposing criminals and lawbreakers," declared a police officer, summing up his satisfaction with these ceremonies.[25]

Lastly, treated with caution, sensational newspaper articles from the early 1960s may afford us a glimpse into drug enforcers' activities, the poor results they yielded, and, significantly, the racialized dimensions of middle-class Jewish attitudes toward local drug dealers. To illustrate these themes, I will specifically draw on two articles that can be regarded as police publicity stunts. The site of both stories is the hashish hub of Beersheba and its Negev desert vicinity. The first article, "A Negro in the Dead of the Night," tells the story of a successful police sting operation, culminating in the arrest of a Bedouin hashish dealer while making a transaction in the Negev area;[26] the second article, "The Shirts Were Too Inflated," sings the praises of a police detective in Beersheba, whose reported ingenuity led not only to the arrest of two Jewish hashish dealers but also to the confiscation of the largest quantity of hashish ever found until that time on Jews in the south of Israel.[27]

Fanfare aside, the first and most obvious thing that comes to mind in considering these two cases is the unimpressive quantity of hashish actually seized in each of them. The story about the sting operation didn't specify any quantities, but did indicate that the transaction involved "one package of hashish." Considering that the hashish dealer passed this package to an undercover police officer playing the role of a criminal accomplice, it must have been small and light enough for just one person to carry. The same can be said regarding "the largest quantity of hashish ever captured on Jewish [drug dealers] in the Negev," which was credited in the second story to a police officer, a Sergeant Yitzhak Berkovitch; it comprised no more than "two 'loaves' [suliyot] of hashish, each weighing 300 grams" (approximately 10.6 ounces, 21.2 ounces altogether). Thus, even if we accept the claim that Berkovitch had "a sharp analytical mind" as well as "many chicaneries up his sleeve," the quantity of hashish that he discovered underneath the two dealers' shirts was not exceptionally large.

Berkovitch, the quintessential Jewish Israeli law enforcer, is described as "a firmly-built man with blond hair and of average height, whose blue eyes emit, when necessary, a spark as cold as steel."[28] Hence, I arrive at the second point that comes to mind in these stories—the social and rhetorical positioning of drug enforcers within the boundaries of "whiteness"—that is, of justice, truth, civilization, purity, and freedom. Drug dealers, on the other hand, stand for absence at best—or ugliness, sin, darkness, and immorality at worst, thus the realm of "blackness." For example, in the story about the police sting, the Bedouin drug dealer is described as "a young . . . negro [kushi] man . . . black as soot, skinny, slender, whose eyes burned like fire"; "in the darkness only his white teeth shone, as though floating in space, disconnected from the body. [These were] sharp monstrous teeth, living of their own accord." Apparently, so ubiquitous was the drug dealer's blackness that when he sensed the looming danger of the police raid, "he blended in the darkness of the night and disappeared." This imputed blackness of the Bedouin also enabled his attorney to come up with a "clever" defense argument, which ran as follows: "From a distance of 50 meters, it would be impossible for the policemen to identify the Negro at night—and not just any night, but a [moonless] night—because he melded into the darkness." The judge, reportedly, accepted this argument and dismissed the charges on account of reasonable doubt: "It is indeed difficult for the human eye to identify a Negro in the dead of the night—surely, [the eye] could not identify the said Negro clearly."[29] Lastly, by claiming that before taking action to disrupt the staged transaction, the police waited for the hashish package "to be transferred from one pair of black hands to another pair of white hands," the writer posited whiteness and blackness, drug enforcer and drug dealer as two irreconcilable opposites.[30] As I will presently demonstrate, blackness and whiteness were also major variables in the history and discourse of hashish consumption in Israel in the post-1948 era. This was made possible by fear of Mizrahi immigrants and the loss of hegemony by the veteran Jewish community, a fear that translated into prejudice and stereotyped perceptions of these immigrants.[31]

"WORN OUT AND FILTHY RIFFRAFF": HASHISH CONSUMERS IN ISRAEL

Throughout the 1950s, official discourse regarding criminal behavior among Mizrahim engaged in doublespeak, or at the very least was defined by ambiguity and irresolution. On the one hand, it was claimed that criminality was not more rampant among these immigrants than among other Jewish groups in Israeli society— that is, Israeli-born Ashkenazim or Jewish immigrants from Europe. Stipulating that it was "nigh possible to determine conclusively the share in criminality of veteran Israelis [*anshei ha-yishuv ha-vatiq*] and that of newly-coming immigrants," a 1955 police report concluded: "It is clear that in certain types [of criminality], new immigrants play a larger role . . . but in the majority of [cases] there is no difference between immigrants and veteran Israelis."[32] The "widespread allegation" that criminality was greater among the "immigrants from the East" was thus totally "unfounded," as police officials opined elsewhere: "Arguably, the percentage of criminals from among the new immigrants does not exceed the percentage among the country's veterans."[33]

At the same time, however, the very same sources were prepared to restate that massive immigration from the Middle East and North Africa did account for the steep rise in criminal activity in Israel. Consider, for example, the following relatively subtle passage from the Police Annual Report for 1951—the year in which Jewish immigration to Israel in general, and to Israel from the Middle East and North Africa in particular, reached a climax:[34]

> The huge wave of immigration has been penetrated by criminal elements. . . . Multitudes of immigrants arrived from countries whose culture is poor and whose political structures are unstable and inferior or built on oppression and coercion. [In these countries] corruption is widespread across all walks of life, and the citizens obey the law out of fear and pressure. [Among these immigrants] there are those for whom liberties and lack of coercion are inappropriately understood as a license to do as they please and . . . as a system of lawlessness [*mishtar shel-hefqerut*].[35]

Despite this doublespeak about criminality, when it came to drug use—mainly of hashish—a wall-to-wall consensus emerged in public and official discourse, that first- and second-generation immigrants from the Muslim world were the main culprits. As a police officer explained: "Since the mass immigration of Jews from the Arab countries, [hashish] consumption has increased. It is easy to explain this [phenomenon]: each wave of immigration to our state has brought with it ways of life, habits, and customs of the immigrants' origin countries, including the habit of using dangerous drugs."[36] This consensus persisted throughout the 1950s and 1960s. A 1966 survey article on drug offenders in Israel, written by two Israeli criminologists, thus confirmed:

> Smoking of drugs (especially hashish and opium) is a relatively widespread practice in the countries of the Middle East, especially in Turkey, Persia, Egypt and Iraq. It can be assumed that . . . there is a relatively large number of people who have brought this custom with them from their country of origin.[37]

The extent of drug abuse or drug addiction during the discussed period is not known, because no reliable data is available.[38] As Jonathan Lewy suggests in his study of drug policy in the Third Reich, the number of drug abusers is invariably difficult to ascertain because, "like many drug statistics, the reported numbers of addicts are mere guesstimates rather than reliable figures, mainly because it is next to impossible to differentiate between addicts and users."[39] Reaching a precise estimation of the number of Jewish hashish smokers in the period discussed here is therefore a difficult task.

However, it can be carefully assumed that the numbers did not exceed a few thousand. This can be gauged from a controversy of sorts sparked in 1960, in the wake of a story about drug addicts in Israel published in the daily *Ha-Aretz*. Among other things, the story included the following excerpt from a separate article written by Avraham Turnau, the chief pharmacist at the Ministry of Health:

In recent years the number of drug addicts [narqomanim] has increased significantly in the Israeli [Jewish] population and their number has now reached a few thousand. More than half of the registered addicts are immigrants from the countries of Islam. . . . (These numbers don't include thousands of hashish smokers.)[40]

The number of Israeli addicts cited by Turnau was far removed from the figures quoted by the Health Ministry in its official reports to the CND. Those reports put the number of registered Israeli drug addicts at around 170 (in the second half of the 1950s), and at around 300 (in the first half of the 1960s).[41] Amazed by the huge discrepancy between the figures submitted to the CND and to Ha-Aretz respectively, Israel's UN representatives in Geneva and New York urged the Ministry of Foreign Affairs to urgently inquire into the matter with the police and the Health Ministry. Kahany, of the Israeli delegation to the European Office of the UN, protested to his superiors in Jerusalem, writing: "I am astonished by these figures because in our reports to the CND we have [always] claimed that the number of addicts in Israel is so small that it shouldn't be treated seriously. . . . I would like to know which figures are the true ones . . . [because] it may be in the interest of the CND."[42] Observed Tamar Eshel, also of the Israeli delegation to the UN, to the Foreign Ministry: "No doubt, we will have to explain [to the CND] this sudden . . . alarming increase in the number of addicts."[43]

Responding to the Foreign Ministry's query, the Health Ministry explained that the number given to the CND consisted of registered addicts only (which at the time of the query amounted to 300); that the total number of opiate addicts in Israel was 1,200; and, more pertinent to my line of inquiry, that "the number of hashish smokers [in Israel] comes close to a few thousand."[44] The police took issue with these figures, however. In a letter to the Foreign Ministry, the Israel Police liaison officer with Interpol claimed that the total number of drug addicts in Israel was actually 50 percent smaller than that reported by the Health Ministry, and that "hashish consumption in the country is relatively small." He did not provide actual numbers of hashish smokers.[45]

Although I could not obtain actual statistics about hashish consumers in Israel, it is likely that smokers of the drug in Israel during the 1950s and 1960s remained limited to no more than a few thousand members of the Mizrahi underclass, and did not make inroads into the Ashkenazi middle class until after the 1967 Arab-Israeli War. A journalist who visited "hashish dens" in Jaffa in the early 1950s thus noted with satisfaction that "very few Ashkenazim smoke hashish, and I did not meet any of them when I toured hashish dens in Jaffa."[46] This profile of hashish users did not change during much of the 1960s. Hence, following a 1963 police raid on a Haifa café that served hashish to its customers, an embedded reporter mused that the patrons were "divided into different types and different ethnic groups ['edot]: about a quarter of them were Arabs. About forty percent of them came from Morocco . . . [and the rest were] immigrants from Iraq and Turkey."[47]

Despite this state of affairs, there were plenty of moral entrepreneurs for whom the hashish-consuming Mizrahim presented a danger to the very Western foundations of the Jewish state, bringing it to the brink of turning into a full-fledged Arab or Levantine space.[48] The primary terms that expressed the state's fears of Mizrahim who smoked hashish were "contagion" (hidabqut) and "plague" (magefah), as though hashish smoking were a disease that might spread to the enlightened, European—not to say white—sectors of Jewish society in Israel. These metaphors are reminiscent of older continental anxieties of reverse colonialism, which spoke of an insidious invasion of Orientals and Oriental drugs disrupting metropolitan life by debilitating and immobilizing its citizens. In 1890s London, for example, "the opium den seemed to contain the threat of the colony infiltrating the imperial capital, and the contagion of the empire staining the mother country."[49] Consider the following ominous warning issued by a police officer in 1956: "What we have here is a national peril, a terrible peril. . . . If something is not done to eliminate this terrible plague, in ten years' time Israel will become a second Egypt."[50] Consider, too, a commentator for the daily Ha-Tzofeh, identified with religious Zionism. Although he was able to reassure his readers that "for the time being the use of intoxicating drugs is confined to Jews of Eastern extraction [bnei 'edot ha-mizrah]," he brought attention to "a few places" where "neighbors started to follow in their footsteps." Specifically, he referred to the northern town of Kiryat Shmona, a transit camp turned into a local council in 1953, where migrant "Romanian Jews . . . have learned the doctrine [torah] of hashish smoking from Eastern Jews, becoming experts in it and infecting others as well."[51]

The fear of Levantinization by way of "hashish contagion" also emerged in the Knesset's Public Services Committee, during discussions over a proposed bill to amend the 1936 Mandatory Dangerous Drugs Ordinance, which, like so many of the young country's laws, remained in force after 1948. The bill, passed by the Knesset in 1952, had nothing to do with hashish. It was directed at eliminating the state's dependence on the importation of narcotics for medicinal use, by removing clauses in the 1936 ordinance that prohibited the cultivation, production, and preparation of the opium poppy and other synthetic drugs.[52] However, opponents to the bill based their arguments on the "quality" of immigrants from the Arab and Muslim world, and their "natural disposition" to hashish smoking. For instance, member of the Knesset Ben-Zion Harel, a physician by training, explained that he would oppose the bill because of "the makeup of our population and all the kinds of immigrants that have come here—this is why I see a great risk here." He then moved on to talk about hashish, unwittingly revealing his fear of Israel's Arabicization or Levantinization resulting from the spread of hashish use:

> As for hashish, I think we need to make sure there is no cultivation [of it] in the country. Countries like Turkey and Lebanon are making profits from cultivating these drugs, but in practice they are killing hundreds and thousands of their own citizens. I believe we should not be partners to this. I strongly insist on this, because [if we allow cannabis cultivation] the morale of our people will be imperiled.[53]

Hashish-smoking venues—where hashish could be shared by Mizrahi and Ashkenazi Jews on the one hand, and between Jews and Arabs on the other—were specifically singled out as a threat to the homogeneity and Eurocentricity of the national project. That these venues were usually located in Israel's ethnically mixed towns, which are basically "bi-national borderlands in which Arabs and Jews live together,"[54] heightened the threat of "mixedness" issuing from them. After all, these very venues, to borrow from Shira Robinson's analysis of the Israeli state's motivation for instituting military rule over Arab-populated regions, ran the risk of crossing

> the social boundaries between native Arabs and immigrant Jews lest they develop political alliances, romantic attachments, or any relationships that could call into question the rationale for Jewish privilege. . . . Many of the new immigrants [grew] up speaking the same mother tongue, reading the same literature, and listening to the same kind of music as the Arabs of Palestine.[55]

Jaffa's hashish dens are a classic case in point. These dens were concentrated in what became known as the "Large Area" (Ha-shetah ha-gadol). Previously part of Jaffa's Old City, the area probably acquired its name at the beginning of the Arab Revolt in the summer of 1936, when the British authorities leveled several hundred houses in the area because they had provided cover for stone throwers and snipers. House demolition was also carried out as a means of punishment and deterrence, and for transforming some of the Old City's alleys into patrol routes.[56] The demolition of this Arab area was resumed during and immediately after the 1948 War; centuries-old buildings were demolished and Jewish immigrants from the Balkans and North Africa were brought in to reoccupy the remaining buildings.[57] By the early 1950s, Jaffa's "Large Area" enjoyed a dubious reputation as Tel Aviv's alter ego or underground self: it "was a location of casual sexual encounters, a casbah of crime, drug dens, and gambling. . . . Under the auspices of the Tel Aviv Municipality, the Large Area became home to orientalist fantasies and ethnic demons that created a place of contamination and revulsion, which is the Jewish antithesis to the White City of Tel Aviv, a UNESCO World Heritage site."[58] Architect Sharon Rotbard further explains:

["The Large Area"] was associated with the dark margins of the white metropolis [Tel Aviv] and it became synonymous with illegal and criminal activity. "The Large Area" was a cultural campaign. . . . Its objective was to blacken the face of Jaffa with dark elements that . . . [the] Labor Party's puritan Zionism found unpalatable: nightlife, underground economy, crime, drugs and alcohol, Orientalism and Arabism. . . . Jaffa became the other, darker side of the white city.[59]

In 1961 the Israeli government and the Tel Aviv municipality joined forces to establish the Old Jaffa Development Company (*Ha-hevra le-fitu'ah Yaffo ha-'atiqah*). Its aim, as the company's present Web page explains, was to "build and rehabilitate the Tel-Jaffa area (also known as the Large Area), a compound that served as a hotbed for crime, prostitution and drugs."[60] By 1964–65 the area, by then known simply as the "Old City," was totally transformed. Toward the end of the construction work, the daily *Yedi'ot Ahronot* described this transformation as follows: "The prostitutes gave way to shiny galleries and glamorous nightclubs. . . . There is no doubt that with the elimination of hashish dens . . . a new page will be opened in the [area]."[61] Rotbard suggests that with the completion of the project, Jaffa, "as a concrete city and an Arab city, had been erased."[62]

In the interval, however, mainstream public discourse cast the area's hashish-smoking spaces to the realms of radical alterity. Patrons of these venues were described as "worn out and filthy riffraff"; "the most revolting figures . . .

ever seen"; "a mixture of malignant diseases, degeneration and the underworld"; and "a prey for bugs and lice."[63] While indulging in hashish, they were said to be "in a state of hallucination—their eyes rolling, their eye pupils wide, their gaze incoherent, their speech tired and unending. And there were those who didn't seem to be conscious of their surroundings."[64]

The interiors of these "Large Area" establishments were also said to be filthy, foul-smelling, depressing, and in a state of utter disrepair: "Everything in this place is dirty and sticky—the furniture, the glasses, the cups, the thick air hanging in space"; "Most of the cafés are very dirty. They are located in ancient, ramshackle one-story buildings," in "quarter[s] of tin shacks," in "pitiable wooden shacks," in "plaster-less buildings, their entrance yawning before you, bringing to mind toothless old women"; "The room is sooty and gloomy. Its windows are shut. The ceiling is high and curved"; "A filthy light bulb flickers, producing very little light and many heavy, depleted, and sickly shadows"; "The paint that was glued to the wooden ceiling peeled off long ago and a few stains remained here and there"; "The stench is discernible in every corner"; "The smell of the manure of beasts is truly nauseating."[65]

Lastly, there was a recurring reminder, at once critical and ridiculing, that these venues were also Arab enclaves at the very heart of a Western space. The décor and the sounds were Arab in each and every respect: in one establishment, "a picture of a smiling King Faruq" of Egypt decorated the wall, and in another there was "a television set which featured Nasser venting malice." In another Jaffa hashish den, "black coffee mixed with cardamom was served, as is customary with the Arabs"; and in yet another hashish den, the guests "were playing—what else—backgammon." In a café by the sea, "a screechy phonograph was playing songs of Umm Kulthum, the famous Egyptian singer, and her seductive voice flowed like fire in the veins of the listeners who were under the influence of the drug."[66]

Unlike Arabs, hashish smoking by Mizrahim was described not as an innate, racial pathology, but rather as something they had picked up over many years of living in a "diasporic" Oriental environment: "Jews who lived among the Arabs . . . were infected by this indecent habit"; it was "from their Arab neighbors that the Jews learned to smoke hashish"; "[these] Jews assimilated [such] unseemly customs in their countries [of origin]."[67]

Yet the fact that they carried this habit over to the *modern* Jewish state was cause for both ridicule and sharp condemnation. Take, for example, a newspaper story about "Mahlul the Moroccan," who "immigrated [to Israel] some time ago and who now lives in one of the transit camps in [Beit She'an] valley" (in northern Israel).[68] From an early age, Mahlul was said to have loved the ways of the Muslims in Morocco; so much so that "when he was a child he used to . . . listen to the . . . muezzin calling the faithful to prayer from the rooftop of the mosque, his voice quavering." And little Mahlul would stand below, "his faint voice quavering and chirping," mimicking the muezzin.

When Mahlul reached adulthood his fear of sin decreased, but his affection for the manners and customs of his Moroccan Muslim compatriots did not wane. And so, instead of practicing piety, Mahlul started to listen to the radio at the local café near his house, ignoring his father's protestations. When he listened to the radio for the first time,

> he was astonished . . . to hear the voice of the Egyptian singer Layla Murad coming out directly from the singing box. A devil's act, a deception, a demon inside [the box]. Stealthily, he tried to remove the [radio's] back lid to take a peek inside. . . . With time, however, he got used to it, and when he started to earn a livelihood he became an important and a permanent patron at this café. After work, he would hasten to [the café]; immediately a hookah with hashish and a cup of coffee were served to him. Mahlul would stretch out on the chair beside the radio and smoke the hookah. Seeing pipe dreams and hearing voices from afar, he enjoyed life.

Joining the great immigrations from the Middle East and North Africa, Mahlul's main goal in Israel was to persist in his previous hashish-induced and leisure-oriented, if not altogether indolent, way of life. Eventually he purchased a radio set, which he paid for in installments, and "the only thing that was missing to make his pleasure whole was a hashish hookah." Fortunately for him, "God [had] left some Arabs in the country"; by socializing with them, he was able to acquire hashish, which he hid—where else?—inside his radio. Since "his experience in removing the back cover of a radio set dated back to his childhood days," he concealed the hashish with great skill; "even the Minister of Police himself would have been unable to find this hashish." At long last, luck was on Mahlul's side: "Returning from work, he would sit by the radio, caressing it with loving eyes, removing the cover, taking out his daily portion . . . and feeling that, despite everything else, not all was bad in the State of Israel."[69]

It is obvious that the feature story about Mahlul is not the ordinary human interest story. Nor should its whimsical intimations be taken at face value. The story has a somber moral value: first and foremost, it is intended to rebuke Mizrahim for embracing a supposedly repulsive, primitive *Arab* habit in their country of origin; and, perhaps more important, for carrying the said habit over to the modern Jewish state. Mahlul was reluctant to give up consuming hashish, an Arab badge of shame and the origin of many unwarranted excesses.

The Mizrahim, Michal Haramati suggests, "were perceived by the state as primitive, backward, and as needing to dispose of their previously established mental constructs and traditional ways of life in order to assimilate into the modern-western nation state."[70] A quintessential "Oriental" Jew who persisted in his old and traditional ways of life in the Jewish state, Mahlul represented an abortive attempt at the transformation that would otherwise make him eligible to join Israeli society. Police Commissioner Yosef Nahmias expressed this sentiment most succinctly in the wake of the "first Mizrahi revolt," the 1959 riots in Wadi Salib, a Haifa neighborhood, sparked by allegations of the prejudicial treatment of its residents, mainly immigrants from North Africa. As part of a massive ideological campaign to delegitimize the protest, Nahmias asserted, "drug addicts are not born in Israel, only in an Arab country"—hence castigating the protest's leaders and its activists, rejecting governmental responsibility for the hardships and grievances of the neighborhood's residents and placing it squarely on the residents' own heads.[71]

I end this section with an episode that may have had the most devastating effect on the reputation of Mizrahim as Arablike, antitransformative "hashishniks" in 1950s and 1960s Israel. This was the discovery in 1954 of cannabis cultivation in transit camps across Israel, which I briefly mentioned in chapter 5. Needless to say, the offenders were all "new immigrants from the Orient," mainly Iran, Turkey, Iraq, and Morocco;[72] "in nearly every transit camp there are immigrants from the Orient who grow this dangerous plant," one observer rebuked.[73] Reportedly "earmarked for personal home consumption only," the crops were grown in open gardens near dwelling places.[74] Ironically, these gardens may have been part of a nationwide project initiated by the Ministry of Agriculture to combat economic strain and austerity measures in the early years of the state. The idea behind this campaign was simple: to encourage families to grow their own produce in private gardens, so as to compensate for shortages in agricultural supplies (fig. 3).[75] The cultivation of hashish in numerous transit camps at the same time may very well have become possible due to the lack of police presence in most of these localities. As the historian Orit Bashkin suggests, "the transit camps were liminal ethnic spaces which, in many ways,

FIGURE 3. Vegetable garden in a transit camp. Photo by Rudi Weissenstein, Pri-Or. PhotoHouse, Israel. Reprinted with permission.

challenged the very essence of the nation-state. The Israeli elites did not see, and did not want to see . . . residents of these camps in their midst."[76] Viewed against this backdrop, the discovery of hashish cultivation in transit camps was in many ways a remarkable event. Once it was discovered, the police embarked on an unprecedented "state-wide campaign" in immigrant camps—from the Galilee and Afula in the north, and from immigrant housing projects in Netanya and south Tel Aviv, to the camps of the Castel (near Jerusalem), Kfar Masmia, and Migdal Ashkelon in the south—in a bid to destroy the cannabis plots and arrest cannabis growers.[77] In the course of the campaign, which put "an immediate and decisive end" to cannabis cultivation in transit camps, a total of 1,089 cannabis plants were destroyed across the country.[78]

The fact that transit camp occupants used their vegetable gardens to grow cannabis was seen in mainstream media as indication of their failure to thrive, as evidence that their problems stemmed from their primitive cultural hinterland rather than from the state's prejudiced policies; they had refused to assimilate, preferring to live in poverty rather than contribute to the Israeli economy. What particularly infuriated observers was that these immigrants, who had been considered unfit for realizing the Zionist ethos of Hebrew labor and self-sufficiency to begin with, were found to be hard-working, motivated toilers of the land—when it came to criminally inclined and harmful enterprises:

> Amid the great song and dance celebrating the tremendous productivity in agriculture—the songs of tomatoes, beetroot and whatnot—this week you will have read that in large swathes of [transit camps] . . . they are growing hashish; and it is very serious because it threatens the souls of hundreds and thousands of this part of our public.[79]

For another critical observer, the revelation of the cannabis plots was reminiscent of the *hashishiyyin* of old, "this sect of devotees and terrifying murderers whose mentor-and-leader would dispatch to perform his command . . . under the influence of the drug of hashish." Alleging that the Mizrahi growers were to blame for a "terrifying murder"—of a child named Rachel Levin, whose body was found near Hiriya, a transit camp close to Tel Aviv and home to Jews of Iraqi provenance—he concluded somberly by warning that "in places where hashish grows . . . a savage youth will also grow."[80] Instructively, when the actual murderer was apprehended, he turned out to be neither an Iraqi immigrant nor a *ma'abarah* resident.[81]

The 1954 cannabis cultivation scandal had a decisive effect on police awareness regarding the challenge of hashish consumption and hashish dealing within Israeli territory. Above everything else, it compelled the force to rethink its drug prevention strategies, and to bring them up to date. The reader may recall that drug enforcement, which had been entrusted to the Police Economic Department, was part of an undifferentiated war on smuggled goods, and that drug use offenses were considered secondary. The discovery of rampant hashish cultivation in transit camps changed all that. Henceforth, a more focused approach to drug control was enforced. While the Economic Department retained its drug prevention responsibilities, the war on drug trafficking, drug dealing, and drug consumption was singled out as a specific field of police activity. As a result, a Dangerous Drugs Section was formed within the Economic Department.[82]

CONCLUSION

> A sweet smell of a heavy drug had already floated in the air. The
> new substances came faster than any other cultural influence.
> Allen Ginsberg had wandered about the Galilee at the time,
> during his first visit in the country [in 1961], and wrote . . .
> about "the thrill of the first Hashish in a holy land."[83]

Thus notes a biographer of the "bohemian" Israeli poet Yona Wallach (1944–85), a member of the "Tel Aviv poets" circle, about her exposure to drug culture in the early 1960s. Indeed, the biography is awash with accounts of Wallach's experimentation with different kinds of mind-altering substances: peyote, LSD, hashish. That is to say, at about the very same time that the Mizrahim were being condemned for hashish smoking, a limited but growing number of Jewish Israeli "bohemians"—literary figures, musicians, singers, artists, and other personalities in the entertainment and intellectual world—were also beginning to experiment with hashish as part of a cultural counter-movement. As will be explained in the concluding chapter, the June 1967 War was a watershed event in the history of hashish and marijuana consumption in Israeli society. Together with the attendant global trends and circumstances, the war unleashed a historical trajectory in which hashish-marijuana culture in the Jewish state transformed, expanded, and underwent a steady process of normalization. In the meantime, however, hashish consumption remained limited mainly to Mizrahim and a handful of the burgeoning, but almost exclusively Ashkenazi, Israeli bohemia.

The antagonistic and paternalistic (not to say racist) reaction to Mizrahim who smoked hashish, as examined above, may be contrasted to the way the same habit was perceived where the Israeli bohemia was concerned. While hashish smoking by Mizrahim and Arabs was viewed as a cultural or even racial deficiency, a symbol of their backwardness, deviancy, and innate criminality, the same behavior by members of the Israeli bohemia was excused, and even described in positive terms (although it too was sometimes condemned as a corrupting practice that might spread among innocent Israeli youngsters). In certain respects, this attitude can be described in terms that the sociologist Howard Becker defined as a "learning by doing" process, in which social interaction plays a role in learning to use and enjoy the effects of the drug.[84] This was the case even when the group's chosen venue for performing the habit was Jaffa—a location which, in the case of hashish-smoking Mizrahim, was singled out as a quintessential regressive *Arab* space. Lastly, hashish use by the bohemia was associated with Western cultural repertoires, unlike with the Mizrahim, where it was linked with the "backward" culture of the Orient.

These themes—the gradual learning about the effects of cannabis, the Western orientation of cannabis consumption, and positive perceptions of the habit—converge in a 1964 story about the Israeli bohemia published in the sensationalist and antiestablishment weekly newsmagazine *Ha-'Olam Ha-Zeh*. Concerned with the extent to which "the forbidden smoke was previously part of the underworld, [but] now . . . has conquered the Israeli bohemia, penetrating into high society," the story follows, inter alia, the writer's own initiation into the world of hashish smoking. She starts her story thusly:

> It was on a cold December night, close to midnight. The house which we entered was one of the old [read: Arab] houses of Jaffa, bordering the sea. Climbing the stairs, we could hear the dim sounds of jazz playing, sounds which gradually became clear as we climbed up.[85]

Note in this particular case how Jaffa's urban *Arab* landscapes and soundscapes, so essential to negative portrayals of hashish-taking by Mizrahim, are totally erased.

Entering a small apartment in which a small band was playing "cool jazz," the host, the writer notes, "picked a black pipe that rested on the piano, filled it with brown and greenish tobacco that had a strange form." He lit it, inhaled the smoke deep into his lungs, and intermittently exhaled streams of thick smoke with a "pungent" smell. "A wide smile spread across his face." The pipe was then passed from hand to hand until it was offered to the writer, who, feeling comfortable in a Western Jaffan enclave, embarked upon her initiation or learning process into the world of cannabis intoxication.

Holding the pipe infirmly in her hand, the writer placed it between her lips and inhaled the smoke, only to find it too strong for "my delicate lungs." She began to cough, and "everybody laughed. The pipe was passed on." The main point is that she felt nothing; in other words, she did not get stoned. Indeed, as Becker explains, "marijuana-produced sensations are not automatically or necessarily pleasurable. The taste for such experience is a socially acquired one, not different in kind from acquired tastes for oysters or dry martinis."[86] Fortunately (or not) for the writer, "a handsome blond young man" named John approached her and suggested instead that she try smoking a hashish-filled cigarette, which, as he explained, was milder to inhale.

> He took a pack of cigarettes from his pocket and emptied the contents of one of the cigarettes on the floor. He dampened the hollow cigarette paper with some saliva and filled it with green leaves like the ones they put in the pipe. . . . [He] lit the cigarette.[87]

John and the writer exchanged the cigarette a few times. "I knew that something grand should happen to me," she recalls, "and I waited for it with great curiosity." Her companion, too, was curious to know if she got "high" (*gavo'ah*), to which she replied: "'I don't know . . . I don't think so." To the readers, however, the writer admitted that she felt "a light dizziness, a dryness of tongue and lips, a stiffening of the hands and feet . . . and nothing but these sensations [*tofa'ot*]."

Were these things pleasurable? The writer was not sure. Becker explains that if the novice "is to continue marijuana use, he must decide that they are. Otherwise, getting high, while a real enough experience, will be an unpleasant one he would rather avoid."[88] And so it was that the writer met again with her bohemian friend in his Jaffa apartment, where they once again shared a spliff. At long last, what was previously distasteful, perhaps frightening, to the writer now became pleasant, desirable, and sought after; she had finally learned how to become a hashish user. All of a sudden, she writes,

> I paid attention to the music that was playing. All my thoughts and faculties were directed to it. I felt as though I was sitting in an orchestra that was playing Brahms' Fourth Symphony. It sounded familiar yet different. The [sounds] were richer and deeper, and I could follow the melodic tunes of the different voices with surprising clarity. I sat fascinated and listened for a very long time.

Listening to the music—Johannes Brahms, mind you, and not, say, Umm Kulthum—the writer realized that it "was brighter and deeper many times over," adding:

> Before my closed eyes there appeared forests and fields covered with flowers and expanses, endless expanses of color, and I was swept into a sea of light with changing colors that could not be defined and were unlike any color I knew. It was now absolutely clear to me that I was someone or something else.

I also had ideas that I was present in another world, in the next world (seriously!) or perhaps on some planet or in the depths of the sea.[89]

These awesome effects of intoxication would eventually lead the writer to experience an epiphany, calling into question the operative social norms according to which hashish was a harmful product. "All my knowledge of drugs was
drawn from newspapers, novels and movies, and I had never seen it first hand
before," she admitted. "It is also clear that I had no yardstick to evaluate the
truth about these stories . . . and I had to assume that they were true." But now,
after processing her psychoactive sensations in a state of sobriety, she could not
"understand why society would impose severe prohibitions on anything if it
was not really harmful and bad."[90] It would not be far-fetched to note that such
a progressively receptive attitude toward hashish use at the time would have
been virtually unthinkable in a Mizrahi, let alone Arab, space or environment.

CONCLUSION

ARGUING THE CASE FOR THE LEGALIZATION of recreational cannabis in Israel, a recent op-ed in the liberal daily *Ha-Aretz* described the country's Jewish citizens as "a nation of stoners." Titled "What Really Unites Israel's Right, Left and Center," the op-ed stated its case thus:

> A love of pot smoking is shared among all populations in Israel. Hilltop settler youth and Tel Aviv radicals, young and old, Knesset members and simple folk, city and country people, religious and secular, everyone loves pot. Marijuana and hashish are the largest common denominator in Israeli society. . . . Despite the common ideals held by hippies, in Israel it turns out that one can be a religious fanatic, a human rights–trampling racist, or a warmongering militarist, and still be incredibly good at rolling joints. No problem. Pot couldn't be any more common in Israel. There aren't enough lungs.[1]

This description of Jewish Israel as "a nation of stoners" is surely an overstatement. However, a 2017 survey conducted by the Israel Anti-Drug Authority validates the general impression, backing it up with hard numbers. The survey found a dramatic surge in the prevalence of cannabis use by Israelis, Jews and non-Jews alike. *Twenty-seven* percent of the adult population reported using cannabis in the past year, in comparison to just under 9 percent in 2009.[2] A comparison with surveys conducted in other countries shows that Israel is probably at the top of cannabis use by adult populations, Iceland and the US lagging behind at 18 and 16 percent respectively.[3] In addition, during the same years, the number of medical cannabis licenses granted in Israel increased more than tenfold, from less than 2,000 in 2009[4] to 28,000 in 2017.[5]

As I have demonstrated in this book, the love of cannabis in Palestine-Israel, among non-Jews and certainly among Jews, is a relatively recent phenomenon. The rise in the recreational use of hashish in Palestine was directly linked to the creation of the trans-Levant hashish trade in the interwar years. There is no doubt that the international legal structures prohibiting and/or regulating drugs in the interwar period, particularly those deployed by the League of Nations, enjoyed "small successes."[6] For the most part, however, these structures proved to be no match for illicit drug flows between states. On the contrary, "international drug diplomacy did little more than to push the drug trade to new markets, prompting traffickers and distributors to search for new sources and consequently catalyzing an evolution in the . . . illicit drug trade."[7] Smugglers moved swiftly across established and incipient political borders to exploit weak points in international law enforcement systems, ensuring that the loss of one drug source would quickly be replaced by another.[8] In a recent study of trafficking across the Arabian Sea from the 1860s to the 1950s, Johan Mathew suggests, "Trafficking, in particular, confounds the desire for a smooth narrative. The opportunistic quality of traffics lends simultaneously erratic and repetitive rhythm to . . . events. . . . New laws were met with new methods of evasion, which elicited even stronger laws and more ingenious evasions. The cycle repeated itself *ad nauseam*."[9] In the setting explored in this book, the disruption of Egypt-bound hashish supplies from Greece was offset by supplies to the same destination from Lebanon and Syria, ensuring that the Levant in general and Palestine in particular (i.e., weak points in the international drug control system) would become new theaters for extensive border-crossing hashish smuggling operations.

Paul Gootenberg suggests that the movement of drugs from their place of origin to their place of destination was born autonomously of political borders; with those borders becoming a "a nuisance" and "an obstacle course," they were destined to be overcome by imaginative smuggling operations.[10] Little wonder, then, that with the establishment of the State of Israel in 1948 and the delineation of the new state's borders, smuggling operations across the Levant, from Lebanon in the north and into Egypt in the south, continued with a vengeance. Hence, after certain adjustments necessitated by border and demographic changes, the territory now ruled by Israel remained an arena for hashish flows to Egypt from Lebanon. What is more, due to the absence of diplomatic relations after 1948 between the State of Israel and its Arab neighbors, coupled with the rising tensions and animosities between them, the Levant evolved into an even weaker point in the system of international drug control than it had been in the preceding interwar period. As a result, additional players joined hashish smuggling operations, including Jews and—allegedly—the Israeli army as well.

As we have seen in this book, Palestine's emergence as a new junction and the most important way station for hashish in the interwar Levant contributed to a significant increase in hashish smoking among the territory's urban working-class Arab population, the British in Palestine lacking the ability and will to enforce the prohibition of the drug. With few exceptions, the nascent Jewish community of interwar Palestine avoided hashish smoking, due to the fear of accommodating an Oriental, "alien" artifact; a similar discourse, framing marijuana as an "alien" Mexican and black substance was also common in the United States of the era. Orientalist stereotypes and interwar colonial knowledge exacerbated the Jewish aversion to hashish, as this knowledge had taught Jews that hashish's unique forms of intoxication were *racially* compatible with the putative deficiencies and pathologies that were an inherent aspect of the Arab mentality—insanity, violence, criminality, hypersexuality, homosexuality, indolence, and manipulability.

Just as hashish flows to Egypt survived the transition from mandatory Palestine to the State of Israel, so too did interwar colonial knowledge about cannabis, albeit by responding to new demographic realities: the country's loss of its Arab population, and its repopulation by Jews from the Muslim world (Mizrahim), who in the years 1948 to 1967 were identified as the main consumers of the drug. Even though hashish smoking in Israel remained limited to no more than a few thousand Mizrahim during this period, it rekindled the dominant Ashkenazi class's apprehension of the Levantinization-cum-Arabicization of the Jewish state. In parallel, this conceptualization served to exacerbate the marginalization and criminalization of Mizrahim in Israeli society.

HASHISH AFTER 1967

What can be said about the hashish trade and hashish consumption after the 1967 War? The latter prompted a significant leap in hashish smoking among Israeli Jews, who had previously stayed clear of the habit; this gradually put an end to the strict construct of hashish as a despicable Arab and Mizrahi vice. Considering that "from Australia, Canada, Columbia, Hong Kong, India, the Philippines, Scotland, Venezuela, West Germany, and other countries came reports of sharply increased cannabis smoking in the 1960s and 1970s,"[11] the expansion of the local hashish market in Israel also derived from structured transformations on a global scale. In particular, the active drug scene in the United States, especially among students, piqued the curiosity of well-to-do Israelis about cannabis, and added a veneer of prestige to its use in the less fortunate sectors in society.[12] At the same time, the 1967 War left an imprint on Israel's role and position in the Levant hashish trade, diverting both local and international market smuggling routes. No doubt, these processes—not at all linear, but some nevertheless persisting through the twenty-first century—deserve to be studied independently. Therefore, in the following passages I comment on these briefly.

The 1967 War trapped within so-called Israel proper large quantities of hashish, no longer with an outlet to Egypt as previously. This supply could no longer be turned over to camel convoys in the Negev to be carried in their journey onward to Egypt; instead, it was now directed to markets inside Israel, specifically the Tel Aviv metropolitan area and its vicinity. Hashish wholesalers from the West Bank and particularly East Jerusalem (formerly under Jordanian rule) continued to maintain networks of trade extending from Jordan to Lebanon, but were similarly unable to direct their contraband in the direction of Egypt. A contemporary Israeli observer described this situation in militaristic and hypernationalistic terms befitting the dominant zeitgeist of the period: "The quantity of hashish that can be found within the walls of Old Jerusalem will most likely stupefy an entire infantry brigade for a full month, and this quantity isn't getting any smaller."[13] As a result, hashish wholesalers pursued new markets inside Israel as well. This newfangled abundance in supply, saturating the Israeli local black market, precipitated a sharp decline in the price of hashish. According to some estimates, that price was the lowest in the Western hemisphere—about half of the price in Europe, and a third of the price in the United States.[14] This precipitous fall in price, coupled with greater accessibility and availability, led to an increase in the number of hashish users (though concrete numbers are frustratingly lacking).[15]

Moreover, in the aftermath of the war, East Jerusalem became the hashish capital of Israel, filching the title from Ramla, Lod, and Jaffa. While the annexation of the city facilitated easier flows of hashish from East Jerusalem to markets across Israel, it also allowed Jewish Israeli consumers and would-be consumers easy access to sources of supply within the city itself. "A border had opened in Jerusalem, a wall came crumbling down. . . . An extensive hashish business was introduced, dealing a decisive death blow to alcoholic beverages."[16] As a result, Israeli Jews were able to make periodic pilgrimages to the city not for spiritual or nationalistic purposes, but for visiting "the Arab coffeehouses that supplied hashish promptly and on the spot for immediate smoking or for smoking at home."[17] In many such cafés, "groups of Hebrew-speaking young-sters constituted the majority of patrons";[18] it was "virtually impossible for any young person to walk through the famed Arab markets of East Jerusalem without being offered 'something special,' Arab code words for hashish," a contemporary observer complained.[19]

If becoming a hashish smoker is a "learning by doing" process à la Howard Becker, new post-1967 Israeli hashish consumers were mentored in the habit by legions of international volunteers—students and tourists, including hippies, from Europe and North and South America who flocked to the country in the wake of the war.[20] An Israeli commentator at the time put it thus:

> It is doubtful whether the average Israeli would have been tempted to indulge in a psychedelic experience if he had not found overseas teachers and instruc-tors who had taught him to take full advantage of [these drugs]. The volunteers who came during the war, and the influx of foreign students who are now vis-iting Israel, spread the drug's popularity and gave it some legitimacy.[21]

No doubt, the multitudes of internationals who arrived in Israel following the 1967 War were generally welcomed and received with open arms by Israeli Jews eager for the attention and love of the outside world. At the same time, however, some of those visitors were vehemently criticized for their poor char-acter qualities and, specifically, for helping to "corrupt" the country's young generation with drugs.[22]

Israel's encounter with hippies is particularly intriguing. Located on the margins of the hippie trail, Israel was not a traditional destination for most hippies.[23] They started arriving in Israel a few years before the 1967 War. De-spite their small number, these hippies were objects of both fascination and consternation. Ideologically mobilized, parsimonious, and still secluded from the outside world, Israeli society was unfamiliar with and sometimes hostile to trends of 1960s Western counterculture, including the hippies—those "bearded, shaggy-haired primitives, unkempt and dirty in dress and table manners, lacking any etiquette or refinement," as a contemporary observer opined.[24]

It is not surprising that these drifters—who were still known as "beatniks" in contemporary Israeli public culture—had a special liking for the local hashish. So much so, that in many discussions of hashish in Israel in the mid-1960s, "beatniks" were often mentioned in the same breath with Mizrahim.[25] At the same time, newspaper readers would often come across stories about "police raids" carried out against "beatnik dens" (me'urot bitnikim) in Eilat and Jaffa, about seizures of "hashish capsules" on the persons of foreign "drifters" (navadim), or about the deportation of "English beatniks" caught red-handed smoking the stuff.[26]

After the 1967 War, hippies began to frequent Israel in greater numbers, in part due to the low cost of hashish, thereby cementing their association with drug consumption in the Israeli imagination. Take, for example, An American Hippie in Israel, known in Hebrew as Ha-trempist (The Hitchhiker), a 1972 Israeli feature film about hippie culture in Israel. The movie is not, it is fair to say, one of the Israeli film industry's proudest moments. On the contrary, it "probably is the worst Israeli movie ever made, and a serious candidate for the worst movie of all time."[27] That is why the movie was unable to find a distributor and was shelved soon after its 1972 debut.[28] Still, the movie provides a vivid testimony to the overall Israeli curiosity with the hippie drug counterculture of the time. It features Mike, a bearded native of New York, who tries to flee traumatic memories of the Vietnam War by traveling to Israel, where he hitchhikes across the country and establishes a utopian commune on an island south of the Red Sea town of Eilat. It is no coincidence that Mike and his new Israeli companions and followers are shown to be heavily predisposed to hashish smoking, nudity, and lovemaking, in scenes accompanied by a psychedelic music soundtrack.

These hippies, alongside international volunteers, tourists, and foreign students, also took part in the hashish trade—and, in the process, diverted its routes and destinations. In fact, the ambition of making an easy profit from the low price of the drug was the motivation for many of these internationals to come to Israel in the first place.[29] Some arrived as ordinary tourists, while others pretended to be students or volunteers.[30] Whatever the case, their objective was one and the same—"to purchase the fresh, high-quality and relatively cheap substance" and "to smuggle the drug to destinations across the sea."[31] American, Australian, Canadian, English, and other European nationals arrived in Israel in large numbers to take advantage of the hashish boom in Israel.

They smuggled consignments of the drug, large and small, to North America and Western Europe sometimes by regular airmail, at other times by concealing the drug inside suitcases with double compartments, tins of canned food, sandals with hollow heels, hollow decorative candles, hollow dolls, and so on.[32]

As discussed in various points in this book, from the outset of the Mandatory period up to 1967 the hashish trade took a north-south trajectory, from Lebanon-Syria to Egypt, via Transjordan (later Jordan) and Palestine-Israel. Accordingly, hashish flows across Palestine-Israel also moved from north to south. The 1967 occupation of the West Bank, the Gaza Strip, and the Sinai Peninsula disrupted this north-to-south commodity chain across Israel, as those places became less accessible and more hazardous. Replacing the north-south trajectory, smuggling routes inside Israel in the immediate post-1967 period ran from East to West—that is, from the West Bank and Jerusalem to metropolitan Tel Aviv.[33] By endeavoring to smuggle hashish out of Israel and across the sea, international guests extended this east-west trajectory to Western Europe and North America.

THE MIDDLE CLASSES, MORAL PANICS, AND NORMALIZATION

As mentioned, after 1967 a marked increase in hashish use occurred in Israel. Writing in 1970, an Israeli journalist described the change as follows: "If until two-three years ago the clouds of illicit smoke obscured the consciousness of Israel's marginal society [hevrat ha-shulayim] and sectors of the underworld, hashish now finds its way into social strata that have thus far been impervious to it."[34] Members of the middle class—particularly high school and university students, "adolescents from good families" (bnei tovim), "bohemian artists' circles" and, generally, "Jews of Western extraction"—were now avid converts to the habit of hashish smoking,[35] a far cry from the stereotypical profile of the Mizrahi and/or Arab hashish smoker.

While at the time Israel had virtually no systematic data regarding the prevalence of drug use in the general population, several studies conducted on the topic between the early 1970s and the early 1980s reveal a more or less consistent picture: "The percentage of young, mainly high school adolescents, who tried illicit psychoactive drugs (mostly hashish) . . . remained stable at between 3–5%."[36] Moreover, a poll conducted among high school–enrolled adolescent Jews in 1972 suggested that a decisive majority, 83 percent, were "strongly opposed to drug use in any shape of form."[37] Be that as it may, reports and perceptions about the spread of hashish use, especially among middle-class Ashkenazi adolescents and young adults, gave rise to moral entrepreneurs who warned that "a nation with the self-image of physical strength and high motivation could become morally weakened by the drug and thus militarily vulnerable."[38] What was at stake was, once again (and see chapters 4 and 6), the degeneration of the country in a manner similar to that perceived in Egypt. To drive this point home, the journalist Aharon Shamir recalled his stay in Egypt during World War II as a soldier in the British army:

> At first the inhabitants seemed to me to be completely feebleminded, and I thought this was the nature of the Egyptian people. When I delved into the issue, however, I realized that everyone was smoking hashish, and that under its influence they became indifferent to everything—work, family, and anything that occurred in their country. I saw entire villages of apathetic people, with bleary eyes, sitting down and dreaming. These were shocking sights. The first thought that came to my mind was this: God forbid that this should also happen to us; and it is happening to us.[39]

This moral panic produced some unusual reactions. Take, for example, the backlash against reports claiming that "more than 1000 [university] students, Israeli and foreign, use drugs on a regular basis"; that "a great part of the drug trade and drug smoking takes place in the student dorms"; and that, consequently, "there is, in the dorms, the constant and pungent smell of hashish."[40] The backlash was amplified by Knesset members demanding that the police storm university compounds to apprehend the offenders.[41] In an attempt to fend off the backlash, Professor Nathan Rotenstreich, rector of the Hebrew University of Jerusalem, promptly vowed that any student caught possessing hashish or consuming the drug would be prosecuted per the university's disciplinary code for "behavior that does not comply with the institution's reputation [kavod] and harms public morality." Rotenstreich warned that accountable students "will be expelled from the university permanently."[42]

The 1968 Dangerous Drugs Ordinance Amendment Law was a direct consequence of this moral panic. Section 16(A) of the law criminalized any person who might "induce" minors, whether directly or indirectly, into using dangerous drugs.[43] As can be gleaned from transcripts of the debates regarding the proposed bill in the Knesset Public Services Committee and the Knesset's general assembly, its supporters and opponents were deeply concerned that increasing drug use would "culminate in social disasters, leading human beings to mental and physical atrophy, insanity, and acts of murder."[44] Special concern was directed to the fate of Israel's young generation. For instance, Knesset Member Shlomo Cohen-Tzidon, sponsor of the bill, justified its necessity, stating:

> Recently, networks of criminals . . . have been discovered enticing underage boys and girls to devote themselves [*lehitmaser*] to dangerous drugs. . . . Their actions might corrupt entire groups of adolescents, in terms of both physical and mental health. Given the seriousness of these acts, I propose the imposition of extraordinary punishments that will serve as a deterrent to anyone who attempts to corrupt boys and girls, young men and young women.[45]

Cohen-Tzidon also described "lustful feasts" (*nishfei hesheq*), "horrible drug orgies," and "parties large and small" (*mesibot ve-nishpiyot*) in which adults supposedly induced adolescents to smoke drugs in order to turn them into dependent addicts.[46] Although the police minister categorically denied such actualities,[47] Cohen-Tzidon remained unimpressed. A short time later, during the initial presentation of his bill before the Knesset, he implored his fellow legislators, with pathos: "Can we, in our right mind, allow these boys and girls [to go to parties] if we do not watch out for them and remove from society these criminals who are nothing but pimps and seducers trying to widen their circle of clients?"[48] But most of all, the concern for the young generation stemmed from the fact that they provided the pool for future soldiers in the Israeli military. The bill's main objective, as stated by its supporters, was to ensure that Egypt's hashish-hazed present realities would not become the dark future of the Jewish state:

> The [June 1967] War has proved beyond a shred of doubt that increased use of intoxicating drugs by the Egyptian army was detrimental [to it]. . . . This was one of [that army's] hallmarks. . . . Hence, should the law not intervene to impose heavy and severe penalties—and even exemplary penalties—our young generation will surely face grave dangers.[49]

While ornate fantasies continued to proliferate about hashish as an insanity-inducing substance and a gateway to stronger drugs, more and more people acquired firsthand experience with hashish after the late 1960s. As a result, they could determine for themselves the nature of hashish intoxication beyond and against accepted notions, and attitudes toward the drug began to shift. In particular, questions began to be asked about the veracity of the conventional wisdom, and calls for the legalization of the substance began to surface for the first time as well. Professor Ezra Zohar, a physician and one of the founders of the Tel Aviv University's medical school, raised the issue of hashish legalization as follows:

> Hashish is an intriguing question. . . . Many people smoke cannabis, but I have neither seen nor read about any severe damage that was caused to them by hashish. If we don't forbid cigarettes and alcohol, there is no reason whatsoever why hashish should be forbidden specifically. If hashish were to be legalized [hofshi] I don't think we'll all become drug addicts. For example, in Israel everyone can buy alcohol, and yet the percentage of drunkards is small. A person doesn't become an alcoholic because he has alcohol, but because he has an internal drive that makes him like that.[50]

Israeli celebrities—authors, intellectuals, entertainers—joined the campaign, albeit cautiously and sometimes begrudgingly. Standing out among them was the acclaimed writer Yoram Kaniuk (1930–2013), who in 1970 put forward the following argument for the legalization of hashish:

> Heroin, cocaine, LSD, mescaline, opium, these are lethal drugs. . . . But let's be honest: to this day it has not been proven anywhere that hashish is truly dangerous. [On the contrary,] it is well known to researchers that hashish is the least dangerous drug. The use of the substance leads to a kind of refined peace of mind [sheqet nafshi], and it does not provoke violent impulses, even if the word "assassin" in European languages derives from the word hashish. . . . It is known that hashish, as opposed to alcohol, . . . is a drug that soothes the bitter passions [tshuqot marot]. While acts of violence are widespread among alcohol drinkers, hashish smokers . . . become tranquil.[51]

The Israeli military's long occupation of Lebanon (1982–2000) further normalized hashish use in Israel. Israel's occupation of southern Lebanon, nearly two decades long, had given great strength and ample human resources to hashish trafficking from Lebanon to the black market in Israel. Israeli military servicemen and civilians with access to occupied Lebanon were crucial intermediaries in this trade—with many of the lower-ranking soldiers concealing hashish in rifle magazines and inside weapons, and military officers concluding lucrative hashish deals with major Lebanese drug lords.

In later years, as Israel became a mecca for the international medical cannabis industry, cannabis consumption was further normalized in public perception. Hence, even though recreational cannabis use is still outlawed in Israel—albeit subject to a fine, not imprisonment[52]—twenty-four-hour street kiosks offer for sale almost every conceivable kind of cannabis paraphernalia: bongs, pipes, vaporizers, filters, rolling paper, and rolling devices of every size and shape—everything except the drug itself. The *Aleh Yarok* (Green Leaf) Party, established in 1999 to push for the legalization of cannabis, is also a part of the cannabis normalization process. Although it has failed to win any seats in the six general Knesset elections in which it has taken part, its very existence is a sign that cannabis has become a permanent fixture of Jewish Israeli society. As for cannabis consumers, despite the fact that supply shortages occur, they are currently offset by homegrown weed,[53] as well as by medical marijuana crossing over to the black market. As a keen observer recently remarked wryly, "Judging by the amount of medical marijuana in circulation, a staggering percentage of the Israeli population is suffering from unbearable back pain."[54]

The normalization of recreational cannabis use in Israel has been building up a head of steam in recent years, as old mythologies about the substance evaporate. Yet remnants of obsolete Oriental fantasies about the drug remain, albeit in reconfigured form. One blatant example is a thirty-three-second video clip prepared by the Israel Anti-Drug Authority in 2006. Designed to dissuade teenagers from using drugs, particularly cannabis, and broadcast on Israel's main public television channel, the clip was produced in the style of the dilet-tantish "last will and testament" videos recorded by Muslim suicide bombers. It shows a teenage boy wielding his bong like a deadly weapon, standing in front of an unsteady camera and reciting the following monologue:

> I, Omer Kandel, aged sixteen, of Raanana, bid goodbye today to my parents Ronit and Shmuel, and to my sister Keren, and am going to a party in Tel Aviv. There's only one way to be truly liberated: to get drunk, take drugs, and get really stoned. Don't cry, mom. I'm going to paradise.[55]

It is easy to see in this short clip echoes of the medieval Assassins myth, dressed in twenty-first century anti-Muslim garb. At the time of the clip's broadcast—during the final days of the al-Aqsa or Second Intifada, and at the height of President George W. Bush's global War on Terror—the suicide bomber had in the United States, Western Europe, and Israel become emblematic of the so-called Islamic death culture.[56] The clip deliberately played on the strings of the anti-Muslim sentiments rampant in Israeli society at the time.[57] But at the same time, it drew upon the vocabulary of nineteenth- and early twentieth-century images of cannabis—namely, that hashish is an Oriental substance used by uncivilized Muslim Arab zealots, who champion a ritual of death rather than a ritual of life.

Of equal note is the fact that the clip's "suicide bomber" is a good middle-class Jewish boy from the "white," prosperous city of Raanana. In terms of his social background and his demographic and ethnic identity, Omer represented something entirely different from the traditional image of hashish consumers in Israel, reflecting contemporary establishment's understandings that hashish had spread to all parts of Israeli society. It may be that Israelis "are a nation of stoners" after all. Or it may be that the Zionist nightmare of assimilation into the Levant, a nightmare that haunted Jews in Palestine-Israel since the 1920s, seems to have materialized—at least to the extent that cannabis consumption is concerned.

NOTES

INTRODUCTION

1. Shimon Ballas, *The Transit Camp*, in Hebrew (Tel Aviv: 'Am 'Oved, 1964), 159–60. Ballas first wrote the novel in Arabic, later rewriting it in Hebrew to appeal to local audiences. Almog Bahar and Yuval Evri, "That Was the Arabic Revenge on Me," *Ha-Aretz*, October 8, 2019. The novel was republished in 2003 as part of a collection of Shimon Ballas's literary works; see Shimon Ballas, *Tel Aviv East: Trilogy*, in Hebrew (Tel Aviv: Hakibbutz Hameuchad, 2003), 8–160. References to the novel are all taken from the latter edition.

2. Yehouda Shenhav-Shahrabani, "Shimon Ballas Was the Spiritual Father of the Mizrahi Left," *Ha-Aretz*, October 6, 2019.

3. See Batya Shimoni, "From Babylon to the Ma'abarah: Iraqi Jewish Women in the Mass Immigration of the 1950s" (in Hebrew), *Sugiyot Hevratiyot be-Israel* 14 (2012), 9–33. One of the novel's protagonists, Eliyahu Eini, vividly expresses the sense of emasculation experienced by transit camp residents, complaining to a transit camp fellow: "This is . . . our fate, our dignity has been trampled. The people . . . have forgotten everything: heritage, family name, status, everything. The morals are not the same morals of our ancestors. The wife is not the same wife, the son is not the same son, the father is not a father. . . . What is there to be added? Everything has been turned on its head." Ballas, *Transit Camp*, 43–44.

4. Though it is that too, as the same protagonist, Eliyahu Eini, laments: "It seems to me that since the Babylonian exile, the Jews of Mesopotamia have not experienced a Holocaust like the Holocaust that has befallen them these days. All that ancient and enlightened Judaism has been crushed, and scattered over the barren and muddy lands called transit camps (*ma'abarot*)"; ibid., 43.

5. Cited in Hannan Hever and Yehouda Shenhav, "Shimon Ballas: Colonialism and *Mizrahiyut* in Israel" (in Hebrew), *Te'oria u-Vikoret* 20 (2002): 299, 297.

6. Hannan Hever, *Producing the Modern Hebrew Canon: Nation Building and Minority Discourse* (New York: New York University Press, 2002), 168.

7. Batya Shimoni, *On the Threshold of Redemption: The Story of the Ma'abarah, First and Second Generation*, in Hebrew (Or Yehuda, Israel: Kinneret Zmora-Bitan Dvir, 2008), 229.

8. For instance, in the novel Ballas makes a few direct and indirect references to the ruins of the Arab village atop which the Oriya transit camp was built; see, e.g., Ballas, *Transit Camp*, 134, 155. Hence, as Hebrew literature scholar Hannan Hever explains in *Producing the Modern Hebrew Canon*, 170: "Instead of a [Zionist-inspired] narrative logic that layers new on old through the erasure of the old, Ballas constructs a space that fuses all the different layers together." On Ballas's subversive gestures in *The Transit Camp*, see also Lital Levy, "Reorienting Hebrew Literary History: The View from the East," *Prooftexts* 29 (2009): 127–72; Ibrahim Taha, "Duality and Acceptance: The Image of the Outsider in the Literary Work of Shimon Ballas," *Hebrew Studies* 38 (1997): 63–87; and Dror Mishani, "Why the Mizrahim Should Return to 'The Transit Camp'" (in Hebrew), *Mi-Ta'am* 3 (2005): 91–98.

9. Ballas, *Transit Camp*, 112, 123.

10. Ibid., 160. Despair and hashish also suffuse Ballas's 1965 short story "Half Asleep" (*BeNim-veLo-Nim*), which depicts the relationship between a prostitute and her client, both Mizrahim and hashish "addicts" in a southern neighborhood of Tel Aviv; see Shimon Balls, *In Front of the Wall: Stories*, in Hebrew (Ramat Gan, Israel: Massada Press, 1969), 90–94.

11. As Shimoni correctly observes in *On the Threshold of Redemption*, 230–31, the "*ma'abara* literature," mainly written by veteran (mostly Ashkenazi) Israeli writers of Ballas's generation, is rich with descriptions of transit camp cafés "as centers of idleness, gambling, drunkenness, drugs and pimping. In the vast majority of them, these cafés are the cultural and social margins of the transit camps and serve as breeding grounds for violence and crime."

12. David Courtwright, *Forces of Habit: Drugs and the Making of the Modern World* (Cambridge, MA: Harvard University Press, 2001), 40.

13. James Gelvin, "Was There a Mandates Period? Some Concluding Thoughts," in *The Routledge Handbook of the History of the Middle East Mandates*, ed. Cyrus Schayegh and Andrew Arsan (New York: Routledge, 2015), 420.

14. William L. Cleveland and Martin Bunton, *A History of the Modern Middle East*, 6th edition (Boulder, CO: Westview Press, 2016), 169; James L. Gelvin, *The Modern Middle East: A History* (New York: Oxford University Press, 2005), 182.

15. Ibid., 186–87.

16. Ibid.; Eugene Rogan, *The Fall of the Ottomans: The Great War in the Middle East, 1914–1920*, Kindle edition (London: Penguin, 2015), ch. 12.

17. Cyrus Schayegh and Andrew Arsan, introduction to *The Routledge Handbook of the History of the Middle East Mandates*, ed. Cyrus Schayegh and Andrew Arsan (New York: Routledge, 2015), 1.

18. Cleveland and Bunton, *A History of the Modern Middle East*, 164. Which is why Schayegh and Arsan ask, in the introduction to *The Routledge Handbook* (14), whether the mandates were "the surest signs of the mutability of imperialism, its ability to shape-shift and transform itself, the better to perpetuate itself in changing circumstances."

19. Cited in Cleveland and Bunton, *A History of the Modern Middle East*, 194.

20. Gelvin, *The Modern Middle East*, 188.

21. Liat Kozma, *Global Women, Colonial Ports: Prostitution in the Interwar Middle East* (Albany: State University of New York Press, 2017), 14–15.

22. Paul Gootenberg, "Talking about the Flow: Drugs, Borders, and the Discourse of Drug Control," *Cultural Critique* 71 (2009): 22.

23. Paul Gootenberg, *Andean Cocaine: The Making of a Global Drug* (Chapel Hill: University of North Carolina Press, 2008), 3; Paul Gootenberg and Isaac Campos, "Toward a New Drug History of Latin America: A Research Frontier at the Center of Debates," *Hispanic and American Historical Review* 95 (2015): 1–35.

24. The following bibliography is by no means exhaustive. Maziyar Ghiabi, *Drugs Politics: Managing Disorder in the Islamic Republic of Iran* (Cambridge: Cambridge University Press, 2019); James Tharin Bradford, *Poppies, Politics, and Power: Afghanistan and the Global History of Drugs and Diplomacy* (Ithaca, NY: Cornell University Press, 2019); Johan Mathew, "Smoke on the Water: Cannabis Smuggling, Corruption and the Janus-Faced Colonial State," *History Workshop Journal* 86 (2018): 67–89; Philip Robins, *Middle East Drugs Bazaar: Production, Prevention and Consumption* (New York: Oxford University Press, 2016); Ryan Gingeras, *Heroin, Organized Crime, and the Making of Modern Turkey* (Oxford: Oxford University Press, 2014); Pierre-Arnaud Chouvy and Kenza Afsahi, "Hashish Revival in Morocco," *International Journal of Drug Policy* 25 (2014): 416–23; Liat Kozma, "White Drugs in Interwar Egypt: Decadent Pleasures, Emaciated Fellahin, and the Campaign against Drugs," *Comparative Studies of South Asia, Africa and the Middle East* 33 (2013): 89–101; Maziyar Ghiabi, Masoomeh Maarefand, Hamed Bahari, and Zohreh Alavi, "Islam and Cannabis: Legalization and Religious Debate in Iran," *International Journal of Drug Policy* 56 (2018): 121–27; Maziyar Ghiabi, "Drugs and Revolution in Iran: Islamic Devotion, Revolutionary Zeal and Republican Means," *Iranian Studies* 48 (2015): 139–63; Liat Kozma, "Cannabis Prohibition in Egypt, 1880–1939: From Local Ban to League of Nations Diplomacy," *Middle Eastern Studies* 47 (2011): 443–60; Jonathan Marshall, *The Lebanese Connection: Corruption, Civil War, and the International Drug Traffic* (Stanford, CA: Stanford University Press, 2012); Ram Baruch Regavim, "The Most Sovereign Masters: The History of Opium in Modern Iran, 1850–1955" (PhD diss., University of Pennsylvania, 2012); Cyrus Schayegh, "The Many Worlds of 'Abud Yasin; or, What Narcotics Trafficking in the Interwar Middle East Can Tell Us about Territorialization," *American Historical Review* 116 (2011): 273–306; Rudi Matthee, *The Pursuit of Pleasure: Drugs and Stimulants in Iranian History, 1500–1900* (Princeton, NJ: Princeton University Press, 2005). See also Robert S. G. Fletcher, *British*

Imperialism and "the Tribal Question": Desert Administration and Nomadic Societies in the Middle East (Oxford: Oxford University Press, 2015), 133–82.

25. On India, see, e.g., Ashley Wright , "Not Just a 'Place for the Smoking of Opium': The Indian Opium Den and Imperial Anxieties in the 1890s," *Journal of Colonialism and Colonial History* 18 (2017): doi:10.1353/cch.2017.0021; Nile Green, "Breaking the Begging Bowl: Morals, Drugs, and Madness in the Fate of the Muslim Faqīr," *South Asian History and Culture* 5 (2014): 226–45; James H. Mills, *Cannabis Britannica: Empire, Trade, and Prohibition, 1800–1928* (Oxford: Oxford University Press, 2003); James H. Mills, *Madness, Cannabis and Colonialism: The "Native Only" Lunatic Asylums of British India, 1857–1900* (New York: Palgrave, 2000). On Egypt, see, e.g., Mathew, "Smoke on the Water"; James H. Mills, *Cannabis Nation: Control and Consumption in Britain, 1928–2008* (Oxford: Oxford University Press, 2013), 35–61; Kozma, "Cannabis Prohibition"; Kozma, "White Drugs"; James H. Mills, "Colonial Africa and the International Politics of Cannabis: Egypt, South Africa and the Origins of Global Control," in *Drugs and Empires: Essays on Modern Imperialism and Intoxication, c. 1500–c. 1930*, ed. James H. Mills and Patricia Barton (London: Palgrave, 2007), 165–84.

26. An interesting, albeit rather brief, exception to this gap is Robins, *Middle East Drugs Bazaar*, 99–118.

27. Sven Beckert, *Empire of Cotton: A Global History* (New York: Vintage, 2015), xxi.

28. Kozma, *Global Women, Colonial Ports*, 5–6.

29. Pierre-Yves Saunier and Akira Iriye, "The Professor and the Madman," in *The Palgrave Dictionary of Transnational History from the Mid-19th Century to the Present Day*, ed. Akira Iriye and Pierre-Yves Saunier (New York: Palgrave, 2009), xviii.

30. Itty Abraham and Willem van Schendel, "Introduction: The Making of Illicitness," in *Illicit Flows and Criminal Things: States: Borders, and the Other Side of Globalization*, ed. Willem van Schendel and Itty Abraham (Bloomington: Indiana University Press, 2005), 1–37.

31. Cyrus Schayegh, *The Middle East and the Making of the Modern World* (Cambridge, MA: Harvard University Press, 2017).

32. Ibid., 138–39.

33. Ibid., 206.

34. Ibid., 152. On this issue, see also Schayegh and Arsan, introduction, 15; Abigail Jacobson and Moshe Naor, *Oriental Neighbors: Middle Eastern Jews and Arabs in Mandatory Palestine* (Waltham, MA: Brandeis University Press, 2016); Abigail Jacobson, "Sephardim, Ashkenazim and the 'Arab Question' in Pre–First World War Palestine: A Reading of Three Zionist Newspapers," *Middle Eastern Studies* 39 (2003): 105–30.

35. Schayegh, *The Middle East*, 271–313.

36. Courtwright, *Forces of Habit*, 1–5.

37. The establishment of a system of international regulation, intended to curtail the legal global economy of drugs and confine it to "legitimate" (read: medical) usage,

originated in the Shanghai Opium Commission of 1909, the Hague Convention of 1912, the post–World War I peace settlement, the 1925 Geneva Convention, and the 1931 League of Nations Convention on the Limitation of Manufactured Drugs. On these and other pre- and interwar international regulation agreements, see William B. McAllister, *Drug Diplomacy in the Twentieth Century* (London: Routledge, 2000), 9–102. For a short review of the establishment of this system, see Virginia Berridge, "Illicit Drugs and Internationalism: The Forgotten Dimension," *Medical History* 45 (2001): 282–88.

38. Magaly Rodríguez García, Davide Rodogno, and Liat Kozma, introduction to *The League of Nations' Work on Social Issues: Visions, Endeavours and Experiments*, ed. idem. (Geneva: United Nations Publications, 2016), 15.

39. See, e.g., ibid.; Kozma, *Global Women, Colonial Ports*; Stephen Legg, "'The Life of Individuals as Well as of Nations': International Law and the League of Nations' Anti-Trafficking Governmentalities," *Leiden Journal of International Law* 25 (2012): 647–64; Susan Pedersen, "Back to the League of Nations: Review Essay," *American Historical Review* 112 (2007): 1091–1117.

40. See, e.g., Kozma, "White Drugs in Interwar Egypt," 89–101; Liat Kozma, "Cannabis Prohibition"; Philippe Bourmaud, "Turf Wars at the League of Nations: International Anti-Cannabis Policies and Oversight in Syria and Lebanon, 1919–1939," in *The League of Nations' Work on Social Issues*, 75–76; Mills, *Cannabis Britannica*; and Mills, *Cannabis Nation*.

41. Kathryn Meyer and Terry Parssinen, introduction to *Webs of Smoke: Smugglers, Warlords, Spies, and the History of the International Drug Trade*, Kindle edition (Lanham, MD: Rowman & Littlefield, 2002); Alan Block, "European Drug Traffic and Traffickers between the Wars: The Policy of Suppression and its Consequences," *Journal of Social History* 23 (1989): 315.

42. Paul Knepper, "Dreams and Nightmares: Drug Trafficking and the History of International Crime," in *The Oxford Handbook of the History of Crime and Criminal Justice*, ed. Paul Knepper and Anja Johansen (Oxford: Oxford University Press, 2016), 208–12; Paul Knepper, *International Crime in the 20th Century: The League of Nations Era, 1919–1939* (London: Palgrave, 2011).

43. Eric Hobsbawm, *Nations and Nationalism since 1780: Program, Myth, Reality* (Cambridge: Cambridge University Press, 1990), 132–33.

44. Jürgen Osterhammel, *The Transformation of the World: A Global History of the Nineteenth Century* (Princeton, NJ: Princeton University Press, 2014), 910–11.

45. Block, "European Drug Traffic and Traffickers"; Knepper, "Dreams and Nightmares."

46. I discuss this issue briefly in Haggai Ram, "On Sleuth Literature, Border-Crossings, and Crime in Mandatory Palestine" (in Hebrew), *Jama'a* 21 (2015): 119–31.

47. Arjun Appadurai, "Introduction: Commodities and the Politics of Value," in

The Social Life of Things: Commodities in Cultural Perspective, ed. Arjun Appadurai (Cambridge: Cambridge University Press, 1986), 48.

48. Mills, *Cannabis Nation*, 61–62; Liat Kozma, "The League of Nations and the Debate over Cannabis Prohibition," *History Compass* 9 (2011): 61–70.

49. Jill Lepore, *These Truths: A History of the United States* (New York and London: W. W. Norton, 2018), 12.

50. Franz Rosenthal, *The Herb: Hashish versus Medieval Muslim Society* (Leiden, Netherlands: E. J. Brill, 1971), 72. See also Haggai Ram, "Middle East Drug Cultures in the Long View," in *OUP Handbook to Global Drug History*, ed. Paul Gootenberg (New York: Oxford University Press, forthcoming).

51. Abraham and van Schendel, "Introduction," 10. This is why Johann Hari, in his study of the War on Drugs in the United States, notes, in jest: "Drug dealers don't keep records: there is no National Heroin Dealers' Archive to consult." Johann Hari, *Chasing the Scream: The First and Last Days of the War on Drugs*, Kindle edition (London: Bloomsbury Circus, 2015), ch. 4.

52. Kozma makes the same point about the absence of prostitutes' voices in her *Global Women, Colonial Ports*, 16.

53. Bradford, *Poppies, Politics, and Power*, 9.

54. Zachary Foster, "Illicit Drug Trafficking and Use in British Mandatory Palestine" (unpublished paper, 2010). I am grateful to Foster for sharing this paper with me.

55. Indeed, delivery "is the most dangerous undertaking. A trafficker's success lies in his ability to penetrate barriers. [At the delivery stage,] contraband becomes vulnerable to government interception or to hijacking by other thieves." Meyer and Parssinen, *Webs of Smoke* (Kindle edition), introduction.

56. Sandeep Chawla and Thomas Pietschmann, "Drug Trafficking as a Transnational Crime," in *Handbook of Transnational Crime and Justice*, ed. Philip Reichel (Thousand Oaks, CA, and London: Sage Publications, 2005), 162.

CHAPTER ONE

1. Jonathan Marshall, *The Lebanese Connection: Corruption, Civil War, and the International Drug Traffic* (Stanford, CA: Stanford University Press, 2012), 136–37.

2. Cited in "Lebanon-Israel Drug Connection," *Journal of Palestine Studies* 13 (1984): 169.

3. Hatice Aynur and Jan Schmidt, "A Debate between Opium, Berş, Hashish, Boza, Wine and Coffee: The Use and Perception of Pleasurable Substances among Ottomans," *Journal of Turkish Studies* 31 (2007): 81.

4. The renowned seventeenth-century Ottoman intellectual and traveler Evilya Çelebi, in his book of travels *Seyahat-name*, enumerates three hundred types of intoxicants for sale in Istanbul, most of them obscure to the author himself. Ibid., 79. See also Marinos Sariyannis, "Law and Morality in Ottoman Society: The Case of Narcotic

Substances," in *The Ottoman Empire, the Balkans, and the Greek Lands: Toward a Social and Economic History*, ed. Elias Kolovos, Phokion Kotzageorgis, Sophia Laiou, and Marinos Sariyannis (Istanbul: Isis Press, 2007), 310; and Ryan Gingeras, *Heroin, Organized Crime, and the Making of Modern Turkey* (Oxford: Oxford University Press, 2014), especially the introduction and ch. 1.

5. See, e.g., John C. Kramer, "Opium Rampant: Medical Use, Misuse and Abuse in Britain and the West in the 17th and 18th Centuries," *British Journal of Addiction* 74 (1979): 377–89.

6. Mehrdad Kia, *Daily Life in the Ottoman Empire* (Santa Barbara, CA: Greenwood Press, 2011), 244–45; Heghnar Zeitlian Watenpaugh, "Deviant Dervishes: Space, Gender, and the Construction of Antinomian Piety in Ottoman Aleppo," *International Journal of Middle East Studies* 37 (2005): 546, 551. See also Benedek Péri, "'It Is the Weed of Lovers': The Use of Cannabis among Turkic Peoples up to the 15th Century," *Acta Orientalia Academiae Scientiarum Hung* 69 (2016): 139–55; Ibrahim Ihsan Poroy, "Expansion of Opium Production in Turkey and the State of Monopoly of 1828–1839," *International Journal of Middle East Studies* 13 (1981): 191–211; Ahmet T. Karamustafa, *God's Unruly Friends: Dervish Groups in the Islamic Later Middle Period, 1200–1550* (Salt Lake City: University of Utah Press, 1994).

7. Fariba Zarinebaf, *Crime and Punishment in Istanbul, 1700–1800* (Los Angeles: University of California Press, 2010), 126–28; Ferdan Ergut, "Policing the Poor in the Late Ottoman Empire," *Middle Eastern Studies* 38 (2002): 152; Ralph Hattox, *Coffee and Coffeehouses: The Origins of a Social Beverage in the Medieval Near East* (Seattle: University of Washington Press, 1985), 110–11; Ali Çaksu, "Janissary Coffee Houses in Late Eighteenth-Century Istanbul," in *Ottoman Tulips, Ottoman Coffee: Leisure and Lifestyle in the Eighteenth Century*, ed. Dana Sajdi (London: I. B. Tauris, 2007); James Grehan, "Smoking and 'Early Modern' Sociability: The Great Tobacco Debate in the Ottoman Middle East (Seventeenth to Eighteenth Centuries)," *American Historical Review* 111 (2006): 1352–77.

8. Cited in Richard Davenport-Hines, *The Pursuit of Oblivion: A Global History of Narcotics* (New York: W. W. Norton, 2003), 34.

9. Ebru Aykut Türker, "Alternative Claims on Justice and Law: Rural Arson and Poison Murder in the 19th-Century Ottoman Empire" (PhD diss., Boğaziçi University, 2011), 233.

10. Rudi Matthee, *The Pursuit of Pleasure: Drugs and Stimulants in Iranian History, 1500–1900* (Princeton, NJ: Princeton University Press, 2005); Rudi Matthee, "Tobacco in Iran," in *Smoke: A Global History of Smoking*, ed. Sander L. Gilman and Zhou Xun (London: Reaktion Books, 2004), 58–67; Ram B. Regavim, "The Most Sovereign of Masters: The History of Opium in Modern Iran, 1850–1955" (Ph.D diss., University of Pennsylvania, 2012); Willem Floor, "The Art of Smoking in Iran and Other Uses of Tobacco," *Iranian Studies* 35 (2002): 47–85.

11. Piero Camporesi, *Bread of Dreams: Food and Fantasy in Early Modern Europe*, trans. David Gentilcore (Chicago: University of Chicago Press, 1996), 25.

12. Franz Rosenthal, *The Herb: Hashish versus Medieval Muslim Society* (Leiden, Netherlands: Brill, 1971), 137–40.

13. Aynur and Schmidt, "A Debate," 51; and see also Sariyannis, "Law and Morality," 315, 316.

14. Maziyar Ghiabi, "Deorientalizing Drugs in the Modern Middle East," in *OUP Handbook to Global Drug History*, ed. Paul Gootenberg (Oxford: Oxford University Press, forthcoming).

15. Sariyannis, "Law and Morality," 315.

16. *Pall Mall Gazette*, May 19, 1876, cited in Charles Hilliard, ed., *Hemp the Joy Giver: Selection of 19th-Century British Press Cuttings on the Subject of Cannabis*, Kindle edition (self-published, 2011).

17. See, e.g., Articles 193–95 of the 1858 Ottoman Penal Code, and subsequent amendments, in *The Imperial Ottoman Penal Code*, trans. and annotated by John A. Strachey Bucknill and Haig Apisoghom S. Utidjian (London: Oxford University Press, 1913), 147–48; Özgur Burçak Gürsoy, "The Opium Problem in Turkey, 1930–1945" (MA thesis, Boğaziçi University, 2007), 13–44.

18. And what is more, the Ottomans kept up their international opium trade to feed European consumption, both on the continent and in the colonies. For this reason, it "remained implacably hostile to the baby steps of the emerging international [drug] regime," e.g., the 1909 Shanghai Opium Commission. Philip Robins, *Middle East Drugs Bazaar: Production, Prevention and Consumption* (Oxford: Oxford University Press, 2016), 9. See also Gürsoy, "The Opium Problem in Turkey," 35–36; Pierre-Arnaud Chouvy, *Opium: Uncovering the Politics of the Poppy* (London: I. B. Tauris, 2009), 82.

19. Cristina Belgiojoso, *Harems, Hashish, and Holy Men*, Kindle edition (Amazon Digital Services, [1858] 2012), ch. 54. On Belgiojoso's sojourn, travels, and experiences in the Ottoman Empire, see Antonio Fabris, ed., *Cristina Trivulzio di Belgiojoso: An Italian Princess in the 19th C. Turkish Countryside* (Venice: Filippi Editore Venezia, 2010).

20. Gingeras, *Heroin, Organized Crime, and the Making of Modern Turkey*, 101.

21. Gabriel Nahas, "Hashish and Drug Abuse in Egypt during the 19th and 20th Centuries," *Bulletin of the New York Academy of Medicine* 61 (1985): 428–44; Gabriel G. Nahas, G. "Hashish in Islam 9th to 18th Century," *Bulletin of the New York Academy of Medicine* 58 (1982): 814–31; and Ahmad M. Khalifa, "Traditional Patterns of Hashish Use in Egypt," in *Cannabis and Culture*, ed. Vera Rubin (The Hague: Mouton, 1975), 195–205.

22. Robins, *Middle East Drugs Bazaar*, 79.

23. Rosenthal, *The Herb*, 131–32.

24. Ibid., 132–35; Li Guo, "Paradise Lost: Ibn Dāniyāl's Response to Baybars'

Campaign against Vice in Cairo," *Journal of the American Oriental Society* 121 (2001): 219–35; Khalifa, "Traditional Patterns of Hashish Use in Egypt," 198–99.

25. "Hashish eaters," according to Franz Rosenthal, "were believed to be low-class people either by nature or by being reduced to that state through their habit which impaired their faculties but in particular those moral and character qualities that determine the individual's standing in society. . . . Hashish was generally branded as something inherently dirty and bestial." Rosenthal, *The Herb*, 140, 150.

26. Maziyar Ghiabi, Masoomeh Maarefand, Hamed Bahari, and Zohreh Alavi, "Islam and Cannabis: Legalization and Religious Debate in Iran," *International Journal of Drug Policy* 56 (2018): 123.

27. Łukasz Kamieński, *Shooting Up: A Short History of Drugs and War* (New York: Oxford University Press, 2016), 54. See also Terry Crowdy, *French Soldier in Egypt, 1798– 1801: The Army of the Orient* (Oxford: Osprey Publishing, 2003), 20–22; David A. Guba, "Antoine Isaac Silvestre de Sacy and the Myth of the Hachichins: Orientalizing Hashish in 19th-Century France," *Social History of Alcohol and Drugs* 30 (2016): 68n8.

28. Liat Kozma, "Cannabis Prohibition in Egypt, 1880–1939: From Local Ban to League of Nations Diplomacy," *Middle Eastern Studies* 47 (2011): 444–45; Philip Robins, "Drugs of Choice, Drugs of Change: Egyptian Consumption Habits since the 1920s," *Third World Quarterly* 39 (2018): 249–50. See also memorandum by A. Caillard, director-general of customs in Egypt, to Lord Cromer, December 1, 1892, in *Reports from Her Majesty's Representatives in Egypt, Greece and Turkey on Regulations Affecting the Importation and Sale of Haschisch*, no. 4 (1893): 2–12.

29. Johan Mathew, "Smoke on the Water: Cannabis Smuggling, Corruption and the Janus-Faced Colonial State," *History Workshop Journal* 86 (2018): 72.

30. Kozma, "Cannabis Prohibition." Heavy hashish use by the urban working classes was also noted by nineteenth-century European travelers in Egypt. See, e.g., Edward William Lane, *An Account of the Manners and Customs of the Modern Egyptians* (The Hague and London: East-West Publications, 1989 [1836]), 335.

31. James L. Gelvin, *The Modern Middle East: A History* (New York: Oxford University Press, 2011), 93.

32. James H. Mills, *Cannabis Britannica: Empire, Trade, and Prohibition* (Oxford: Oxford University Press, 2003), 48.

33. Cited in James H. Mills, *Cannabis Nation: Control and Consumption in Britain, 1928–2008* (Oxford: Oxford University Press, 2013), 49.

34. Ibid.; Ronen Shamir and Daphna Hacker, "Colonialism's Civilizing Mission: The Case of the Indian Hemp Drug Commission," *Law & Social Inquiry* 26 (2001), 438; Kozma, "Cannabis Prohibition," 448–49.

35. Kozma, "Cannabis Prohibition," 449.

36. National Archives (hereafter NA), UK, FO/407/164, Cromer to Marquess of

Lansdowne, in *Further Correspondence Respecting the Affairs of Egypt* (hereafter FCRAE), March 15, 1905, 111.

37. NA, U.K., FO/407/182, Kitchener to Sir Edward Grey, in FCRAE, 1914, January 3, 1914, 2–3.

38. Kozma, "Cannabis Prohibition," 446. All in all, the *effendiya* were crucial to the evolution of public discourse and the public sphere in late-nineteenth- and early-twentieth-century Egypt; see Lucie Ryzova, *The Age of the Effendiyya: Passages to Modernity in National-Colonial Egypt* (Oxford: Oxford University Press, 2014).

39. Memorandum by A. Caillard, director-general of customs in Egypt, to Lord Cromer, December 1, 1892, in *Reports from Her Majesty's Representatives in Egypt, Greece and Turkey on Regulations Affecting the Importation and Sale of Haschisch*, 4.

40. Kozma, "Cannabis Prohibition," 446; Robert Kendell, "Cannabis Condemned: The Proscription of Indian Hemp," *Addiction* 98 (2003): 143–51; Mills, *Cannabis Britannica*, 152–87.

41. League of Nations Archive (hereafter LNA), box 797, dossier 40538, document 41142, annex to report concerning Indian hemp, note by Indian delegation, Second Opium Conference, November–December 1924, 4; LNA, box 797, dossier 40538, document 45844, Indian hemp: summary of the replies received from the various governments regarding this drug, August 26, 1925.

42. Liat Kozma, "The League of Nations and the Debate over Cannabis Prohibition," *History Compass* 9 (2011): 63.

43. Liat Kozma, "White Drugs in Interwar Egypt: Decadent Pleasures, Emaciated Fellahin, and the Campaign against Drugs," *Comparative Studies of South Asia, Africa and the Middle East* 33 (2013): 89–101; Gabriel G. Nahas, "Hashish and Drug Abuse in Egypt," 433–34.

44. Sir Thomas Russell Pasha, *Egyptian Service, 1902–1946* (London: J. Murray, 1949), 222.

45. Ibid., 231.

46. Baron Harry D'Erlanger, *The Last Plague of Egypt* (London: L. Dickson and Thompson, 1936), 11. See also Walter Lewis Treadway, "The Abusive Use of Narcotic Drugs in Egypt," *Public Health Reports* 45 (1930): 1239–41.

47. As Philip Robins succinctly explains in *Middle East Drugs Bazaar*, 16: "The surge in hard-drugs supply [to Egypt in the interwar years] owed much to a combination of European drugs producers identifying a potentially large and unpenetrated market, and the exploitation of the Capitulations by such criminals in order to escape the rule of law." See also Kozma, "White Drugs," 90. Among the European master craftsmen of contraband trading, Jews and Greeks stood out as the prime traffickers in white drugs; Alan Block, "European Drug Traffic and Traffickers between the Wars: The Policy of Suppression and Its Consequences," *Journal of Social History* 23 (1989): 315–27.

48. Tom Carnwath and Ian Smith, *Heroin Century* (London and New York: Routledge, 2002), 55.

49. LNA, OAC, box 3165, dossier 1476, document 2609, extract from the report of the Cairo City police for 1926, March 26, 1928.

50. Cyrus Schayegh, *The Middle East and the Making of the Modern World* (Cambridge, MA: Harvard University Press, 2017), 185.

51. Mills, *Cannabis Nation*, 38.

52. LNA, OAC, Traffic in Opium and Other Dangerous Drugs, annual reports by government for 1937, C.195 M.105.1938 (O.C./A.R.1937/5), May 20, 1938.

53. Ibid., ix. However, as Kozma notes in "White Drugs," 93, though heroin and cocaine were now too expensive for the *fellahin*, they became middle-class problems.

54. LNA, OAC, Annual Reports of Governments on the Traffic in Opium and Other Dangerous Drugs for the Year 1938, C.134.M.86.1939, O.C./A.R 11939(2), May 3, 1939, 211.

55. LNA, OAC, Subcommittee on Cannabis; report presented by Dr. J. Bouquet, April 12, 1939, 87; Schayegh, *The Middle East*, 257.

56. Mills, *Cannabis Nation*, 40.

57. Cited in ibid., 40–41.

58. More will be said about this proposition in chapter 4.

59. LNA, Opium Advisory Committee (OAC), Subcommittee to Study Questions in Regard to Indian Hemp and Indian Hemp Drugs, O.C./S/C. Can.Sat.Indian/4th session, 3rd meeting, June 18, 1938, 4.

60. Paul Gootenberg, "Talking about the Flow: Drugs, Borders, and the Discourse of Drug Control," *Cultural Critique* 71 (2009): 36.

61. Harry J. Anslinger with Courtney Ryley Cooper, "Marijuana: Assassin of Youth," *American Magazine,* July 1937. The article can be accessed at https://www.redhousebooks.com/galleries/assassin.htm (accessed April 9, 2020).

62. On Anslinger's war on marijuana, see, e.g., Johann Hari, *Chasing the Scream: The First and Last Days of the War on Drugs* (New York: Bloomsbury, 2015); Marcus Boon, *The Road of Excess: A History of Writers on Drugs* (Cambridge, MA: Harvard University Press, 2002), 154–69; Jerome L. Himmelstein, "From Killer Weed to Drop-Out Drug: The Changing Ideology of Marihuana," *Contemporary Crises* 7 (1983): 13–38; H. Wayne Morgan, *Drugs in America: A Social History, 1800–1980* (Syracuse, NY: Syracuse University Press, 1981), 118–48.

63. LNA, OAC, O.C./s/c.Cann.Sat.Ind./3rd Session, Special Committee to Study Questions in Regard to Indian Hemp and Indian Hemp Drugs, June 2, 1937, 9–10.

64. Cited in Tom Blickman, Dave Bewley-Taylor, and Martin Jelsma, *The Rise and Decline of Cannabis Prohibition: The History of Cannabis in the UN Drug Control System and Options for Reform* (Amsterdam: Transnational Institute 2014), 14.

65. LNA, OAC, O.C./s/c.Cann.Sat.Ind./3rd Session, Special Committee to Study Questions in Regard to Indian Hemp and Indian Hemp Drugs, June 2, 1937, 9–10.

66. Robert S. G. Fletcher, *British Imperialism and "the Tribal Question": Desert Administration and Nomadic Societies in the Middle East* (Oxford: Oxford University Press, 2015), 139.

67. See, e.g., NA (UK), FO/407/155, Lord Cromer to Marquees of Salisbury, in FCRAE, 1900, March 5, 1900, 41; NA (UK), FO/407/157, Cromer to Marquess of Lansdowne, in FCRAE, 1901, March 1, 1901, 45.

68. NA (UK), FO/407/182, Kitchener to Sir Edward Grey, in FCRAE, 1914, January 3, 1913, 3.

69. Henry De Monfreid, *Hashish: A Smuggler's Tale* (London: Penguin, 2007 [1935]), 167.

70. NA (UK), FO/407/159, Cromer to the Marquess of Lansdowne, in FCRAE, 1902, February 21, 1902, 62.

71. In his memoir *Hashish: A Smuggler's Tale*, Henry De Monfreid, who smuggled hashish from Greece to Egypt, provides detailed accounts of his smuggling methods and routes; see also Mathew, "Smoke on the Water."

72. N.A. (UK), FO/407/172, Sir E. Gorst to Sir Edward Grey, in FCRAE, 1908, March 7, 1908, 98.

73. N.A. (UK), FO/407/182, Viscount Kitchener to Sir Edward Grey, in FCRAE, 1914, January 3, 1914, 3.

74. N.A. (UK), FO/407/155, Cromer to Marquees of Salisbury, in FCRAE, 1900, March 5, 1900, 41.

75. N.A. (UK), FO/407/157, Cromer to Marquess of Lansdowne, in FCRAE, 1901, March 1, 1901, 45.

76. N.A. (UK), FO/407/164, Cromer to Marquess of Lansdowne, in FCRAE, 1905, March 15, 1905, 111.

77. Johan Mathew, "Smoke on the Water," 72.

78. Edwin H. Egerton, British ambassador to Greece, to Earl of Rosebery, 26 November 1892, in *Reports from Her Majesty's Representatives in Egypt, Greece and Turkey on Regulations Affecting the Importation and Sale of Haschisch*, 13; N.A. (UK), FO/407/182, Kitchener to Sir Edward Grey, in FCRAE, 1914, January 3, 1914, 2.

79. De Monfreid, *Hashish*, 31. For more detail about de Monfreid's career as a hashish smuggler, see Mathew, "Smoke on the Water."

80. N.A. (U.K.), FO/407/164, Cromer to the Marquess of Lansdow, in FCRAE, 1905, March 15, 1905, 110–11; N.A. (UK), FO/407/165, Cromer to Sir Edward Grey, in FCRAE, 1906, March 8, 1906, 135.

81. N.A. (UK), FO/407/165, Cromer to Sir Edward Grey, in FCRAE, 1906, March 8, 1906, 135.

82. N.A. (UK), FO/407/182, Kitchener to Grey, in FCRAE, 1914, January 3, 1914, 1–2.

83. N.A. (U.K.), FO/407/180, memorandum communicated by Mr. Cheetham, in FCRAE, 1913, April 21, 1913, 154.

84. Mathew, "Smoke on the Water," 76.

85. De Monfreid, *Hashish*, 38, 56.

86. Mills, *Cannabis Nation*, 38.

87. LNA, OAC, Traffic in Opium and other dangerous drugs, annual reports by government for 1937, C.195 M.105.1938 (O.C./A.R.1937/5), May 20, 1938, 68.

88. Russell Pasha, *Egyptian Service*, 228.

89. Russell Pasha, "Introductory Note," in LNA, OAC, Traffic in Opium and other Dangerous Drugs, Annual Reports by Covernment for 1937, C.195 M.105.1938 (O.C./A.R.1937/5), May 20, 1938, x. See also Fletcher, *British Imperialism and "the Tribal Question,"* 138.

90. Marshall, *Lebanese Connection*, 1.

91. Ghiabi, "Deorientalizing Drugs in the Modern Middle East."

92. LNA, OAC, box 3204, dossier 8003, document 12735, Production of Hashish in Syria; Russell Pasha, "Report on Hashish Cultivation in Syria," June 11, 1929, x, 2–3. See also Cyrus Schayegh, "The Many Worlds of 'Abud Yasin; or, What Narcotics Trafficking in the Interwar Middle East Can Tell Us about Territorialization," *American Historical Review* 116 (2011): 274n3.

93. As Gabriel Nahas concludes in "Hashish and Drug Abuse in Egypt," 437: Owing, among other things, to the abolition of the Capitulations, "Syria and Lebanon . . . became the main areas of cultivation and production of hashish and the principal suppliers of Egypt." See also Fletcher, *British Imperialism and "the Tribal Question,"* 139.

94. LNA, OAC, box 3204, dossier 8003, document 8003, Hashish: Various Correspondence; Note on the Drug Traffic in the Levant States under French Mandate, November 18, 1929.

95. Ibid.

96. Philippe Bourmaud, "Turf Wars at the League of Nations: International Anti-Cannabis Policies and Oversight in Syria and Lebanon, 1919–1939," in *The League of Nations' Work on Social Issues*, ed. Magaly Rodríguez García, Davide Rodogno, and Liat Kozma (Geneva: United Nations Publications, 2016), 75–76.

97. Ibid., 77; Schayegh, "Many Worlds," 276.

98. Schayegh, "Many Worlds," 277. "Many [Lebanese] officials are themselves partners in hasheesh farms," as John Carlson reminisced in his *Cairo to Damascus* (New York: Knopf, 1951), 442.

99. Accounts of Lebanese hashish kingpins with immense political power—including those groomed by the French to fill the position of president of Lebanon—run through Norman Phillips, *Guns, Drugs and Deserters: The Special Investigation Branch in the Middle East* (London: Werner Laurie, 1954). See also "Hashish in Lebanon," *Al-Mukattam*, February 24, 1932; Imam 'Amer, "An Order Preventing Commerce in

Narcotics," *Umm al-Qura*, September 21, 1934; and "Idde Expected to Resign President of Lebanon: Hashish in High Places," *Palestine Post*, August 8, 1939.

100. LNA, OAC, box 3204, dossier 8003, document 12735, Production of Hashish in Syria; Russell Pasha, "Report on Hashish Cultivation in Syria," June 11, 1929, 2–3.

101. LNA, OAC, C.75.M68, Annual Reports by Governments for 1939; Central Narcotics Intelligence Bureau, June 6, 1940, 101.

102. Schayegh, "Many Worlds," 277; Bourmaud, "Turf Wars," 79.

103. LNA, OAC, box 3204, dossier 8003, document 12735, "Hashish: Various Correspondence; Note on the Drug Traffic in the Levant States under French Mandate," November 18, 1929.

104. LNA, OAC, box 3204, dossier 8003, document 12735, "Report of the Minister of Finance, Public Works and Agriculture of the Lebanese Republic to the Delegate of the High Commissioner Regarding Destruction of Indian Hemp," August 29, 1929.

105. Kozma, "Cannabis Prohibition," 453.

106. Schayegh, *The Middle East*, 257, 334.

107. "The Modern Plague: Russell Pasha's Drug Traffic Review at Geneva," *Palestine Post*, July 3, 1933.

108. LNA, OAC, box 4928, dossier, 6043, document 24058, Situation as Regards the Control of Cannabis (Hemp) and Drugs Derived from Cannabis, May 15, 1936; LNA, OAC, O.C. 1542(b), Position in Regard to Indian hemp, New Decree Relating to the Regulations Applicable to Narcotic Drugs in Syria and Lebanon, November 7, 1934, 6. See also Mills, *Cannabis Nation*, 41–42.

109. LNA, OAC, O.C. 1542(d), Note on Indian hemp as it effects Egypt; statement presented to the Advisory Committee by the representative of Egypt, November 16, 1934, 4.

110. Ibid.

111. LNA, Sub-Committee on Cannabis, box 4927, dossier 6043, document 20827, Indian hemp, Sub-Committee of Experts, services and correspondence with Dr. Bouquet; report by Dr. J. Bouquet, April 12, 1939, 87.

112. LNA, OAC, C.75.M68, annual reports by governments for 1939; Central Narcotics Intelligence Bureau, June 6, 1940, xiii.

113. Ibid., xiv.

114. Ziad Abu-Rish, "Review of Jonathan Marshall, 'The Lebanese Connection,'" *International Journal of Middle East Studies* 46 (2014): 415.

115. N.A. (UK), FO/484/2, Houstoun-Boswall to Ernest Bevin, Changes in the Lebanese cabinet, in FCRAE, 1948, 6.9.1948, 15. In the same year, an American diplomat in Beirut commented on the "alarming" increase in hashish production from cannabis fields, clearly visible along one of the country's northern highways. He also cited evidence that "persons in the President's entourage are prominent in this traffic"; Marshall, *Lebanese Connection*, 2.

116. Gootenberg, "Talking about the Flow," 22–23.

117. Ibid., 23.

118. Ibid., 13–46.

119. Arjun Appadurai, "Introduction: Commodities and the Political Value," in *The Social Life of Things: Commodities in Cultural Perspective*, ed. Arjun Appadurai (Cambridge: Cambridge University Press, 1986), 24, 26.

120. LNA, Subcommittee on Cannabis; observations on the causes of drug addiction in North Africa by Dr. Jules Bouquet, O.C. 1724, January 24, 1939, 89.

CHAPTER TWO

1. Elias Khoury, *Bundle of Secrets*, in Arabic (Beirut: Dar al-Adab, 1994). Sami al-Khouri's cabbage ploy is related on pp. 113–14.

2. Ryan Gingeras, *Heroin, Organized Crime, and the Making of Modern Turkey* (Oxford: Oxford University Press, 2014), 104.

3. Jonathan Marshall, *The Lebanese Connection: Corruption, Civil War, and the International Drug Traffic* (Stanford, CA: Stanford University Press, 2012), 41. Al-Khoury gained this reputation through playing a key role in Lebanon's integration into the wider world of the transatlantic heroin trade, which consequently became known as the "French Connection." Hence, in the 1950s, al-Khoury would have been busy securing raw opium from Turkey, overseeing its conversion into morphine base in Lebanon, and sending it along to laboratories in Sicily and Marseilles for its final conversion into heroin. In the process, al-Khoury entered into a business partnership with the infamous Charles "Lucky" Luciano. See also Alexander Cockburn and Jeffrey St. Clair, *Whiteout: the CIA, Drugs, and the Press* (London: Verso, 1998), 131.

4. Arjun Appadurai, "Introduction: Commodities and the Political Value," in *The Social Life of Things: Commodities in Cultural Perspective*, ed. Arjun Appadurai (Cambridge: Cambridge University Press, 1986), 18.

5. Itty Abraham and Willem van Schendel, "Introduction: The Making of Illicitness," in *Illicit Flows and Criminal Things: States, Borders, and the Other Side of Globalization*, ed. Willem van Schendel and Itty Abraham (Bloomington: Indiana University Press, 2005), 13.

6. Cyrus Schayegh, "The Many Worlds of 'Abud Yasin; or, What Narcotics Trafficking in the Interwar Middle East Can Tell Us about Territorialization," *American Historical Review* 116 (2011): 278; Robert S. G. Fletcher, *British Imperialism and "'the Tribal Question": Desert Administration and Nomadic Societies in the Middle East* (Oxford: Oxford University Press, 2015), 136–37.

7. Colonial authorities faced the same problem in stopping cross-border trafficking in women and prostitutes in the interwar years; and see Liat Kozma, *Global Women, Colonial Ports: Prostitution in the Interwar Middle East* (Albany: State University of New York Press, 2017), 96–101.

8. In fact, the only time Britain tried to police a border strictly was during the 1936–39 Palestinian revolt, relating to Lebanon and Syria; Cyrus Schayegh, *The Middle East and the Making of the Modern World* (Cambridge, MA: Harvard University Press, 2017), 198.

9. Lauren Banko, "Keeping Out the 'Undesirable Elements': The Treatment of Communists, Transients, Criminals, and the Ill in Mandate Palestine," *Journal of Imperial and Commonwealth History* (2019): 1–28.

10. Undoubtedly, "individuals and social groups that systematically contest or by-pass state controls do not simply flout the letter of the law; with repeated transgressions over time, they bring into question the legitimacy of the state itself by questioning the state's ability to control its own territory"; Abraham and van Schendel, "Introduction," 14.

11. Joseph F. Broadhurst, *From Vine Street to Jerusalem* (London: Stanley Paul, 1936), 193–94.

12. Israel State Archive (hereafter ISA), M-24/322, "Report by the Inspector General of the Palestine Police for the Calendar Year 1947 on the Traffic in Dangerous Drugs," February 23, 1948.

13. The names and professions of hashish offenders in Palestine were provided in annual British reports to the League of Nations on "important seizures of narcotic drugs." Most of those arrested and/or indicted for hashish offences bore distinctly Arabic names. This information was also gathered from regular reports by Shai, the intelligence and counterespionage arm of the Haganah; see, e.g., Haganah History Archive (hereafter HHA), div. 47, file 201, roll 331, 51–100, Lists of Convicted Criminals; HHA, div. 47, file 203, roll 331, 151–200; Lists of convicted criminals, HHA, C.I.D. Information, drug smuggling, 26.1.1943, 21.

14. Sir Thomas Russell Pasha, *Egyptian Service, 1902–1946* (London: J. Murray, 1949), 254.

15. Douglas V. Duff, *Sword for Hire: The Saga of a Modern Free-Companion* (London: John Murray, 1934), 117. Duff's contemptuous attitude is not at all surprising. Duff was notorious for his harsh treatment of Arabs, on account of which his surname became an epithet for Palestine police brutality (e.g., "Duff them up"); Matthew Kraig Kelly, *The Crime of Nationalism: Britain, Palestine, and Nation-Building on the Fringe of Empire* (Oakland: University of California Press, 2017), 26–27.

16. League of Nations Archives (hereafter LNA), OAC, box 4930, dossier 6043, document 36534, Subcommittee on Cannabis; report presented by Dr. J. Bouquet, April 12, 1939, 90.

17. Ibid., 131.

18. Henry De Monfreid, *Hashish: A Smuggler's Tale* (London: Penguin, 2007 [1935]), 32–33.

19. Barbara Ehrenreich, *Blood Rites: Origins and History of the Passions of War* (London: Virago, 1997), 11. See also Łukasz Kamieński, *Shooting Up: A Short History*

of Drugs and War (New York: Oxford University Press, 2016); and David Courtwright, *Forces of Habit: Drugs and the Making of the Modern World* (Cambridge, MA: Harvard University Press, 2001), 140–41.

20. National Archives (hereafter NA), US, 0660 Palestine, Dr. Zdeněk Frank König to Harry J. Anslinger, February 1, 1948.

21. Norman Phillips, *Guns, Drugs and Deserters: The Special Investigation Branch in the Middle East* (London: Werner Laurie, 1954), 17.

22. ISA, M-24/322, Important seizures of narcotic drugs effected during 1947; "The Juke Box Trial," *Palestine Post*, June 1, 1947; "Juke Box Actress Turns King's Evidence," *Palestine Post*, August 19, 1947.

23. "Jewish Soldiers in Egypt Accused of Hashish Smuggling," *Davar*, December 27, 1945; "How to Inflate," *Ha-Tzofeh*, December 27, 1945.

24. See, e.g., "Police Discovers Trails of a Large Group of Intoxicating Drugs," *Ha-Mashqif*, November 9, 1947; "On the Possession of Hashish," *Ha-Mashqif*, October 3, 1941. See also Zachary Foster, "Illicit Drug Trafficking and Use in British Mandatory Palestine" (unpublished paper, 2010).

25. NA, U.S, 867N.111- 867N.114 Narcotics/12-3044, Traffic in Opium and Other Dangerous Drugs, Seizures in Palestine by Customs Department, March–June 1940; ISA, M 24/322, Report by the Government of Palestine for the Calendar Year 1946 and 1947 on the Traffic in Opium and other Dangerous Drugs.

26. John Knight, "The Successful Failure of Reform: Police Legitimacy in British Palestine," in *The Routledge Handbook of the History of Middle East Mandates*, eds. Cyrus Schayegh and Andrew Arsan (New York: Routledge, 2015), 202.

27. In some cases, Jews even helped the authorities in apprehending the Palestinian Arabs dealing in hashish in their neighborhoods. Such antihashish services rendered to the police by Jews—for which no satisfactorily conclusive information exists—usually took place in Palestine's "mixed cities," such as Jaffa, and frontier neighborhoods, where Jews and Arabs lived side by side. For instance, Abigail Jacobson and Moshe Naor—in *Oriental Neighbors: Middle Eastern Jews and Arabs in Mandatory Palestine* (Waltham, MA: Brandeis University Press, 2016), 122—tell the story of Moshe Levi Nachum, the head (*mukhtar*) of Tel Aviv's Yemenite Quarter (Kerem Hatemanim), and consequently the Jewish representative in the Jaffa municipality during the Mandate era, who was instrumental in helping the police track down thieves, hashish traders, and murderers active in the quarter.

28. As Alan Block contends in "European Drug Traffic and Traffickers between the Wars: The Policy of Suppression and Its Consequences," *Journal of Social History* 23 (1989), 323–24: "Their long exclusion from European civil society forced them into the most extreme social and economic statuses. Pushed into borderline commercial ventures by the vagaries of Jewish existence in an alien, hostile world, dealing in contraband was inevitable." For an engaging discussion of the Jewish Viennese underworld,

see Bernard Wasserstein, *On the Eve: The Jews of Europe before the Second World War* (London: Profile Books, 2012).

29. Gabriel Nahas, "Hashish and Drug Abuse in Egypt during the 19th and 20th Centuries," *Bulletin of the New York Academy of Medicine* 61 (1985): 433; Liat Kozma, "White Drugs in Interwar Egypt: Decadent Pleasures, Emaciated Fellahin, and the Campaign against Drugs," *Comparative Studies of South Asia, Africa and the Middle East* 33 (2013): 90.

30. Paul Knepper, "Dreams and Nightmares: Drug Trafficking and the History of International Crime," in *The Oxford Handbook of the History and Crime and Criminal Justice*, eds. Paul Knepper and Anja Johansen (Oxford: Oxford University Press, 2016), 216; Paul Knepper, *International Crime in the Twentieth Century: The League of Nations Era, 1919–1939* (London: Palgrave, 2011), 133.

31. Baron Harry D'Erlanger, *The Last Plague of Egypt* (London: L. Dickson and Thompson, 1936), 125.

32. Knepper, "Dreams and Nightmares," 216.

33. See, e.g., LNA, OAC, O.C. 1284, Illicit Traffic between Austria and Egypt, November 27, 1930; LNA, OAC, O.C. 1284, Additional Information on the Chaskes, Glickmann and Friedman Organization, January 14, 1931; LNA, box S212-17, Black List of Traffickers and Persons Implicated in the Illicit Traffic in Heroin, Cocaine, Morphine and Allied Drugs, prepared by the CNIB, 1930.

34. Phillips, *Guns, Drugs and Deserters*, 18. See also "Jewish Terrorists Are Smuggling Hashish to Egypt," *Ma'ariv*, May 11, 1948. That Zionist organizations smuggled arms from Lebanon and Syria is established beyond doubt; see Schayegh, *The Middle East*, 276. See also "How to Inflate," *Ha-Tzofeh*, December 27, 1945, which reports about a "Jewish military gang" arrested in Cairo for "smuggling hashish and opium on a large scale."

35. See e.g. HHA, div. 47, file 95, roll 354, Personality Sheet on David Vaknin, 1944–47; HHA, div. 47, file 76, Personality Sheet on Haim Ben Shmuel Arusi Levi, 1945–47; HHA, div. 47, file 37, Smuggling by Plane between Egypt and Palestine, November 10–December 31, 1945. In 1964, the Israeli daily *Yedi'ot Ahronot* confirmed "rumors" that "the Irgun was engaged in hashish smuggling to Egypt to finance its war"; Aviezer Golan, "Those Who Drug Themselves to Unconsciousness," *Yedi'ot Ahronot*, May 8, 1964.

36. HHA, 178.00034, Shimshon Mashbetz's Testimony, November 18, 1970.

37. Schayegh, *The Middle East*, 152.

38. HHA, 178.00034, Shimshon Mashbetz's Testimony, November 18, 1970.

39. Ibid.

40. Yirmiyahu Halpern, *The Revival of Hebrew Shipping*, in Hebrew (Tel Aviv: Hadar, 1960), 49.

41. NA, U.S., 867N.111–867N.114, Report by the Government of Palestine for the Year 1937 on the Traffic in Opium and Other Dangerous Drugs.

42. "Hashish: The Curse of the Middle East," *Davar*, May 29, 1952.

43. Schayegh, "Many Worlds," 293.

44. Ibid, 289.

45. Foster, "Illicit Drug Trafficking."

46. Cited in Schayegh, *The Middle East*, 259.

47. Cited in Schayegh, "Many Worlds," 288n56.

48. Zachary Lockman, *Comrades and Enemies: Arab and Jewish Workers in Palestine, 1906–1948* (Berkeley: University of California Press, 1996), 112–13; Shereen Khairallah, *Railways in the Middle East, 1856–1948: Political and Economic Background* (Beirut: Librairie du Liban, 1991), 142–43.

49. Lockman, *Comrades and Enemies*, 112. See also Paul Cotterell, *The Railways of Palestine and Israel* (Abingdon, UK: Tourret Publishing, 1984), 32–67. As Cyrus Schayegh observes in *The Middle East*, 158, the British Qantara–Haifa railroad "slashed traveling from Haifa to Egypt's Suez Canal to a mere ten hours."

50. "Hashish and Opium Smuggling via Haifa," *Davar*, May 3, 1937.

51. Schayegh, *The Middle East*, 174.

52. Lockman, *Comrades and Enemies*, 112.

53. Schayegh, *The Middle East*, 252.

54. Foster, "Illicit Drug Trafficking." See also Zachary Foster, "Are Lod and Ramla the Drug Capitals of Israel and Palestine?" *Palestine Square*, December 30, 2015, https://www.palestine-studies.org/en/node/232329 (accessed April 9, 2020).

55.. "Hashish in the High Commissioner's Train Car," *Davar*, July 1, 1929.

56. *Al-Karmil*, July 12, 1929.

57. LNA, OAC, C.134.M.86.1939.XI (O.C./A.R. 1938/2), Traffic in Opium and Other Dangerous Drugs, Annual Reports by Governments for 1938, May 3, 1939, 50. See also "From the Courts," *Do'ar ha-Yom*, February 17, 1931, for a brief account of "an Arab train engine worker" standing trial for attempting to smuggle hashish by train.

58. "Hashish Hidden in Axle-Box of Railway Truck," *Palestine Post*, March 31, 1933.

59. Lockman, *Comrades and Enemies*, 12.

60. Ibid., 130, 164.

61. See, e.g., "Case of Shaker Mohamed El-Shewehi and others," in LNA, OAC, C.75.M.68.1940.XI (O.C./A.R. 1030/5), in annual reports by governments for 1939, June 6, 1940, 54.

62. "Drug Trafficking in Palestine," in *The King's Royal Rifle Corps Chronicles, 1936* (Winchester: Warren & Son, 1937), 166. I thank the National Army Museum, London, for making this source available to me.

63. "Hashish, Opium, Revolver and Bullets Found in Car Wheels and in House Staircase," *Davar*, April 25, 1937; "Alleged Smugglers of Opium Arrested," *Palestine Post*, April 25, 1937. Concealing hashish inside wheels loaded onto Egypt-bound

trains was a ploy used repeatedly by smugglers in Palestine; and see, e.g., LNA, OAC, C.134.M.86.1939.XI (O.C./A.R. 1938/2), Traffic in Opium and other Dangerous Drugs, Annual Reports by Governments for 1938, May 3, 1939, 13–14.

64.   LNA, Traffic in Opium and Other Dangerous Drugs, Annual Reports by Governments for 1941, C.3.M.e.1943.XI (O.C./A.R.1941), February 24, 1943, 12. John Roy Carlson, in *Cairo to Damascus* (New York: Knopf, 1951), writes: "Hasheesh smugglers, after crossing Palestine, often met here [Deir al-Balah]."

65.   Phillip, *Guns, Drugs, and Deserters*, 70.

66.   LNA, OAC, C.373.M.251.1937.XI (O.C./A.R. 1936/7), Annual Reports for Governments for 1936, November 13, 1937; NA, US, 867N.111–867N.114 Narcotics/75, May 23, 1937, Seizures of Opium and Hashish in Palestine during 1937; HHA, div. 105, file 80, Criminal Activities and Firearms, August 10, 1943–February 15, 1944; "How to Smuggle Drugs," *Davar*, August 29, 1934; "A New Drug Menace: Palestine as a Market," *The Times*, July 20, 1939.

67.   Schayegh, "Many Worlds," 291–92.

68.   See e.g. NA, U.S., 867N.111–867N.114, Seizures of Opium and Hashish in Palestine during 1937, May 23, 1937.

69.   NA, UK, Foreign Office (hereafter FO) 141/764, Telegram to the High Commissioner for Egypt, April 5, 1933; NA, UK, FO-141/764, H. G. Jakins, British Vice-Consulate, Constanta, April 11, 1933; NA, UK, FO-141/764, Mr. Palairet, Bucharest, to R. I. Campbell, high commissioner for Egypt, April 5, 1933.

70.   Broadhurst, *From Vine Street to Jerusalem*, 197–98.

71.   Knepper, *International Crime*, 37.

72.   Cited in ibid., 40.

73.   Hillel Cohen, *Good Arabs: The Israeli Security Agencies and the Israeli Arabs, 1948–1967* (Berkeley: University of California Press, 2011), 191.

74.   Details of this failed smuggling operation can be gleaned from ISA, P-9/195, Henry Cattan: Smuggling of Hashish; and LNA, OAC, C.195.M.105.1938.XI (O.C./A.R. 1937/5), Annual Reports by Governments for 1937, Smuggling of Drugs into Egypt from Syria and Palestine by Air, May 20, 1938, 28–31. For a detailed account of this foiled smuggling operation, see Haggai Ram, "Travelling Substances and Their Human Carriers: Hashish-Trafficking in Mandatory Palestine," in *A Global Middle East: Mobility, Materiality and Culture in the Modern Age, 1880–1940*, eds. Liat Kozma, Avner Wishnitzer, and Cyrus Schayegh (London: I. B. Tauris, 2014), 209–10.

75.   NA, U.K., CO-814/9–0012, Palestine Police Force, Annual Administrative Report for 1934, 26–27.

76.   Schayegh, *The Middle East*, 250.

77.   Knepper, *International Crime*, 1, 35.

78.   Fletcher, *British Imperialism and "the Tribal Question,"* 141; Emanuel Marx,

"Hashish Smuggling by Bedouin in South Sinai," in *Organized Crime: Culture, Markets and Policies*, eds. Dina Siegel and Hans Nelen (New York: Springer, 2008), 30.

79.   LNA, OAC, box 4927, dossier 6043, document 20830, Subcommittee on Cannabis; report presented by Dr. J. Bouquet, April 12, 1939, 89; Clinton Bailey, *The Magic of Camel-Mares: Bedouin Poetry from Sinai to the Negev*, in Hebrew (Beit Berl, Israel: Institute for Israeli Arab Studies, 1993), 55–56.

80.   "The Modern Plague: Russell's Pasha Drug Traffic Review at Geneva," *Palestine Post*, July 3, 1933; Russell, *Egyptian Service*, 271–72.

81.   Ibid. See also NA, US, 867N.01/606–740, Report by His Majesty's Government in the UK of Great Britain and Northern Ireland to the Council of the League of Nations on the Administration of Palestine and Trans-Jordan for 1932, August 1931–March 1937.

82.   NA, US, 867N.01/606–740, Report by His Majesty's Government in the UK of Great Britain and Northern Ireland to the Council of the League of Nations on the Administration of Palestine and Trans-Jordan for 1932, August 1931–March 1937; Broadhurst, *From Vine Street to Jerusalem*, 191–93.

83.   Ibid., 195.

84.   Guy Arnold, *The International Drugs Trade* (New York: Routledge, 2005), vii.

85.   Russell Pasha, *Egyptian Service*, 279.

86.   LNA, OAC, C.75.M.68.1940 (O.C./A.R.1939/3), Traffic in Opium and Other Dangerous Drugs, Annual Reports by Government for 1939; Smuggling through Sinai, June 6, 1940, 42–47; see also Russell Pasha, *Egyptian Service*, 276–78.

87.   Ibid., 278. A smuggling camel could be identified by wounds to the mouth, caused by the forced introduction of cylinders filled with the drug. Martin Booth, *Opium: A History* (New York: St. Martin's Griffin, 1996), 232.

88.   LNA, OAC, C.75.M.68.1940.XI (O.C./A.R. 1030/5), in annual reports by governments for 1939, June 6, 1940, 44.

89.   HHA, div. 105, file 298, Report of Current Events; Methods of Smuggling Hashish, February 23, 1943. See also "Hashish Smuggled in Camel's Interiors," *'Al ha-Mishmar Ha-Mashkif*, October 13, 1947; "Hashish Worth 10,000 PP Revealed in a Living Camels' Stomach," *HaMashkif*, October 13, 1947.

90.   NA, U.K., CO-814/40–0008, Palestine Police Annual Administrative Report for 1946; ISA, M-326/37, Discovery of Area of Land Planted with Indian Hemp (Hashish), June 1946; ISA, M-18/15, Cultivation of Hashish in Deir Tarif, Ramla Sub-District, June–September 1946; ISA, M-6482/6, Agriculture: Cultivation of Hashish, May 1947; ISA, M-858/67, Cultivation of Hashish, May 1947. See also Foster, "Illicit Drug Trafficking."

91.   ISA, M-18/7, Plantation of Hashish in Jenin, July–October 1946; letter to the High Commissioner, July 31, 1946.

92.   Major C. S. Jarvis, OBE, "Sinai," *Journal of the Royal Central Asian Society* 22 (1935), 45.

93. *Official Gazette O.E.T.A (South)*, November 1919, 2.

94. Robert Kendell, "Cannabis Condemned: The Proscription of Indian Hemp," *Addiction* 98 (2003): 143–51; James Mills, *Cannabis Britannica: Empire, Trade, and Prohibition, 1800–1928* (Oxford: Oxford University Press, 2003), 152–87.

95. "Dangerous Drugs Ordinance 1925," *Palestine Gazette* 140 (June 1925): 249–52; Joshua Caspi, *Dangerous Drugs: Policy, Control, Enforcement and Trial*, in Hebrew (Haifa: Tamar, 1996), 129–30; Mills, *Cannabis Britannica*, 189.

96. Virginia Berridge, "Drugs and Social Policy: The Establishment of Drug Control in Britain 1900–30," *Addiction* 79 (1984): 17–29.

97. "Dangerous Drugs Ordinance 1925."

98. LON, [Opium] Advisory Committee on the Traffic in Opium and other Dangerous Drugs (hereafter OAC), Extract from the Report of the Cairo City Police for 1926; and Extracts from the Annual Report of the Cairo City Police for 1927, box 3165, dossier 1476, document 2609, March 26, 1928.

99. LON, Traffic in Opium and other Dangerous Drugs, Annual Reports by Government for 1936, C.373 M.251.1937 (O.C./A.R.1936/7), September 20, 1937.

100. NA, US (867N.111–867N.114 Narcotics/75), Dangerous Drugs Ordinance, Number 17, of 1936, 9; LNA, OAC, C.373 M.251.1937 (O.C./A.R.1936/7), Traffic in Opium and other Dangerous Drugs, Annual Reports by Government for 1936, November 20, 1937.

101. Yoav Alon, "Bridging Imperial, National, and Local Historiographies: Britons, Arabs, and Jews in the Mandate Palestine Police," *Jerusalem Quarterly* 75 (2018): 65.

102. LNA, OAC, O.C. 1542, Preliminary Notes on the Chief Aspects of the Problem of Indian Hemp and the Laws Relating Thereto in Force in Certain Countries, March 25, 1934, 35.

103. Elizabeth Bartels, "Policing Politics: Crime and Conflict in British Mandate Palestine (1920–1948)" (PhD diss., New York: City University of New York, 2004).

104. Edward Horne, *A Job Well Done (Being a History of the Palestine Police Force 1920–1948)* (Essex: Anchor Press, 1982), 463–79; Eldad Harouvi, *Palestine Investigated: The CID in Eretz Yisrael, 1920–1948*, in Hebrew (Tzur Yigal: Porath Publishing, 2011), 39–79; Martin Kolinsky, *Law, Order and Riots in Mandatory Palestine, 1928–35* (London: St. Martin's Press, 1993), 101.

105. Horne, *Job Well Done*, 470; Knight, "Successful Failure of Reform," 200.

106. Broadhurst, *From Vine Street*, 193–94.

107. Eugene Rogan, "The Palestine Police Oral History Project," *CBRL Bulletin* 2 (2007): 37; Alon, "Bridging Imperial, National, and Local Historiographies," 64.

108. Horne, *Job Well Done*, 463. This statement by Horne is inaccurate, to say the least, as recent works clearly indicate that by the 1860s, and certainly after the 1870s, Ottoman police carried detective work that included collecting forensic evidence, interrogating suspects and the like. See, e.g., Omri Paz, "Crime, Criminals, and the Ottoman

State: Anatolia between the Late 1830s and the Late 1860s" (PhD diss., Tel Aviv University, 2011); Noémi Levy-Aksu, *Ordre et désordres dans l'Istanbul ottoman, 1879–1909* (Paris: Karthala, 2012); Ferdan Ergut, "Policing the Poor in the Late Ottoman Empire," *Middle Eastern Studies* 38 (2002): 149–64.

109. Marx, "Hashish Smuggling by Bedouin," 32–33; Jarvis, "Sinai," 45–46; Fletcher, *British Imperialism and "the Tribal Question,"* 147ff.

110. Mansour Nasasra, *The Naqab Bedouins: A Century of Politics and Resistance* (New York: Columbia University Press, 2017), 83–87.

111. "Cable from Jerusalem," *Palestine Post*, November 8, 1945.

112. Horne, *Job Well Done*, 413. See also Mansour Nasasra, "Bedouin Tribes in the Middle East and the Naqab: Changing Dynamics and the New State," in *The Naqab Bedouin and Colonialism: New Perspectives*, ed. Mansour Nasasra, Sophie Richter-Devroe, Sarab Abu-Rabia-Queder, and Richard Ratcliffe (New York: Routledge, 2015), 44.

113. Horne, *Job Well Done*, 401.

114. Ibid., 421.

115. Ibid., 415; Nasasra, *Naqab Bedouins*, 87.

116. Fletcher, *British Imperialism and "the Tribal Question,"* 151–52.

117. Horne, *Job Well Done*, 427.

118. Douglas V. Duff, *Galilee Galloper* (London: John Murray, 1935), 28–29. For additional information on the unit's failure to apprehend hashish smuggling at sea, see "Attempt to Smuggle Hashish," *Do'ar ha-Yom*, July 21, 1930.

119. Duff, *Sword for Hire*, 122.

120. Horne, *Job Well Done*, 427.

121. In 1933 Britain completed the massive deep-water port construction project, started in 1929; Schayegh, *The Middle East*, 250.

122. Horne, *Job Well Done*, 431.

123. "LP. 50,000 Worth of Drugs," *Palestine Post*, February 18, 1941.

124. N.A. (US), 867N.114, Narcotics/90, Secretary of State to the Secretary of the Treasury, March 10, 1941.

125. Horne, *Job Well Done*, 429.

126. Ibid., 428–29.

127. Ibid., 428.

128. Eric Tagliacozzo, *Secret Trade, Porous Borders: Smuggling and States along a Southeast Asian Frontier, 1865–1915* (New Haven, CT: Yale University Press, 2005), 1–22.

129. Schayegh, "Many Worlds," 292.

130. Horne, *Job Well Done*, 428–29; Harouvi, *Palestine Investigated*, 164.

131. NA, U.K., CO 814/11–0014, Palestine Police Force, Annual Administrative Report, 1936, 25; ISA, M-24/322, Report by the Government of Palestine for the Calendar Year 1946 on the Traffic in Opium and other Dangerous Drugs.

132. Schayegh, *The Middle East*, 257.

133. Ibid., 186. This latter catalogue is available in LNA, box S212–17, blacklist of traffickers and persons implicated in the illicit traffic in heroin, cocaine, morphine and allied drugs, published by the NCIB, 1930.

134. Broadhurst, *From Vine Street*, 194–95.

135. LNA, OAC, box 3204, dossier 8003, document 12735, Note on the Drug Traffic in the Levant States under French Mandate, Communicated by the French Government, November 18, 1929.

136. Ibid.

137. LNA, OAC, C.715.M.303.1930 (O.C. 23 (g) 20), Traffic in Opium and Other Dangerous Drugs, Annual Reports by Governments for 1929, December 8, 1930; LNA, OAC, C.494.M.307.1936 (O.C./A.R.1935/29), Traffic in Opium and Other Dangerous Drugs, Annual Reports by Government for 1935, December 2, 1936, 4.

138. ISA, M 24/322, Report by the Government of Palestine for the Calendar Year 1946 and 1947 on the Traffic in Opium and other Dangerous Drugs.

139. LNA, OAC, C.3.M.3.1943 (O.C../A.R.1941/44), Annual Reports by Governments for 1941, February 24, 1943, 3.

140. Ibid.

141. See, in particular, NA, UK, CO 814/1–CO 814/7, the Government of Palestine Annual Reports of the Department of Health for the Years 1923–32; and NA, UK, CO 814/7–CO 814/40, the Palestine Police and Prisons Annual Administrative Reports for the Years 1932–46.

142. Phillips, *Guns, Drugs and Deserters*, 58–59.

143. Russell Pasha, *Egyptian Service*, 282. The same figures are provided in Phillips, *Guns, Drugs and Deserters*, 41.

144. Schayegh, *The Middle East*, 185.

145. Martin Edwards, *The Golden Age of Murder: The Mystery of the Writers Who Invented the Modern Detective Story* (London: HarperCollins, 2015).

146. "One of the indications of the increasing anxiety about crime is that crime stories started to be published and read extensively at this period." Thus argues Ferdan Ergut with respect to the Ottoman Empire in the early 1900s. Ferdan Ergut, "Policing the Poor in the Late Ottoman Empire," *Middle Eastern Studies* 38 (2002): 153. See also Knepper, *International Crime*, 32.

147. Pablo Piccato, *A History of Infamy: Crime, Truth, and Justice in Mexico* (Oakland: University of California Press, 2017), 194. For a detailed discussion of crime fiction in interwar Palestine, see Haggai Ram, "On Sleuth Literature, Border-Crossings, and Crime in Mandatory Palestine" (in Hebrew), *Jama'a* 21 (2015): 119–31.

148. Shlomo Gelper, *The Blue Crosses: The Tales of Hashish Smugglers*, in Hebrew (Tel Aviv: HaBalash Publishers, 1932).

149. Gad Magen's battle against a ring of hashish smugglers unfolds across three

consecutive booklets: *The Adventures of Gad Magen: Hashish and Murder; The Adventures of Gad Magen: Abdul Ma'ti's Emissary;* and *The Adventures of Gad Magen: Gad Escapes Trouble*, all three in Hebrew (Tel Aviv: Hotza'a ha-Me'a ha-'Esrim, 1947). The writers of the Gad Magen series are unknown.

150. Yoram Kaniuk, "David Tidhar and the Hebrew Book Fair," *Davar*, June 6, 1975; Moshe Dor, "The Return of the Hebrew Detective," *Ma'ariv*, January 13, 1984; Dalia Karpel, "David Tidhar Looking for a Successor," *Ha-Aretz Weekly Supplement*, September 15, 2016; Yaakov Shavit and Zohar Shavit, "History of the Hebrew 'Crime Story' in the Land of Israel" (in Hebrew), *HaSifrut* 18–19 (1974): 30–73.

151. Gelper, *Blue Crosses*, 23–24.

152. *Gad Escapes Trouble*, 4.

153. *Hashish and Murder*, 6.

154. Ibid., 6–7.

155. *Abdul Ma'ti's Emissary*, 8.

156. *Gad Escapes Trouble*, 7.

157. Ibid.

158. *Abdul Ma'ti's Emissary*, 5.

159. Ibid., 6.

160. LNA, OAC, C.59.M.59.1946.XI (O.C/A.R.1944/60), Annual Reports for Governments for 1944, July 18, 1946, 24–25.

161. *Gad Escapes Trouble*, 8–9.

162. ISA, M. 58/11, E. Mills to the Secretary of State, August 13, 1928.

CHAPTER THREE

1. Leon Uris, *Exodus* (London: Corgi Books, [1958] 1983), 213.

2. Leon Uris, *The Haj* (London: Book Club Associates, 1984), 17, 516.

3. Jeremy Salt, "Fact and Fiction in the Middle Eastern Novels of Leon Uris," *Journal of Palestine Studies* 14 (1985): 55.

4. Ibid., 61–62.

5. Ibid., 62. In the same vein, Elise Salem Manganaro opines—in "Voicing the Arab: Multivocality and Ideology in Leon Uris's 'The Haj,'" *MELUS* 15 (1988): 12—that the Arab emerging in Uris's fiction "is an ugly misrepresentation, a spectre to fill the essential absence regarding the Arab psyche and Arab aspirations. And since Uris' popular novel [*The Haj*] offers no forum for debate or objection, the political consequences of such representations are collectively enormous."

6. Salt, "Fact and Fiction," 58.

7. Sebastian Conrad, *What Is Global History?* (Princeton, NJ: Princeton University Press, 2016), 122–23.

8. See, e.g., Virginia Berridge, *Opium and the People: Opiate Use and Drug Control Policy in Nineteenth- and Early Twentieth-Century England* (London: Free Association

Books, 1999), 193–94; Stanton Peele, *The Meaning of Addiction: An Unconventional View* (New York: Lexington Books, 1985).

9. Frank Dikötter, Lars Peter Laamann, and Zhou Xun, *Narcotic Culture: A History of Drugs in China* (Chicago: University of Chicago Press, 2004), 7–8. The same writers come out strongly against the availability-consumption paradigm by observing that, although India was to become the world's largest exporter of opium from the seventeenth to the nineteenth century, "[opium] use in India was . . . generally moderate, rarely leading to excessive consumption." Ibid., 21.

10. David Courtwright, *Forces of Habit: Drugs and the Making of the Modern World* (Cambridge, MA: Harvard University Press), 95.

11. Liat Kozma, "White Drugs in Interwar Egypt: Decadent Pleasures, Emaciated Fellahin, and the Campaign against Drugs," *Comparative Studies of South Asia, Africa and the Middle East* 33 (2013): 93.

12. Berridge, *Opium and the People*, 192,

13. Yitzhak Shami, *Vengeance of the Fathers*, in Hebrew (Jerusalem: Mitzpeh, 1927).

14. Salim Tamari, "Ishaq al-Shami and the Predicament of the Arab Jew in Palestine," *Jerusalem Quarterly File* 21 (2004): 11.

15. At the same time, Shami was highly critical of Arab life in Palestine, voicing this criticism in flagrantly Orientalist terms. Hence, in *Vengeance of the Fathers* he describes the lust for murder and blood as an essentially Arab trait, draws analogies between Arabs and animals and insects, and stresses the oppressive treatment of women by Arab men. See Hannan Hever, "Yitzhak Shami: Ethnicity as an Unresolved Conflict," *Shofar* 24 (2006): 132–33.

16. Eliyahu Shamir and Joseph Zernik, "The Jewish-Arab Writer Who Was Forgotten in Israel and Adopted by Palestinians," *Ha-Aretz*, July 26, 2013.

17. Yitzhaq Shami, *Life's Mill*, in Hebrew, ed. Yigal Schwartz and Joseph Zernik (Or Yehuda, Israel: Kinneret Zmora-Bitan Dvir, 2015).

18. Cited from the back cover of ibid. On the restoration of Shami's name and works, see Yigal Schwartz and Joseph Zernik, "Epilogue," in Shami, *Life's Mill*, 305–65; Uri Cohen, "Yitzhak Shami: The First Mizrahi Writer," *Ha-Aretz*, December 17, 2015, http://www.haaretz.co.il/literature/prose/.premium-1.2798388 (accessed October 13, 2019); Hannan Hever, "A Literary Challenge to Separating Jews from Arabs," *Ha-Aretz*, March 14, 2016, http://www.haaretz.co.il/literature/prose/.premium-1.2879961 (accessed October 13, 2019).

19. Schwartz and Zernik, "Epilogue," 305.

20. Shami, *Vengeance of the Fathers*, 93.

21. E.g., a "Turkish officer" is mentioned a few times in the story (as in ibid., 85), and at one point the protagonist, a reluctant murderer, is warned that he might be tried and "hanged in the streets of Stambul [Istanbul]"; ibid., 99.

22. Daniella Talmon-Heller, "Job (Ayyūb), al-Husayn, and Saladin in Late Ottoman Palestine: The Memoirs of Nuʿmān al-Qasāṭlī, the Arab Scribe of the PEF Team," in *Exploring the Holy Land: 150 Years of the Palestine Exploration Fund*, ed. David Gurevich and Anat Kidron (Sheffield, UK: Equinox, 2019), 123–49; Amnon Cohen, "Al-Nabi Musa: An Ottoman Festival (*Mawsim*) Resurrected," in *Mamluks and Ottomans: Studies in Honour of Michael Winter*, ed. David Wasserstein and Ami Ayalon (London: Routledge, 2013), 44–54; Roger Friedland and Richard Hecht, "The Nebi Musa Pilgrimage and the Origins of Palestinian Nationalism," in *Pilgrims and Travelers to the Holy Land*, ed. B. F. Le Beau and M. Mor (Omaha, NE: Creighton University Press, 1996), 89–118.

23. Merle Rubin, "Luminous Tales of a Bygone Middle East," *Los Angeles Times*, January 22, 2001, http://articles.latimes.com/2001/jan/22/news/cl-15491(accessed October 13, 2019).

24. Schwartz and Zernik, "Epilogue," 336.

25. Shami, *Vengeance of the Fathers*, 110, 131.

26. Ibid., 121–22.

27. Ibid., 121.

28. Hever, "Yitzhak Shami," 125.

29. Michal Haramati, "The Theory of Autochthonous Zionism in Political Discourse in Israel, 1961–1967," *Journal of Spatial and Organizational Dynamics* 6 (2018): 123.

30. Schwartz and Zernik, "Epilogue," 344.

31. Shami, *Vengeance of the Fathers*, 105.

32. Here I draw on the Hebrew edition of the book *Criminals and Crimes in the Land of Israel* (Jerusalem: Tzion, 1924). The English edition, *Crime and Criminals in Palestine* (Jerusalem: Kahane Press, 1924), as the translator explains (pp. 10–11), was edited according to the requirements of English readers, but "retained the salient features of the Hebrew work."

33. Tidhar, *Criminals and Crimes in the Land of Israel*, 22–23. Nevertheless, in line with his hierarchal disposition, Tidhar makes a distinction between Jews of Ashkenazi and Jews of Sephardi descent, saying that the former "are better than [the latter] in matters concerning shrewdness [*harifut*], aptitude and ingenuity"; ibid., 24.

34. Ibid., 18–20.

35. Ibid., 21.

36. These reports also claim that "occasional patients who have been admitted to the Government Mental Hospital suffering from its effects have invariably been Egyptian." See League of Nations Archives (LNA), Opium Advisory Committee (OAC), box 4894, dossier 1072, document 10146, Summary of Annual Reports of Governments on the Traffic in Opium and Other Dangerous Drugs for 1932, July 17, 1934; and National Archives (NA), UK, CO 814/2-0014, Department of Health Annual Report for 1928.

37. David A. Guba, "Antoine Isaac Silverstre de Sacy and the Myth of the Hachich-ins: Orientalizing Hashish in Nineteenth-Century France," *Social History of Alcohol and Drugs* 30 (2016): 52.

38. A. E. Harwich, "A Method of Detecting Hashish," *Palestine Police Magazine* 1 (1933): 14. I thank the Middle East Center Archive at St. Antony's College, Oxford, UK, for making this article available to me.

39. Edward Horne, *A Job Well Done (Being a History of the Palestine Police Force 1920–1948)* (Essex, UK: Anchor Press, 1982), 472. In principle, cannabis use is known to be more prevalent in urbanized than in rural areas; and see Dirk J. Korf, "Dutch Cof-fee Shops and Trends in Cannabis Use," *Addictive Behaviors* 27 (2002): 856.

40. By the 1930s, Hauranis were the most numerous labor migrants in Palestine. A drought that started in 1929 and would not let off for half a decade, as well as the Great Depression, compelled them to move in increasing numbers to Beirut, Damascus, and Palestine. See Cyrus Schayegh, *The Middle East and the Making of the Modern World* (Cambridge, MA: Harvard University Press, 2017), 192–96.

41. "Readers' Letters: Cure for Hashish Addiction," *Palestine Post*, February 26, 1935.

42. "Hashish Smokers in Jaffa," *Al-Khamis*, November 1, 1936. The italics are mine.

43. "A Misfortune," *Do'ar ha-Yom*, August 9, 1928. See also *Al-Karmil*, May 6, 1937.

44. See, e.g., NA, US, 867N.111-867N.114 Narcotics/75, Seizures in Palestine dur-ing May 1938, August 28, 1938.

45. LNA, OAC, C.402.M.140; O.C. 279, Traffic in Opium; Seizures in Palestine, August 18, 1925.

46. See e.g. NA, US, 867N.111-967n.114 Narcotics/75, 1928 Dangerous Drugs Or-dinance, in Annual Reports by the Governments for 1935; NA, UK, CO 814/4-0008, Department of Health Annual Report for the Year 1930.

47. Itamar Radai, "The Rise and Fall of the Palestinian-Arab Middle Class under the British Mandate, 1920–1939," *Journal of Contemporary History* 51 (2016): 497–98.

48. Salim Tamari, "Wasif Jawhariyyeh's Jerusalem," in *The Storyteller of Jerusalem: The Life and Times of Wasif Jawhariyyeh, 1904–1948*, Kindle edition, ed. Salim Tam-ari and Issam Nassar (Northampton, MA: Olive Branch Press, 2014). James L. Gelvin suggests—in *The Modern Middle East: A History* (New York: Oxford University Press, 2011), 105–6—that in Jerusalem during Jawhaiyyeh's time, hashish would be smoked in "bachelor apartments" kept by notable families. According to Menachem Klein—in *Lives in Common: Arabs and Jews in Jerusalem, Jaffa and Hebron* (Oxford: Oxford Uni-versity Press, 2014), 45—"Liquor and hashish were served at these parties, with mem-bers of both faiths [Jews and Muslims] partaking," though, as will be seen in chapter 4, Jews in Palestine rarely indulged in the forbidden drug.

49. See, e.g., "Smuggling Hashish and Opium through Haifa," *Davar*, May 3, 1937; "Two Months for Hashish," *Palestine Post*, November 27, 1936; "A Club of Hashish Smokers in Jaffa," *Davar*, March 22, 1936; *Al-Karmil*, April 6, 1938.

50. This information is provided in LNA, OAC, box 3204, dossier 8003, document 8003, Malcolm Delevingne to Madam [Rachel Eleanor Crowdy], October 23, 1926.

51. Ralph S. Hattox, *Coffee and Coffeehouses: The Origins of a Social Beverage in the Medieval Near East* (Seattle: University of Washington Press, 1988), 28.

52. Jordan Goodman, *Tobacco in History: The Cultures of Dependence* (London and New York: Routledge, 2005), 54.

53. Rudolph Matthee, *The Pursuit of Pleasure: Drugs and Stimulants in Iranian History, 1500–1900* (Princeton, NJ: Princeton University Press, 2005), 130. The same can be said about the relationship between tobacco and coffee in the context of European coffeehouses in the seventeenth and eighteenth centuries. See also Brian Cowan, *The Social Life of Coffee: The Emergence of the British Coffeehouse* (New Haven, CT: Yale University Press, 2008), 82; Wolfgang Schivelbusch, *Tastes of Paradise: A Social History of Spices, Stimulants, and Intoxication* (New York: Vintage Books, 1993), 110.

54. James Grehan, "Smoking and 'Early Modern' Sociability: The Great Tobacco Debate in the Ottoman Middle East (Seventeenth to Eighteenth Centuries)," *American Historical Review* 111 (2006): 1357.

55. Ibid., 1373. According to Schivelbusch, in *Tastes of Paradise*, 103, "Tobacco-drinking" was a term sometimes used in seventeenth-century France as well, when tobacco was still regarded as a "dry inebriant."

56. Ram Baruch Regavim, "The Most Sovereign Masters: The History of Opium in Modern Iran, 1850–1955" (PhD diss., University of Pennsylvania, 2012); Ibrahim Ihsan Poroy, "Expansion of Opium Production in Turkey and the State Monopoly of 1828–1839," *International Journal of Middle East Studies* 13 (1981): 191–211; Ahmad M. Khalifa, "Traditional Patterns of Hashish Use in Egypt," in *Cannabis and Culture*, ed. Vera Rubin (The Hague: Mouton, 1975), 195–205.

57. Martin Booth, *Opium: A History* (New York: St. Martin's Griffin, 1996), 105.

58. Grehan, "Smoking and 'Early Modern' Sociability," 1374. See also Matthee, *Pursuit of Pleasure*, 210–13. More than tobacco and opium, tobacco and cannabis were highly complementary. "They have been smoked together in virtually every culture in which they have taken root. . . . Tobacco was a gateway to cannabis experimentation." Courtwright, *Forces of Habit*, 105.

59. Matthee, *Pursuit of Pleasure*, 131.

60. Hattox, *Coffee and Coffeehouses*, 110–11; Relli Shechter, *Smoking, Culture and Economy in the Middle East: The Egyptian Tobacco Market, 1850–2000* (London and New York: I. B. Tauris, 2006), 18, 125.

61. Cowan, *Social Life of Coffee*, 18.

62. Eminegül Karababa and Güliz Ger, "Early Modern Ottoman Coffeehouse Culture and the Formation of the Consumer Subject," *Journal of Consumer Research* 37 (2011): 737–60; Hattox, *Coffee and Coffeehouses*, 6, 109–10.

63. Alan Mikhail, "The Heart's Desire: Gender, Urban Space and the Ottoman

Coffee House," in *Ottoman Tulips, Ottoman Coffee: Leisure and Lifestyle in the Eighteenth Century*, ed. Dana Sajdi (London: I. B. Tauris, 2014), 135–36. See also Alon Tam, "Cairo's Coffeehouses in the Late 19th and Early 20th Centuries: An Urban and Socio-Political History" (PhD diss., University of Pennsylvania, 2018); Ami Ayalon, *The Arabic Print Revolution: Cultural Production and Mass Readership* (Cambridge: Cambridge University Press, 2016), 177–84.

64. Cemal Kafadar, "A History of Coffee," *The XIIIth Congress of the International Economic History Association (IEHA),* (2002); Cengiz Kirli, "Coffeehouses: Leisure and Sociability in Ottoman Istanbul," in *Leisure Cultures in Urban Europe, c. 1700–1870: A Transnational Perspective*, ed. Peter Borsay and Jan Hein Furnée (Manchester, UK: Manchester University Press, 2016), 161–82; Hagai Ram, "Middle East Drug Cultures in the Long View," in *OUP Handbook to Global Drug History*, ed. Paul Gootenberg (London: Oxford University Press, forthcoming).

65. Cowan, *Social Life of Coffee*, 18.

66. Liat Kozma, "Cannabis Prohibition in Egypt, 1880–1939: From Local Ban to League of Nations Diplomacy," *Middle Eastern Studies* 47 (2011): 446.

67. Ibid.

68. And, like consuming cannabis, drinking coffee is a habit that must be learned and assimilated into one's dietary consumption routine, in a manner not unlike the process Howard Becker has described for marijuana smoking in "Becoming a Marijuana User," *American Journal of Sociology* 59 (1953): 235–42. Hence, acquiring a taste for coffee requires a process of socialization and habituation "in which the novice user learns to make sense of, and enjoy, their psychoactive effects and its taste." Cowan, *Social Life of Coffee*, 6.

69. Schivelbusch, *Tastes of Paradise*, 34.

70. Ibid., 15–84; Woodruff D. Smith, "From Coffeehouses to Parlour: The Consumption of Coffee, Tea and Sugar in North-Western Europe in the Seventeenth and Eighteenth Centuries," in *Consuming Habits: Drugs in History and Anthropology*, ed. Jordan Goodman, Paul Lovejoy and Andrew Sherratt (London: Routledge, 1995), 149-63.

71. Cowan, *Social Life of Coffee*, 32.

72. See, e.g., Salim Tamari, *Mountain against the Sea: Essays on Palestinian Society and Culture* (Berkeley: University of California Press, 2008), especially ch. 11; Deborah Bernstein, *Women on the Margins: Gender and Nationalism in Mandatory Tel Aviv*, in Hebrew (Jerusalem: Yad Ben Zvi, 2008), 59–83; Manar Hasan, *Hidden from View: Women and Palestinian Cities*, in Hebrew (Tel Aviv: Van Leer and Hakibbutz Hameuchad, 2017), especially ch. 3; and Yael Buchman, *Pashas, Fellahs, and Pirates: A Window to the Ways of Life in the Land of Israel from the 16th to the 18th Centuries*, in Hebrew (Sde Ilan, Israel: Yeda ha-Aretz, 2013), 193–204.

73. Tamari, *Mountain against the Sea*, 178.

74. Ibid., 178.

75. Cited in ibid. A story about male sex involving, inter alia, "hashish bars" in Acres is mentioned in Orna Darr Alyagon, *Plausible Crime Stories: The Legal History of Sexual Offences in Mandate Palestine* (Cambridge: Cambridge University Press, 2019), 87.

76. "A New Drug Menace: Palestine as a Market," *The Times*, July 20, 1939; "A Center for Smuggling Hashish Revealed in Tel Aviv," *'Iton Meyuhad*, October 3, 1945.

77. Anat Helman, *Young Tel Aviv: A Tale of Two Cities*, trans. Haim Watzman (Waltham, MA: Brandeis University Press, 2010), 128.

78. "Hashish Smokers Revealed," *Davar*, March 26, 1930; *Filastin*, August 20, 1930; *Filastin*, August 29, 1933; "Two Months for Hashish," *Palestine Post*, November 27, 1936; "Hashish," *Davar*, April 14, 1937; "Hashish and Opium," *Davar*, April 21, 1937; "Hashish," *Davar*, April 6, 1938; "Charge of Running Place for Smoking Hashish," *Palestine Post*, June 2, 1941; "The Hashish Crop," *Palestine Post*, February 5, 1942.

79. NA, UK, CO 814/7-0005, The Palestine Police and Prisons Annual Administrative Report for 1932, 20; *Palestine Post*, July 9, 1940; Joshua Caspi, *Dangerous Drugs: Policy, Control, Enforcement and Trial* (Haifa: Tamar, 1996), 115.

80. Besides hashish dens and coffeehouses, there were additional hashish-smoking venues in interwar Palestine which did not fit the definition of the former establishments but nevertheless aroused the concern of the authorities. For instance, in 1940 a man was prosecuted for "permitting his house in Jaffa to be used for smoking hashish, and for being in possession of vessels for the smoking of the drug." *Palestine Post*, July 9, 1940.

81. NA, US, 867N.111-867N.114 Narcotics/75, Dangerous Drugs Ordinance, number 17, of 1936, 9.

82. Mahmoud Yazbak argues, "The state of Israel confiscated all of the lands that belonged to the Nabi Rubin *waqf*. . . . The mosque was destroyed, the minaret, initially left standing, was torn down in 1991, and the huge mulberry trees in the tomb courtyard uprooted. The shrine itself survived but was now turned into an exclusively Jewish religious site." "The Muslim Festival of Nabi Rubin in Palestine: From Religious Festival to Summer Resort," *Holy Land Studies* 10 (2011): 195.

83. Ibid.; Tamari, *Mountain against the Sea*, 27–31.

84. Tamari, *Mountain against the Sea*, 31. See also Yazbak, "Muslim Festival of Nabi Rubin," 179–89; Hasan, *Hidden from View*, 131–32; Meron Benvenisti, *Sacred Landscape: The Buried History of the Holy Land since 1948* (Berkeley: University of California Press, 2002), 274–77; Andrew Petersen, "A Preliminary Report of Three Muslim Shrines in Palestine," *Levant* 28 (1996): 97–113.

85. Here I borrow from the title of Mahmoud Yazbak's article, "The Muslim Festival of Nabi Rubin."

86. Tamari, *Mountain against the Sea*, 30. The relaxation of strict gender boundaries during the festival is demonstrated by the saying "Either take me to Rubin or I will

have you divorce me" (*Ya bitrubini ya bitaliqni*), which was very popular at the time. See also p. 31; Hasan, *Hidden from View*, 43n37; Yazbak, "Muslim Festival of Nabi Rubin," 190; Benvenisti, *Sacred Landscape*, 275.

87.   *Filastin*, August 20, 1933; *Filastin*, August 27, 1933.

88.   Yazbak, "Muslim Festival of Nabi Rubin," 191.

89.   "Smoking Hashish and Chivalrous Murder in Honor of the Prophet Reuven," *'Iton Meyuhad*, September 26, 1934.

90.   Ofri Ilany, "'An Oriental Vice': Representations of Homosexuality in the Hebrew Press of the British Mandate Era," in *Sexuality in Transregional Perspective: The Homophobic Argument*, ed. Achim Rhode, Christina von Braun, and Stefanie Schüler-Springorum (New York: Routledge, 2017), 126.

91.   Menachem Kapeliuk, "Nightly Visit to Camp Rubin," *Davar*, November 26, 1934. See also Klein, *Lives in Common*, 89.

92.   NA, UK, CO 814/2-0002, Annual Report of the Department of Health for the Year 1926.

93.   NA, US, 867N.111–867N.114, Report by the Government of Palestine for the Year 1937 on the Traffic in Opium and Other Dangerous Drugs.

94.   ISA, M-24/322, Report by the Inspector General of the Palestine Police for the Calendar Year 1947 on the traffic in dangerous drugs, March 11, 1948.

95.   See, e.g., NA, UK, CO 814/4-0008, Annual Report of the Department of Health for the Year 1930; NA, UK, CO 814/7-0004, Annual Report of the Department of Health for the Year 1932.

96.   Joseph F. Broadhurst, *From Vine Street to Jerusalem* (London: Stanley Paul, 1936), 194.

97.   Zachary Foster, "Illicit Drug Trafficking and Use in British Mandatory Palestine" (unpublished paper, 2010).

98.   Liat Kozma, *Global Women, Colonial Ports: Prostitution in the Interwar Middle East* (Albany: State University of New York Press, 2017), 19–20.

99.   James Mills demonstrates, in *Madness, Cannabis and Colonialism: The "Native Only" Lunatic Asylums of British India, 1857–1900* (London: Palgrave, 2000), 47, that the British in India associated cannabis use with rampant insanity, "infanticide, immorality, suicide and murder of Christians, and even the revolt against British authority of 1857." See also Nile Green, "Breaking the Begging Bowl: Morals, Drugs, and Madness in the Fate of the Muslim Faqir," *South Asian History and Culture* 5 (2014): 226–45; and Ashley Wright, "Not Just a 'Place for the Smoking of Opium': The Indian Opium Den and Imperial Anxieties in the 1890s," *Journal of Colonialism and Colonial History* 18 (2017): doi:10.1353/cch.2017.0021. The British in Egypt espoused similar outlandish ideas about hashish-smoking Egyptians. See, for example, John Warnock (director of the Egyptian Hospital for the Insane in the 1890s and 1900s) in "Insanity from Hasheesh," *Journal of Mental Science* 49 (1903): 96–110. To

the best of my knowledge, no such ideas about hashish smoking were espoused by the British in Palestine.

100.   NA, US, 867N.01/606-740, Report by His Majesty's Government in the UK of GB and Northern Ireland to the Council of the League of Nations on the Administration of Palestine and Trans-Jordan for 1933, Trade in and Manufacture of Drugs, Arms, and Liquors, August 1931–March 1937.

101.   Kozma, "Cannabis Prohibition," 404.

102.   Maziyar Ghiabi, *Drugs Politics: Managing Disorder in the Islamic Republic of Iran* (Cambridge: Cambridge University Press, 2019), 36.

103.   Muhammad Baader al-Khatib, "Drugs in Palestine," *Mir'at al-Sharq,* October 9, 1926. The editorial claimed that there were three hundred cocaine, opium, morphine, and hashish users in Haifa, who were either partially or completely insane. The editorial implored the government to take action against the distribution of these "poisons." I thank Zachary Foster for bringing this editorial to my attention.

104.   Radai, "Rise and Fall of Palestinian-Arab Middle Class," 488.

105.   See, e.g., James Gelvin, "The League of Nations and the Question of National Identity in the Fertile Crescent," *World Affairs* 158 (1995): 40.

106.   Ibid., 498. See also Itamar Radai, "The Collapse of the Palestinian-Arab Middle Class in 1948: The Case of Qatamon," *Middle East Journal* 43 (2007): 961–82.

107.   D. Zismann, "The Country's Gangs and Hashish," *Davar,* March 30,1938.

108.   Ibid.

CHAPTER FOUR

1.   See, e.g., Michal Haramati, "The Theory of Autochthonous Zionism in Political Discourse in Israel, 1961–1967," *Journal of Spatial and Organizational Dynamics* 6 (2018): 112–39; Abigail Jacobson and Moshe Naor, *Oriental Neighbors: Middle Eastern Jews and Arabs in Mandatory Palestine* (Waltham, MA: Brandeis University Press, 2016); Yehouda Shenhav, ed., *Zionism and Empires,* in Hebrew (Tel Aviv: Van Leer and Hakibbutz Hameuchad, 2015); Michelle U. Campos, *Ottoman Brothers: Muslims, Christians, and Jews in Early Twentieth-Century Palestine* (Stanford, CA: Stanford University Press, 2011); Abigail Jacobson, *From Empire to Empire: Jerusalem between Ottoman and British Rule* (Syracuse, NY: Syracuse University Press, 2011); Salim Tamari, *Mountain against the Sea: Essays on Palestinian Society and Culture* (Berkeley: University of California Press, 2009); Deborah Bernstein, *Women on the Margins: Gender and Nationalism in Mandate Tel Aviv,* in Hebrew (Jerusalem: Yad Ben-Zvi, 2008); Salim Tamari, "Ishaq al-Shami and the Predicament of the Arab Jew in Palestine," *Jerusalem Quarterly* 21 (2004): 10–26.

2.   Jacobson and Naor, *Oriental Neighbors,* 4.

3.   Hillel Cohen, *Year Zero of the Arab Israeli Conflict, 1929,* trans. Haim Watzman (Lebanon, NH: Brandeis University Press, 2015), 49. See also Mark LeVine,

Overthrowing Geography: Jaffa, Tel Aviv, and the Struggle for Palestine, 1880–1948 (Los Angeles: University of California Press, 2005), 84–120.

4. See note 67 for references on this issue. In the meantime, Isaac Campos, in a recent compelling intervention, argued that "the role of Mexican immigrants in the history of U.S. marijuana prohibition has surely been overstated." Isaac Campos, "Mexicans and the Origins of Marijuana Prohibition in the United States: A Reassessment," *Social History of Alcohol and Drugs* 32 (2018): 7.

5. Cited in "Ze'ev Jabotinsky Smoking Hashish and Writing about It" (in Hebrew), *The Marker Café*, July 16, 2014. I thank Jonathan Stoppi for graciously translating the poem from Hebrew to English.

6. Mike Jay, *Emperors of Dreams: Drugs in the Nineteenth Century* (Sawtry, UK: Dedalus, 2000), 73–104.

7. Cyrus Schayegh, *The Middle East and the Making of the Modern World* (Cambridge, MA: Harvard University Press, 2017), 81.

8. Boaz Lev Tov, *Leisure and Popular Cultural Patterns of Eretz Israeli Jews in the Years 1882–1914 as a Reflection of Social Changes*, in Hebrew (PhD diss., Tel Aviv University, 2009), 19.

9. Gil Eyal, *The Disenchantment of the Orient: Expertise in Arab Affairs and the Israeli State* (Stanford, CA: Stanford University Press, 2006).

10. Lev Tov, *Leisure and Popular Cultural Patterns*, 167–68. See also Abigail Jacobson, "Practices of Citizenship and Loyalty to Empire: The Movement of Ottomanization as a Case Study" (in Hebrew), in *Zionism and Empires*, ed. Yehouda Shenhav, in Hebrew (Tel Aviv: Van Leer and Hakibbutz Hameuchad, 2015), 159–82.

11. Dafna Hirsch, "'Hummus Is Best When It Is Fresh and Made by Arabs': The Gourmetization of Hummus in Israel and the Return of the Repressed Arab," *American Ethnologist* 38 (2011): 617–30. Hirsch goes on to suggest (p. 618), "Since the late 1980s, the Arab identity of hummus has gradually reemerged in culinary discourse, [a] development due to the interaction between social transformations and political processes, as they articulate in the culinary field."

12. Ofri Ilany, "'An Oriental Vice': Representations of Sodomy in Early Zionist Discourse," in *National Politics and Sexuality in Transregional Perspective*, ed. Achim Rhode, Christina von Braun, and Stefanie Schüler-Springoruml (New York: Routledge, 2018), 113.

13. Ibid., 119.

14. The British in Palestine, too, "who had explicitly set out to overthrow the Ottoman norms that previously governed male-to-male sex in Palestine, utilized criminalization, and the stereotypes surrounding male-to-male sex in the 'East' to distinguish themselves from their subjects and bolster their superiority." Orna Alyagon-Darr, "Narratives of 'Sodomy' and 'Unnatural Offences' in the Courts of Palestine (1918–1948)," *Law and History Review* 35 (2017): 236.

15. On the feminizing conception of drug use in the United States and Europe, see, e.g., Susan Zieger, *Inventing the Addict: Drugs, Race, and Sexuality in Nineteenth-Century British and American Literature* (Amherst: University of Massachusetts Press, 2008); and Mara L. Keire, "Dope Fiends and Degenerates: The Gendering of Addiction in the Early Twentieth Century," *Journal of Social History* 31 (1998): 809–22. On the Zionist project of creating a "new Jewish man" as a transformative move, directed toward salvaging the body of the exilic Jew from its putative passive and effeminate state, see, e.g., Daniel Boyarin, *Unheroic Conduct: The Rise of Heterosexuality and the Invention of the Jewish Man* (Berkeley: University of California Press, 1997); Sander Gilman, *The Jew's Body* (New York: Routledge, 1991); and Michael Gluzman, *The Zionist Body: Nationalism, Gender and Sexuality in Modern Hebrew Prose*, in Hebrew (Tel Aviv: Hakibbutz Hameuchad, 2007).

16. Ilany, "An Oriental Vice," 114.

17. National identity and crime fiction are often mutually constitutive, as Reeva S. Simon argues in *Spies and Holy Wars: The Middle East in 20th-Century Crime Fiction* (Austin: University of Texas Press, 2010), 9–10.

18. Shlomo Gelper, *The Blue Crosses: The Tales of Hashish Smugglers*, in Hebrew (Tel Aviv: Ha-Balash Publishers, 1932), 25–26.

19. Timothy Mitchell, "The World as Exhibition," *Comparative Studies in Society and History* 31 (1989): 227–28.

20. League of Nations Archive (hereafter LNA) Subcommittee on Cannabis, O.C./Cannabis/8, Cannabis Addiction in Turkey, report submitted by Mazhar Osman Uzman, April 27, 1939, 3.

21. LNA, Opium Advisory Committee (hereafter OAC), O.C. 1542, Preliminary Notes on the Chief Aspects of the Problem of Indian Hemp and the Laws Relating Thereto in Force in Certain Countries, 11; LNA, Subcommittee on Cannabis, O.C./Cannabis/3, Present State of Documentation Concerning Cannabis and the Problems to Which It Gives Rise, April 12, 1939, 69.

22. Liat Kozma, *Global Women, Colonial Ports: Prostitution in the Interwar Middle East* (Albany: State University of New York Press, 2017), 9.

23. D. Zismann, "The Country's Gangs and Hashish," *Davar*, March 30, 1938.

24. Ted Swedenburg, *Memories of Revolt: the 1936–1939 Rebellion and the Palestinian National Past* (Minneapolis: University of Minnesota Press, 1995), xix. Deploying twenty thousand troops and imposing collective punishments on villages suspected of sheltering terrorists, as well as commando-style special night squads and Zionist and Palestinian collaborators—not to mention assassinations, mass arrests, deportations, and the dynamiting of homes of suspected guerillas and their sympathizers—by 1939 the British crushed the revolt. The revolt took a heavy toll: more than three thousand Arabs, two thousand Jews, and six hundred British were killed; Palestine's economy was in chaos; and the Arab leaders were in exile or under arrest. See James Gelvin, "The

League of Nations and the Question of National Identity in the Fertile Crescent," *World Affairs* 158 (1995): 40.

25. James L. Gelvin, *The Modern Middle East: A History* (New York: Oxford University Press, 2005), 109.

26. Zismann, "Country's Gangs." In this marginalization and diminution of the Arab Revolt, the Zionists saw eye to eye with the British authorities in Palestine. As Matthew Kraig Kelly suggested in *The Crime of Nationalism: Britain, Palestine, and Nation-Building on the Fringe of Empire* (Oakland: University of California Press, 2017), 4, British officials presented the rebellion as the work of a criminal minority masquerading as a national army, and in this they had the full support of mainstream Zionist opinion.

27. Zismann, "Country's Gangs." This excerpt, no doubt, echoes colonial gender ideologies about the oppression of women in Muslim societies, and the uncontrollable sexuality of Muslim men, which "stood as an index of civilization and served to justify colonial rule and policies." Kozma, *Global Women, Colonial Ports*, 9.

28. This causal link between cannabis use and madness was commonplace at the time, not only in Palestine but the world over. See Isaac Campos, *Home Grown: Marijuana and the Origins of Mexico's War on Drugs* (Chapel Hill: University of North Carolina Press, 2012); and James H. Mills, *Madness, Cannabis and Colonialism: The "Native Only" Lunatic Asylums of British India, 1857–1900* (New York: Palgrave 2000).

29. Zismann, "Country's Gangs." For additional interwar Jewish expressions of the putative link between hashish, insanity, and loss of agency, see Deborah Eilon-Sireni, "Hashish," *Davar*, June 21, 1942.

30. Zismann, "Country's Gangs."

31. Amin Maalouf, *The Crusades through Arab Eyes* (New York: Schocken Books, 1987), 98.

32. David A. Guba, "Antoine Isaac Silvestre de Sacy and the Myth of the Hachichins: Orientalizing Hashish in Nineteenth-Century France," *Social History of Alcohol and Drugs* 30 (2016): 50–74; Juliette Wood, "The Old Man of the Mountain in Medieval Folklore," *Folklore* 99 (1988): 78–87.

33. Farhad Daftary, "'Order of the Assassins': J. von Hammer and the Orientalist Misrepresentations of the Nizari Ismailis," *Iranian Studies* 39 (2006): 75.

34. The scholarly prominence of de Sacy is scrutinized by Edward Said: "Every major Arabist in Europe during the nineteenth century traced his intellectual authority back to him [de Sacy]. Universities and academics in France, Spain, Norway, Sweden, Denmark and especially Germany were dotted with the students who formed themselves at his feet"; Edward W. Said, *Orientalism* (New York: Vintage, 1978), 129.

35. Guba, "Silvestre de Sacy," 51.

36. Zismann, "Country's Gangs." Compare this excerpt with Bruce Lincoln's summary of Marco Polo's fourteenth-century account: "The Old Man is said to have built splendid gardens in his mountain redoubt and filled them with beautiful maidens. After

giving his *Fedayeen* a drink that rendered them unconscious, he had them carried into his garden. When they awoke, they believed they were in paradise and as long as they remained there, the women—favored Orientalist trope of Muslim concupiscence—were constantly at their service. When the Old Man wanted to send a *fida'i* on a mission . . . the lad was drugged once more and carried out." Bruce Lincoln, "An Early Moment in the Discourse of 'Terrorism': Reflections of a Tale from Marco Polo," *Comparative Studies in Society and History* 48 (2006): 252. For a similar account of the Assassins myth in interwar Palestine, see Trevor Williams, "Hashish Menace a Thousand Years Old," *Palestine Post*, November 18, 1947.

37. Zismann, "Country's Gangs."

38. Alex Winder, "Abu Jilda, Anti-Imperial Antihero: Banditry and Popular Rebellion in Palestine," in *The Routledge Handbook of the History of the Middle East Mandates*, ed. Cyrus Schayegh and Andrew Arsan (New York: Routledge, 2015), 308; Ziad Abu-Amr, "Hamas: A Historical and Political Background," *Journal of Palestine Studies* 22 (1993): 6; Swedenburg, *Memories of Revolt*, 2.

39. M. Zinger, "The Causes for the Clashes' Resumption," *Davar*, April 5, 1937.

40. Daftary, "Order of the Assassins," 74.

41. Franz Rosenthal, *The Herb: Hashish versus Medieval Muslim Society* (Leiden, E. J. Brill, 1971), 43.

42. Ibid. The apparent misinterpretation by de Sacy is also confirmed by the fact that "dope intoxication, a markedly pacific state characterized by impaired concentration, would be a positive liability in a man who had been commissioned to plunge a dagger into somebody's heart." Stuart Walton, *Intoxicology: A Cultural History of Drink and Drugs*, Kindle edition (London: Dean Street Press, 2016), ch. 3.

43. Lincoln, "Early Moment in the Discourse of 'Terrorism,'" 242.

44. Łukasz Kamieński, *Shooting Up: A Short History of Drugs and War* (New York: Oxford University Press, 2016), 38.

45. For instance, in the 1930s and 1940s, Harry J. Anslinger, the first commissioner of the US Federal Bureau of Narcotics (FBN), enthusiastically embraced the Assassins myth to advance his antimarijuana crusade. In fact, Anslinger's most famous tract, "Marijuana: Assassin of Youth," published in 1937, makes explicit reference to the sect to buttress his "killer weed" and "reefer madness" propositions. See Emily Dufton, *Grass Roots: The Rise and Fall and Rise of Marijuana in America* (New York: Basic Books, 2017), 3–4; Marcus Boon, *The Road of Excess: A History of Writers on Drugs* (Cambridge, MA: Harvard University Press, 2002), 123–32; Campos, *Home Grown*; and James H. Mills, *Cannabis Nation: Control and Consumption in Britain, 1928–2008* (Oxford: Oxford University Press, 2013), 28–29.

46. E.g., James H. Mills, *Cannabis Britannica: Empire, Trade, and Prohibition, 1800–1928* (Oxford: Oxford University Press, 2003), 152–87; James H. Mills, "Colonial Africa and the International Politics of Cannabis: Egypt, South Africa and the Origins

of Global Control," in *Drugs and Empires: Essays in Modern Imperialism and Intoxication, c. 1500–c. 1930*, ed. James H. Mills and Patricia Barton (London: Palgrave, 2007); Liat Kozma, "Cannabis Prohibition in Egypt, 1880–1939: From Local Ban to League of Nations Diplomacy," *Middle Eastern Studies* 47 (2011): 444–45. A neglected but highly informative study of how and why cannabis found its way onto the 1925 Opium Convention's list of dangerous drugs is Robert Kendell, "Cannabis Condemned: The Proscription of Indian Hemp," *Addiction* 98 (2003): 143–51.

47. Liat Kozma, "The League of Nations and the Debate over Cannabis Prohibition," *History Compass* 9 (2011): 61–70. See also James H. Mills, *Cannabis Nation: Control and Consumption in Britain, 1928–2008* (Oxford: Oxford University Press, 2013), 35–61.

48. Bernard S. Cohn, *Colonialism and Its Forms of Knowledge: The British in India* (Princeton, NJ: Princeton University Press, 1996), 3–15.

49. See, e.g., Kozma, *Global Women, Colonial Ports*; Magaly Rodríguez García, Davide Rodogno and Liat Kozma, eds., *The League of Nations' Work on Social Issues: Visions, Endeavors and Experiments* (Geneva: United Nations Publications, 2016); Keith David Watenpaugh, "The League of Nations' Rescue of Armenian Genocide Survivors and the Making of Modern Humanitarianism, 1920–1927," *American Historical Review* 115 (2010): 1315–39; Susan Pedersen, "Back to the League of Nations," *American Historical Review* 112 (2007): 1091–1117.

50. Magaly Rodríguez García, Davide Rodogno and Liat Kozma, introduction to *The League of Nations' Work on Social Issues*, 27.

51. Kozma, *Global Women, Colonial Ports*, 24. See also García, Rodogno, and Kozma, introduction, 24–25.

52. The exclusion of colonial subjects from the League was not unique to the interwar period, however. For instance, previously in India, "colonial officials increasingly disparaged the scholarly participation of Indians in favor of consolidating scientific capital by a select, if often seriously deficient, European elite"; Nicholas B. Dirks, foreword to Cohn, *Colonialism and Its Forms of Knowledge*, xvi.

53. Cyrus Schayegh, *The Middle East and the Making of the Modern World* (Cambridge, MA: Harvard University Press, 2017), 135; Klaas Dykmann, "How International Was the Secretariat of the League of Nations?" *International History Review* 37 (2015): 727.

54. Kozma, *Global Women, Colonial Ports*, 8.

55. Kozma, "Cannabis Prohibition," 455.

56. Mills, *Cannabis Nation*, 61.

57. In Britain, for example, "negligible numbers of white British subjects were convicted in [the interwar] period, mainly because very few of them had any contact with the drug." Mills, *Cannabis Nation*, 20.

58. Cited in Mills, *Cannabis Britannica*, 171.

59. John Warnock, "Twenty-Eight Years' Lunacy Experience in Egypt (1895–1923)," *British Journal of Psychiatry* 70 (1924): 579–612; see also John Warnock, "Insanity from Hasheesh," *Journal of Mental Science* 49 (1903): 96–110.

60. Mills, *Cannabis Britannica*, 183–84.

61. Warnock, "Twenty-Eight Years' Lunacy Experience," 595–96. See also Mills, *Cannabis Britannica*, 170.

62. Richard C. Keller, *Colonial Madness: Psychiatry in French North Africa* (Chicago: University of Chicago Press, 2007), 22. The same is true as regards British colonial psychiatry in India; and see Mills, *Madness, Cannabis and Colonialism*, 43–65.

63. Kozma, "Cannabis Prohibition," 449–50.

64. LNA OAC, box 3237, dossier 27405, document 36624, Note Prepared on Seizures and Cases of Illicit Traffic Incorporated in the Summary of Illicit Transactions and Seizures for the Use of the Sub-Committee on Seizures, April 9, 1932.

65. Mills, *Cannabis Nation*, 44.

66. Kozma, "League of Nations," 64.

67. Boon, *Road of Excess*, 154–66; Susan L. Speaker, "'The Struggle of Mankind against its Deadliest Foe': Themes of Counter-Subversion in Anti-Narcotic Campaigns, 1920–1940," *Journal of Social History* 34 (2001): 591–610; Jerome L. Himmelstein, "From Killer Weed to Drop-Out Drug: the Changing Ideology of Marihuana," *Contemporary Crises* 7 (1983): 13–38; Larry Sloman, *Reefer Madness: The History of Marijuana in America* (Indianapolis: Bobb-Merrill Company, 1979).

68. Marty Roth, "Victorian Highs: Detection, Drugs, and Empire," in *High Anxieties: Cultural Studies in Addiction*, ed. Janet Farrell Brodie and Marc Redfield (Berkeley: University of California Press, 2002), 86.

69. Paul Knepper, "Dreams and Nightmares: Drug Trafficking and the History of International Crime," in *The Oxford Handbook of the History and Crime and Criminal Justice*, eds. Paul Knepper and Anja Johansen, (Oxford: Oxford University Press, 2016), 212.

70. Mills, *Cannabis Nation*, 47. For a detailed account of "the main problems with which the Subcommittee faced," see LNA, OAC, O.C./Cannabis/7, Subcommittee on Cannabis, Advisory Committee on Traffic in Opium and Other Dangerous Drugs, April 22, 1939.

71. Kozma, "League of Nations," 63. For the identity and expertise of these experts, see LNA, OAC, box 4928, dossier 6043, Situation as Regards the Control of Cannabis (Hemp) and Drugs Derived from Cannabis, O.C. 1542 (K), 1.

72. This move, from diplomats to scientists and experts, seems to have been symptomatic of the League in the early 1930s; in the same period, the body's work against prostitution was also taken up by the latter, as "they could criticize national governments more freely in the League's institutions." Kozma, *Global Women, Colonial Ports*, 41.

73. LNA, OAC, O.C. 1542, Preliminary Notes on the Chief Aspects of the Problem of Indian Hemp and the Laws Relating Thereto in Force in Certain Countries, 4, 12.

74. Mills, *Cannabis Nation*, 48.

75. Tom Blickman, Dave Bewley-Taylor and Martin Jelsma, *The Rise and Decline of Cannabis Prohibition: The History of Cannabis in the U.N. Drug Control System and Options for Reform* (Amsterdam: Transnational Institute 2014), 14.

76. LNA, Subcommittee on Cannabis, O.C./Cannabis/12, Cannabis Addiction in Algeria, May 8, 1939, 4.

77. LNA, Subcommittee on Cannabis, O.C./Cannabis/3, Present State of Documentation Concerning Cannabis and the Problems to Which It Gives Rise, April 12, 1939, 5.

78. Nile Green, "Breaking the Begging Bowl: Morals, Drugs, and Madness in the Fate of the Muslim Faqīr," *South Asian History and Culture* 5 (2014): 232.

79. LON, Subcommittee on Cannabis, O.C./Cannabis/8, 3.

80. LNA, Subcommittee on Cannabis, O.C./Cannabis/3, Present State of Documentation Concerning Cannabis and the Problems to Which It Gives Rise, April 12, 1939, 69; LNA, Subcommittee on Cannabis, O.C./Cannabis/8, Cannabis Addiction in Turkey, report submitted by Mazhar Osman Uzman, April 27, 1939, 1–2.

81. LNA, Subcommittee on Cannabis, O.C./Cannabis/3, Present State of Documentation Concerning Cannabis and the Problems to Which It Gives Rise, April 12, 1939, 80.

82. LNA, Subcommittee on Cannabis, O.C./Cannabis/12, Cannabis Addiction in Algeria, May 8, 1939, 4.

83. LNA, Subcommittee on Cannabis, O.C./Cannabis/8, Cannabis Addiction in Turkey, report submitted by Mazhar Osman Uzman, April 27, 1939, 3–4.

84. Anne McClintock, *Imperial Leather: Race, Gender, and Sexuality in the Colonial Contest* (New York: Routledge, 1995); Ann L. Stoler, *Carnal Knowledge and Imperial Power: Race and the Intimate in Colonial Rule* (Berkeley: University of California Press, 2002).

85. LNA, Subcommittee on Cannabis, O.C.1724, Observations on the Causes of Drug-Addiction in North Africa, January 24, 1939, 5.

86. LNA, Sub-Committee on Cannabis, O.C./Cannabis/3, Present State of Documentation Concerning Cannabis and the Problems to Which It Gives Rise, April 12, 1939, 73.

87. LNA, Subcommittee on Cannabis, O.C./Cannabis/7, Present Position in Regard to Cannabis: Results Obtained and Problems Solved, April 4, 1939, 2; LNA, OAC, O.C. 1542, Preliminary Notes on the Chief Aspects of the Problem of Indian Hemp and the Laws Relating Thereto in Force in Certain Countries, 11; LNA, Subcommittee on Cannabis, O.C./Cannabis/3, Present State of Documentation Concerning Cannabis and the Problems to Which It Gives Rise, April 12, 1939, 69.

88. Ibid., 68.

89. Ibid., 74–75; LNA, OAC, O.C.s/c Cannabis Sat./Indian/4th session/P.V.1, Subcommittee to Consider Questions in Regard to Indian Hemp and Indian Hemp Drugs, June 15, 1938, 5.

90. LNA, Subcommittee on Cannabis, O.C./Cannabis/7, Present Position in Regard to Cannabis: Results Obtained and Problems Solved, April 22, 1939, 8. French perceptions of opium use in the colonies during the interwar years rested on similar racial assumptions. See Aro Velmet, "From Universal Relaxant to Oriental Vice: Race and French Perceptions of Opium Use in the Moment of Global Control," in *Prohibitions and Psychoactive Substances in History, Culture and Theory*, ed. Susannah Wilson (New York and London: Routledge, 2019), 33–50.

91. LNA, OAC, O.C. 1542, Preliminary Notes on the Chief Aspects of the Problem of Indian Hemp and the Laws Relating Thereto in Force in Certain Countries, 11.

92. LNA, Subcommittee on Cannabis, O.C./Cannabis/3, Present State of Documentation Concerning Cannabis and the Problems to Which It Gives Rise, April 12, 1939, 74.

93. Kozma, "League of Nations," 66–67.

94. Sir Thomas Russell Pasha, *Egyptian Service, 1902–1946* (London: J. Murray, 1949); P. J. V. Rolo, "Russell, Sir Thomas Wentworth (1879–1954)," *Oxford Dictionary of National Biography* (Oxford: Oxford University Press, 2004), https://www.oxforddnb.com/view/10.1093/ref:odnb/9780198614128.001.0001/odnb-9780198614128-e-35886;jsessionid=918EB24AE0425EA0E7F5EEE4B0C0A624 (accessed April 7, 2020).

95. Mills, *Cannabis Nation*, 36–49.

96. LNA, Subcommittee on Cannabis, O.C. 1724 Addendum, January 24, 1939; LNA, OAC, OC/cannabis/4th session/P.V.1, Subcommittee to Consider Questions in Regard to Indian Hemp and Indian Hemp Drugs, Provisional Minutes, Forth Session, First Meeting, June 15, 1938.

97. LNA, OAC, C.l95. M. l05.1938 .XI. (O.C./A.R.l937/5), Traffic in Opium and Other Dangerous Drugs, Annual Reports by Government for 1937, May 20, 1938, 192.

98. LNA, OAC, O.C.s/c Cannabis Sat./Indian/4th session/P.V.1, Subcommittee to Consider Questions in Regard to Indian Hemp and Indian Hemp Drugs, June 15, 1938, 11–12.

99. Kozma, "League of Nations," 67.

100. Sally Falk Moore, "Explaining the Present: Theoretical Dilemmas in Processual Ethnography," *American Ethnologist* 14 (1987): 727–36.

101. Ibid., 730.

102. LNA, OAC, O.C./S/C Cannabis Sat./Indian/4th Session/P.V.1, Subcommittee to Consider Questions in Regard to Indian Hemp and Indian Hemp drugs, Provisional Minutes, June 15, 1938, 17.

103. Y. Sheffi, "Hashish in Tel Aviv," *Davar*, August 26, 1948.

CHAPTER FIVE

1. Israel Police, *Annual Report for 1948*, in Hebrew (Tel Aviv, 1949), 22.

2. Israel Police, *Annual Report for 1949*, in Hebrew (Tel Aviv, 1950), 21. Also see Sh. Yachin, "Hashish, the Curse of the Middle East," *Davar*, May 29, 1952, which

ascertained that "the resurrection [*tquma*] of Israel" has made "the business of smuggling drugs across the country practically impossible."

3. Michal Haramati, "The Theory of Autochthonous Zionism in Political Discourse in Israel, 1961–1967," *Journal of Spatial and Organizational Dynamics* 6 (2018), 119.

4. Cyrus Schayegh, *The Middle East and the Making of the Modern World* (Cambridge, MA: Harvard University Press, 2017), 294.

5. Israel State Archives (hereafter ISA), HZ-7/1994, Annual Report on Illicit Traffic for 1950.

6. ISA, HZ-11/1994, Yaacov Ginosar, head of Police Economic Department, to International Organizations Division of the Israeli Ministry of Foreign Affairs, August 19, 1956. For similar expressions, see ISA, HZ-4/2633, Police Report on Illicit Traffic in Narcotic Drugs for 1962; ISA, G-5/5102, Police Report on Illicit Commerce in Intoxicating Drugs for 1958; Amos Carmeli, "Drug-Smuggling Routes," *Davar*, September 21, 1965. See also Philip Robins, *Middle East Drugs Bazaar: Production, Prevention and Consumption* (Oxford and New York: Oxford University Press, 2016), 100–101.

7. Hashish consumption during the first two decades of the State of Israel is the main topic of chapter 6.

8. See annual reports to the police minister for the years 1950 to 1967, and reports on illicit traffic for the same years prepared by Israel Police for the CND, in ISA, G-1/4279; G-1/5421; G-45/5576; HZ-14/2613; HZ-11/21; HZ-11.2613; HZ-4/2633; HZ-4/2659; and HZ-9/4847.

9. Benny Morris, *Israel's Border Wars, 1949–1956: Arab Infiltration, Israeli Retaliation, and the Countdown to the Suez War* (Oxford: Oxford University Press, 1993), 1–2; Avi Shlaim, *The Iron Wall: Israel and the Arab World* (New York: W. W. Norton, 2001), 41–47.

10. Shira Robinson, *Citizen Strangers: Palestinians and the Birth of Israel's Liberal Settler State* (Stanford, CA: Stanford University Press, 2013), 10.

11. ISA, HZ-5/2633, Israel Police, CID, Memorandum on Illicit Drug Trafficking, October 1963.

12. ISA, HZ-16/2082, Deputy Superintendent of Police Yaacov Genossar, Seizures of Dangerous Drugs within Israel's Borders, September 25, 1959; Mansour Nasasra, *The Naqab Bedouins: A Century of Politics and Resistance* (New York: Columbia University Press, 2017), 164.

13. ISA, HZ-12/2613, Special Police Report on the Problem of Dangerous Drugs in Israel, October 4, 1960. See also IDF Archives, 1954/405/135, Military Governor of the Negev, The State of the Bedouin in Israel, October 1952, 1–2.

14. This point was made in many a police report in the years 1949 to 1967. See, e.g., ISA, HZ-12/2613, Special Police Report on the Problem of Dangerous Drugs in Israel, October 4, 1960.

15. Ilan Pappé, *The Forgotten Palestinians: A History of the Palestinians in Israel* (New Haven, CT: Yale University Press, 2011), 18.

16. Mohammed Afifi, Mahmoud Al-Zuheiri, Violet Fasheh, and Salah El-Sousi, "Drug Abuse: Problems, Policies, and Programs in Palestine," in *Drug Problems: Cross-Cultural Policy and Program Development*, Kindle edition, ed. Richard Isralowitz, Mohammed Afifi, and Richard Rawson (Westport, CT: Auburn House, 2002).

17. On the paucity of hashish and opium seizures in Transjordan during the 1930s and 1940s, see, e.g., League of Nations Archive (hereafter LNA), Opium Advisory Committee (hereafter OAC), C.420.M.284 (O.C./A.R. 1936/28), Traffic in Opium and Other Dangerous Drugs, Annual Reports by Governments for 1936, Trans-Jordan, September 23, 1937; LNA, OAC, C.64.M.64.1942.XI. (O.C./A.R. 1941/28), Traffic in Opium and Other Dangerous Drugs, Annual Reports by Governments for 1941, Trans-Jordan, August 18, 1942.

18. Morris, *Israel's Border Wars*, 37, 40.

19. Literature on the PANB in any language is scarce. For a very brief passage on the Arab League's Anti-Narcotics Bureau, see Mahsan Abd al-Hamid Ahmad, *Arab Security Collaboration and the Security Challenges*, in Arabic (Riyadh: Markaz al-dirasat wa-al-buhuth, 1999), 17.

20. ISA, G-5/189, UN Economic and Social Council (ECOSOC), CND, 7th Session, A Report by the Director of the Arab League PANB Together with a Supplementary Note, May 22, 1952. See also ISA, HZ-9/1994, Report from the Director of the Permanent Anti-Narcotics Bureau of the Arab League to the CND, March 28, 1955.

21. ISA, G-12/5102, UN, ECOSOC, 15th CND Session, Report of the Middle East Narcotics Survey Mission, November 16, 1959.

22. Morris, *Israel's Border Wars*, 1.

23. Cited in ibid., 2.

24. IDF Archives, 2009/22/12, Head of the Israeli Military Intelligence, Survey of Intelligence Directorate, December 14, 1959, 4.

25. Shira Pinhas, "Road, Map: Partition in Palestine from the Local to the Transnational," *Journal of Levantine Studies* 10 (forthcoming); Matthew Kraig Kelly, *The Crime of Nationalism: Britain, Palestine, and Nation-Building on the Fringe of Empire* (Oakland: University of California Press, 2017), 45.

26. Morris, *Israel's Border Wars*, 4.

27. Hillel Cohen, *Good Arabs: The Israeli Security Services and the Israeli Arabs*, trans. Haim Watzman (Berkeley: University of California Press, 2011).

28. ISA, G-5/5102, Department of Pharmacy of the Israel Health Ministry, Internal Report on the Problem of Drug Addicts in the Country for the Year 1958, 1.

29. Shlaim, *Iron Wall*, 82.

30. Cohen, *Good Arabs*, 67–68. See also Orit Rozin, "Infiltration and the Making of

Israel's Emotional Regime in the State's Early Years," *Middle Eastern Studies* 52 (2016): 448–72.

31. Morris, *Israel's Border Wars*, 48; Cohen, *Good Arabs*, 67–68. On Israel's dealings with Palestinian "infiltrators," see IDF Archives, 1957/626/10, IDF Operations Directorate, Lessons from IDF Operational Activity (Land Forces), August 19,1955; IDF Archives, 1960/610/81, Military Governor of the Negev, Supply of Cattle from Jordan, August 18, 1953.

32. I thank Matthew Sparks for this latter formulation.

33. Benny Morris, *The Birth of the Palestinian Refugee Problem Revisited* (Cambridge: Cambridge University Press, 2004), 507.

34. This was decided in addition to parallel efforts to "Judaize the Galilee." See Dan Rabinowitz, *Overlooking Nazareth: The Ethnography of Exclusion in Galilee* (Cambridge: Cambridge University Press, 1997); Oren Yiftachel, *Ethnocracy: Land and Identity Politics in Israel/Palestine* (Philadelphia: University of Pennsylvania Press, 2006).

35. Itty Abraham and Willem van Schendel, "Introduction: The Making of Illicitness," in *Illicit Flows and Criminal Things*, ed. Willem van Schendel and Itty Abraham (Bloomington: Indiana University Press, 2005), 4, 14.

36. ISA, G-12/5102, Annual Police Report on Illicit Traffic of Narcotic Drugs for 1958.

37. Morris, *Israel's Border Wars*, 44–45; Robinson, *Citizen Strangers*, 38–39.

38. The following examination of Isa's hashish trade ventures draws on the text of his eight-page confession, which was originally given in Arabic, and recorded on June 28, 1956, in highly irregular Hebrew. See ISA, L-27/2480.

39. Akram Fouad Khater, "'House' to 'Goddess of the House': Gender, Class, and Silk in 19th-Century Mount Lebanon," *International Journal of Middle East Studies* 28 (1996): 325.

40. ISA, HZ-7/1994, Police Report on Illicit Traffic for 1950. See also "Smugglers of Intoxicating Drugs Arrested, among Them a Jewish Policeman from Jerusalem," *Herut*, October 28, 1951.

41. ISA, HZ-9/1994, Foreign Ministry to Mission of Israel to the UN, Intoxicating Drugs, April 26, 1955.

42. Y. Yaakobi, "Hashish Plantations Revealed," *Davar*, August 17, 1954; Yigal Lev, "Police Can't Tell the Line between a Drug Addict and a Criminal," *Ma'ariv*, December 30, 1964.

43. "Cooperation in Hashish Smuggling," *Ma'ariv*, April 24, 1956; Ephraim Hopshteter, "International Police and Israel Police" (in Hebrew), *999* 3 (April 1953): 23. The periodical *999* was an Israel Police mouthpiece for reaching out to the Israeli public in the 1950s; it was named after the telephone number for the emergency services in Israel at the time. Some information on *999* is provided in Bryan K. Roby, *Mizrahi Era*

of Rebellion: Israel's Forgotten Civil Rights Struggle, 1948–1966 (Syracuse, NY: Syracuse University Press, 2015), 36–37.

44. Joe Alex Morris, Jr., "The Middle East Drug Traffic," *New York Herald Tribune*, October 22, 1960.

45. ISA, L-17/2278, First Inspector Yehuda Kaufman, Second Report on Dangerous Drugs, February 12, 1953.

46. ISA, L-17/2278, Sub-Inspector A. Zelinger, Dangerous Drugs, March 3, 1953.

47. Roby, *Mizrahi Era of Rebellion*, 21.

48. Tom Segev, *Palestine under the British*, in Hebrew (Jerusalem: Keter, 1999), 415–16.

49. Yoav Alon, "Bridging Imperial, National, and Local Historiographies: Britons, Arabs, and Jews in the Mandate Palestine Police," *Jerusalem Quarterly* 75 (2018): 62–63.

50. Israel Police, "The First Decade of Israel Police" (in Hebrew), *Annual Report for 1957* (Tel Aviv, 1958): 8.

51. Israel Police, "Twenty Years of Israel Police" (in Hebrew), *Annual Report for 1968* (Tel Aviv: Yefet Publishing, 1969): 9. See also "Ten Years" (in Hebrew), *Israel Police Quarterly* 7–8 (April 1958): 129–30, which claimed that before leaving, the Mandatory authorities "did the best they could to maliciously destroy the structure of government. . . . [Therefore, the fledgling police force] experienced difficulties in finance, recruitment, expertise, and stability. . . . Massive immigration during the period of construction and economic strain added to [existing] complications and difficulties." Copies of *The Israel Police Quarterly* were sent to court libraries, lawyers, judges, prison wardens, government ministers, and police officers. Roby, *Mizrahi Era of Rebellion*, 37.

52. Nomi Levenkron, "Between the Manifest and the Hidden: Historiography of Israel Police in the First Decade" (in Hebrew), *Mishtara ve-Historia* 1 (2019): 18–19.

53. The Knesset, Protocol 9/B of the Meeting of the Committee of Internal Affairs, Police Commissioner Review of Conditions in the Police, December 4, 1956, 1–2. A chapter titled "Manpower" in the Israel Police *Annual Report for 1957*, 20, stated that "From day one to this very day, the problem of manpower has been and remains the main problem of the police force."

54. Roby, *Mizrahi Era of Rebellion*, 28, 36.

55. Bechor-Shalom Sheetrit, "The Police and the Merging of Exiles" (in Hebrew), *999* 2 (March 1953): 4.

56. The Knesset, Protocol 2 of Meeting of the Committee of Internal Affairs, November 21, 1951, 4.

57. The Knesset, Protocol 6 of Meeting of the Committee of Internal Affairs, Police Minister Review of Police Issues, December 10, 1951, 5.

58. See, e.g., Israel Police, "Twenty Years of Israel Police," *Annual Report for 1968*, 12.

59. The Knesset, Protocol 9/B of Meeting of the Committee of Internal Affairs, Police Commissioner Review of Conditions in the Police, December 4, 1956, 3.

60. Bryan, *Mizrahi Era of Rebellion*, 36.

61. Israel Police, *Annual Report for 1953*, 65.

62. Ibid.

63. Elie Hod and Erella Shadmi, *History of Israel Police, Vol 1: The Foundation Stage, 1948–1958*, in Hebrew (Jerusalem: Israel Police Human Resources Division, History Department, 2004), 167, 363; Israel Police, *Annual Report for 1958*, in Hebrew (Tel Aviv, 1959), 56.

64. Israel Police, *Annual Report for 1953*, in Hebrew (Tel Aviv, 1954), 61–62; Israel Police, *Annual Report for 1954*, in Hebrew (Tel Aviv, 1955), 49; Aryeh Heshbaya, "Infiltration by Sea" (in Hebrew), *999* 9 (October 1953): 9–10. In 1977, the duties of the police coast guard were transferred to the Israeli Navy.

65. Israel Police, *Annual Report for 1957*, in Hebrew (Tel Aviv, 1958), 56.

66. Israel Police, *Annual Report for 1953*, 65.

67. Orit Rozin, *The Rise of the Individual in 1950s Israel: A Challenge to Collectivism* (Waltham, MA: Brandeis University Press, 2011), 3–64; Orit Rozin, "Food, Identity, and Nation-Building in Israel's Formative Years," *Israel Studies Review* 21 (2006): 52–80.

68. Roby, *Mizrahi Era of Rebellion*, 39.

69. "Intoxicating Drugs," *Ha-'Olam Ha-Zeh* 987, September 12, 1956.

70. ISA, HZ-11/21, UN Conference for the Adoption of a Single Convention on Narcotic Drugs, Statement by Ambassador Michael Comay, January 27, 1961.

71. Kaufman made these remarks in a lecture on dangerous drugs given to 120 navy servicemen; and see ISA, L-17/2278.

72. Yehuda Kaufman and David Ginsburg, "Smuggling Dangerous Drugs" (in Hebrew), *999* 6 (July 1955): 12.

73. Y. Ariel, "The Tricks of Concealment and Discovery" (in Hebrew), *Israel Police Quarterly* 5 (April 1957): 52.

74. Ibid., 51, 53.

75. ISA, HZ-16/2082, Deputy Superintendent of Police Yaacov Genossar, Seizures of Dangerous Drugs within Israel's Borders, September 25, 1959.

76. See, e.g., ISA, HZ-8/1994, Israel Police CID Dispatch to Interpol Regarding Drug Trafficking in Israel, January 15, 1953; ISA, HZ-12/2613, Police Report on the Problem of Dangerous Drugs in Israel, October 4, 1960.

77. Shlomo Giv'on, "Seven Loaves of Hashish Rolled Out," *Ma'ariv*, June 4, 1962.

78. Ariel, "Tricks of Concealment and Discovery," 51.

79. Ibid., 51–52. See also "Animals: First-Rate Criminals" (in Hebrew), *999* 7 (August 1956): 16.

80. Morris, "Middle East Drug Traffic."

81. The Knesset, Protocol 9/B of the Meeting of the Internal Affairs Committee, Police Commissioner Review on Conditions in the Police Force, December 4, 1956, 1.

82. The Knesset, Protocol 12/B of the Meeting of the Internal Affairs Committee, Issue of Police Manpower, December 25, 1956, 7.

83. See, e.g., ISA, L-24/2278, Merhavim Police Station, Report on Drug Seizures, July 13, 1953; ISA, L-31/2480, Ofakim Police Station, Drug Seizure Report, March 1, 1957; ISA, L-28/2480, Beersheba Police Station, Seizure of Dangerous Drugs, February 17, 1958; ISA, L-28/2480, Beersheba Police Station to CID Headquarters, Seizure of Dangerous Drugs, February 12, 1958; Gad Yagul, "The Path of Hashish," *Davar*, November 20, 1959.

84. Ibid.

85. Kaufman and Ginsburg, "Smuggling Dangerous Drugs," 12.

86. ISA, HZ-12/2613, Special Police Report on the Problem of Dangerous Drugs in Israel, October 4, 1960; ISA, HZ-5/2633, Israel Police, CID Memorandum on Illicit Drug Trafficking, October 1963; Carmeli, "Drug-Smuggling Routes."

87. ISA, HZ-9/1994, Police Report on the War on Intoxicating Drugs, March 1, 1955; Yachin, "Hashish." See also Robins, *Middle East Drugs Bazaar*, 100–101.

88. Carmeli, "Drug-Smuggling Routes." See also HZ-12/2613, Police Report on the Problem of Dangerous Drugs in Israel, October 4, 1960; ISA, HZ-16/2082, Police Report on Illicit Traffic of Narcotic Drugs for the Year 1959.

89. See, e.g., ISA, L-31/2480, Assistant District Commander Yaacov Genossar to Commander of CID Economic Department, Discovery of 70 kg of Hashish and Opium at Sea, June 23, 1957; L. Riseman, "Went Fishing and Caught Bags of Hashish," *Yedi'ot Ahronot*, February 2, 1959; "Forty KG of Hashish Pulled Out by Fishermen," *Davar*, August 9, 1959.

90. "Thirteen Tires Containing Hashish Emitted from the Sea," *Davar*, July 6, 1955; "Another Tire Containing Hashish Was Found Near Migdal Ashkelon," *Herut*, August 16, 1955.

91. See, e.g., Peter Dale Scott, *American War Machine: Deep Politics, the CIA Global Drug Connection, and the Road to Afghanistan* (Lanham, MD, and Boulder, CO: Rowman & Littlefield, 2014); Mahmood Mamdani, *Good Muslim, Bad Muslim: America, the Cold War, and the Roots of Terror* (New York: Pantheon Books, 2004), 66–69.

92. Cited in Maziyar Ghiabi, *Drug Politics: Managing Disorder in the Islamic Republic of Iran* (Cambridge: Cambridge University Press, 2019), 82.

93. "Not on Hashish Alone," *Ma'ariv*, November 4, 1966.

94. R. Musari, "Criminal Way of Life under the Naguib Regime" (in Hebrew), *999* 6 (July 1953): 23.

95. Ibid; Yigal Lev, "Police Can't Tell the Difference between a Drug Addict and a Criminal," *Ma'ariv*, December 30, 1964.

96. Sh. Itur, "In the Underground of Hashish Smokers," *Ma'ariv*, September 7, 1955; "Hashish: The Plague of Egypt," *Davar*, November 20, 1966. The figures given reflect a third of Egypt's total population. The proportion of the adult population who consumed hashish was presumably greater than a third.

97. Yachin, "Hashish"; Musari, "Criminal Way of Life"; K. Greenbaum, "Colonel Mahrawi: Nasser is Smoking Hashish," *Ma'ariv*, March 19, 1959.

98. Jacqueline (Shohat) Kahanoff, "Tragedy of the Woman in the Orient," *Ma'ariv*, July 30, 1965. Kahanoff is the Egyptian-born Israeli novelist, essayist, and journalist who reintroduced the term *Levantinism* to the Israeli lexicon, determined to transform its derogatory and colonialist connotations into a new radical sociopolitical and cultural identity in Israeli society. In the quoted *Ma'ariv* article, Kahanoff traces the excessive use of hashish among Egyptian men to the genital mutilation of women. In addition to other traumatic effects of such acts, Kahanoff explains, it leaves "the majority of women handicapped from a sexual point of view." Faced with "a lack of responsiveness on the part of their wives, who remain cold and passive," Egyptian men "have recourse to hashish in order to intensify their own sexual potency." As they use this drug more frequently, she says, "their attachment to it increases."

99. Kokhva, "On 'Successes' in Hashish Growing," *'Al ha-Mishmar*, September 1, 1954.

100. Ibid.; Yachin, "Hashish."

101. As a matter of fact, reports concerning such allegations by Arab nations against Israel had already began to surface in the Israeli press by 1952. See, for example, "The Arabs Are Blaming Israel for 'Disseminating Drugs in the Arab World,'" *'Al ha-Mishmar*, December 8, 1952; "A New Arab Libel: Israel Is Smuggling Intoxicating Drugs to the Arab World," *Ha-Tzofeh*, December 7, 1952.

102. ISA, HZ-9/1994, Summary of Meeting # 21 of the Mission of Israel to the UN, February 25, 1955.

103. ISA, HZ-9/1994, League of Arab States, a Report from the Director of PANB, March 28, 1955; HZ-9/1994, Abdel Aziz Safwat, Note Submitted to the Secretary-General of the League of Arab States, n/d; Mordechai Kidron, Israel UN Mission in New York, 10th CND Session, 11.5.1955. See also Sh. Gavriel, "Hashish War between Israel and Egypt," *Ma'ariv*, May 27, 1956.

104. ISA, HZ-9/1994, League of Arab States, a Report from the Director of Permeant Anti-Narcotic Bureau.

105. ISA, HZ-9/1994, Mordechai Kidron, Israel UN Mission in New York, to the Foreign Ministry International Organizations Division (hereafter IOD), 10th CND Session, May 11,1 955. See also HZ-9/1994, Abdel Aziz Safwat, Note Submitted to the Secretary-General of the League of Arab States, 1955.

106. See e.g. ISA, HZ-11/1994, Foreign Ministry, IOD to Israel UN Mission in New York, 12th CND Session on Dangerous Drugs, April 1, 1957; ISA, HZ-15/2082, Zvi

Neeman, IOD, to Menachem Kahany, Israel Mission to the European Office of the UN, April 8, 1959; ISA HZ-11/21 Nissim Yaish, Israel Mission to the European Office of the UN, to IOD, CND 16th Session, April 24, 1961.

107. "Israel Smuggling Hashish to Egypt," *Al-Ahram*, February 5, 1957.

108. "Israel Smuggling Poisoned Cigarettes," *Filastin*, May 26, 1956.

109. These arguments are taken from an English-language "memorandum" prepared by Israel police to help the Foreign Ministry refute the Arab League's allegations. ISA, HZ-9/1994.

110. ISA, HZ-11/1994, Sima Rapaport, IOD, to Israeli Mission to UN in New York, the 12th Session for Intoxicating Drugs, April 30, 1957.

111. ISA, HZ-11/1994, Southern Command Field Security to Commander of Southern Command, Survey of the Smuggling of Intoxicating Drugs to Egypt under the Protection of the Egyptian Military, December 28, 1956.

112. Ibid.

113. Ilana Feldman, *Police Encounters: Security and Surveillance in Gaza under Egyptian Rule* (Stanford, CA: Stanford University Press, 2015), 77–78; 170n11.

114. See, e.g., ISA, HZ-9/1994, Research Department, Intoxicating Drugs in the Middle East, May 3, 1954; ISA, HZ-9/1994, Research Department to the IOD, Intoxicating Drugs, July 6, 1957; ISA, HZ-9/1994, IOD to Israeli UN Mission in New York, CND 12th Session, April 9, 1957.

115. Jonathan Marshall, *The Lebanese Connection: Corruption, Civil War, and the International Drug Traffic* (Stanford, CA: Stanford University Press, 2012), 37–38; Ryan Gingeras, *Heroin, Organized Crime, and the Making of Modern Turkey* (Oxford: Oxford University Press, 2014).

116. "The Middle East Narcotics Survey Mission (September–October 1959) of the UN," January 1, 1960, *UNODC*, https://www.unodc.org/unodc/en/data-and-analysis/bulletin/bulletin_1960-01-01_4_page006.html (accessed April 8, 2020). See also ISA, G-12/5102, European Office of the UN, Geneva, Narcotics Survey Mission to the Middle East Appointed by the UN Secretary-General, August 7, 1959; ISA, G-12/5102, ECOSOC, CND 15th Session, Report of the Middle East Narcotics Survey Mission, November 16, 1959; ISA, G-12/5102, European Office of the UN, Narcotics Survey Mission to the Middle East Appointed by UN Secretary General, Press Release, August 7, 1959.

117. Uzi Mahnaimi, "Revealed: Israel Made the Egyptian Army Go to Pot," *The Times* (London), December 22, 1996; Benny Lévy, "Opération Toto," *Revue XXI* (July-September 2010), 58–66. This charge has also been mentioned, albeit in passing, in a handful of scholarly works; see, e.g., Cohen, *Good Arabs*, 191; Ted Swedenburg, "Sa'ida Sultan / Danna International: Transgender Pop and the Polysemiotics of Sex, Nation, and Ethnicity on the Israeli-Egyptian Border," in *Mass Mediations: New Approaches to Popular Culture in the Middle East and Beyond*, ed. Walter Armbrust (Berkeley: University of California Press, 2000), 111; Marshall, *Lebanese Connection*, 137.

118. Unless stated otherwise, my discussion below of the alleged Israeli involvement in the illicit Levant hashish trade draws heavily on these two reports, and particularly the 2010 French report, which is more detailed and based on extensive research.

119. An interview I conducted in October 2018 with a highly knowledgeable informant who requested to remain anonymous.

120. Yossi Melman, "Operation 'Addictive Candy': How Israel Silenced a Spy Privy to One of Its Darkest Intelligence Debacles," *Ha-Aretz*, May 20, 2020, https://www.haaretz.com/israel-news/.premium.MAGAZINE-how-israel-silenced-a-spy-privy-to-one-of-its-darkest-intelligence-debacles-1.8864069 (accessed May 22, 2020).

121. The following additional Israeli press reports refer to the veil of secrecy surrounding the hashish-smuggling affair, albeit indirectly and vaguely so as to elude censorship: Yossi Melman, "When Young Israel Meddled Deep into the Nile's Waters," March 5, 2020; Yossi Melman, "A Top Secret for Eternity under the Cover of Quotation Marks," *Ha-Aretz*, January 28, 2020.

122. Herzog held this position twice, from 1948 to 1950 and from 1959 to 1962.

123. Mahnaimi, "Revealed"; Lévy, "Opération Toto," 61.

124. Ibid.

125. Yossi Melman, "Unit 504 and the Success in the Six Day War: The Untold Story," *Ma'ariv*, June 5, 2013.

126. Yossi Melman, "With No Shame: Is Israel Abandoning Agents' Relatives Who Have Risked their Lives for It?" *Ma'ariv*, November 11, 2017. For more information about the unit's operations, see Ronen Bergman and Gil Meltzer, *The Yom Kippur War: Moments of Truth*, in Hebrew (Tel Aviv: Miskal-Yedi'ot Ahronot Books, 2003), 324; Yossi Melman, "The Tales of the 504 Intelligence Unit in Lebanon," *Ha-Aretz*, May 22, 2009; Yossi Melman, "With or without Tahini, Unit 504 Must Be Shut Down," *Ha-Aretz*, February 4, 2020.

127. Melman, "Operation 'Addictive Candy.'"

128. Lévy, "Opération Toto," 63. Managed by Lebanese traffickers, the cannabis and the poppy were processed in laboratories in Lebanon.

129. On the death in 2018 of Eli Avivi, owner of the Achziv hippie camp, the Israeli press reported that "over the years, [he had] cooperated with various security officials who were active near the northern border, " but did not elaborate on the issue. See Ofer Aderet, "Eli Avivi, 'Head of Achziv State', Dies," *Ha-Aretz*, May 16, 2018. It is possible that this cooperation included assisting the army in offloading hashish supplies to the shore.

130. These smuggling routes are confirmed in PANB reports to the CND. See, e.g., ISA, HZ-11/2613, Nissim Yaish, Deputy Permanent Representative in the Israeli Geneva UN Mission, to the Foreign Ministry's IOD, April 24, 1961.

131. ISA, HZ-10/1994, Kahany to Director of IOD, 11th session of CND, May 18, 1956.

132. ISA, HZ-9/1994, Foreign Ministry Research Department to IOD, Intoxicating Drugs, July 6, 1954.

133. Israel Shahak, "The Real Israeli Interests in Lebanon," *Washington Report on Middle East Affairs* (July 1996), http://www.bintjbeil.com/E/occupation/shahak2.html (accessed April 8, 2020).

CHAPTER SIX

1. Andrew Sherratt, "Introduction: Peculiar Substances," in *Consuming Habits: Drugs in History and Anthropology*, ed. Jordan Goodman, Paul E. Lovejoy, and Andrew Sherratt (London and New York: Routledge, 1995), 5.

2. Lorenzo Veracini, "The Other Shift: Settler Colonialism, Israel, and the Occupation," *Journal of Palestine Studies* 42 (2013): 26–42; see also Patrick Wolfe, "Settler Colonialism and the Elimination of the Native," *Journal of Genocide Research* 8 (2006): 387–409; Marcelo Svirski and Ronnen Ben-Arie, *From Shared Life to Co-Resistance in Historic Palestine* (London: Rowman & Littlefield, 2018).

3. Aziza Khazzoom, "The Great Chain of Orientalism: Jewish Identity, Stigma Management, and Ethnic Exclusion in Israel," *American Sociological Review* 4 (2003): 500. Daniel Boyarin, in his *Unheroic Conduct: The Rise of Heterosexuality and the Invention of the Jewish Man* (Berkeley and Los Angeles: University of California Press, 1997), 302, puts it more succinctly: "Zionism is . . . itself the civilizing mission, first and foremost directed by Jews at other Jews."

4. Arik Cohen, "Hashish and Hashishniks in Acre" (in Hebrew), *'Avaryanut ve-Hevra* 3 (1968): 37.

5. Michal Haramati, "The Theory of Autochthonous Zionism in Political Discourse in Israel, 1961–1967," *Journal of Spatial and Organizational Dynamics* 6 (2018): 123.

6. Here I paraphrase Maziyar Ghiabi's analysis of drug control in 1960s monarchical Iran, in *Drug Politics: Managing Disorder in the Islamic Republic of Iran* (Cambridge: Cambridge University Press, 2019), 55.

7. The great masses, about 680,000, arrived in 1948–51, about half Ashkenazi/Oriental. After that the immigration was always of a substantial Oriental majority. By 1955 approximately 80,000 more arrived; Haramati, "Theory of Autochthonous Zionism," 119n11.

8. Orit Bashkin, *Impossible Exodus: Iraqi Jews in Israel* (Stanford, CA: Stanford University Press, 2017).

9. Haramati, "Theory of Autochthonous Zionism," 120.

10. David Elisha, Jorge Gleser, and Michael Reiter, "Patterns, Policies, and Treatment Strategies of Substance Abuse in Israel: Past and Present," in *Drug Problems: Cross-Cultural Policy and Program Development*, ed. Richard Isralowitz, Mohammed Afifi, and Richard Rawson, Kindle edition (Westport, CT: Auburn House, 2002).

11. Amos Carmeli, "Drug-Smuggling Routes," *Davar*, September 21, 1965. See also Rachel Adiv, "They Are Called Criminals," *Davar*, August 9, 1957; Gad Yagul, "Path of Hashish," *Davar*, November 20, 1959.

12. Israel State Archives (ISA), G-5/5102, Department of Pharmacy of the Israel Health Ministry, Internal Report on the Problem of Drug Addicts in the Country for the Year 1958, 1. See also "Police Undertakes to Fight Hashish Cultivators and Commerce in Intoxicating Drugs," *Herut*, November 8, 1954.

13. Israel Drapkin and Simha F. Landau, "Drug Offenders in Israel: A Survey," *British Journal of Criminology* 6 (1966), 383.

14. Cohen, "Hashish and Hashishniks," 35. A short story written by Israeli novelist Yeshayahu Koren, titled "Mars Le Fou," tells the story of such transactions, intended for the local hashish market in the Beersheba region. The story was published in Yeshayahu Koren, *Those Who Stand at Night*, in Hebrew (Tel Aviv: Hakibbutz Hameuchad, 1992), 201–18.

15. ISA, L-17/2278, First Inspector Yehuda Kaufman, Second Report on Dangerous Drugs, Feburary 12, 1953; ISA, HZ-16/2082, Deputy Superintendent Yaacov Genossar, Seizures of Dangerous Drugs within Israel's Borders, September 25, 1959.

16. Binyamin Blum, "The Hounds of Empire: Forensic Dog Tracking in Britain and Its Colonies, 1888–1953," *Law and History Review* 35 (2017): 621–65.

17. Yehuda Kaufman, "Dangerous Drugs" (in Hebrew), *999* 4 (May 1953): 15. See also Adiv, "They Are Called Criminals."

18. Israel Police, *Annual Report for 1960*, in Hebrew (Tel Aviv, 1961), 15; Raphael Razin, "Helping the Investigator with Police Dogs" (in Hebrew), *Israel Police Quarterly* 20–21 (December 1965): 23–26.

19. M. Ben Gavriel, "Interview with Lassie," *Davar*, December 25, 1953.

20. Kaufman, "Dangerous Drugs," 15.

21. ISA, L-17/2278, Israel Police, Shfela Regional Headquarters, the Smoking and Selling of Hashish in Lod, November 26, 1953; ibid., Israel Police, Head of the Animal Section, Report on the Activities of the Dog Lassie, December 6, 1953.

22. Ben Gavriel, "Interview with Lassie."

23. "The Risk of Intoxicating Drugs Increases," *Davar*, November 8, 1954.

24. "Awards to Children Who Helped the Police," *Davar*, September 14, 1964; "The 9-Year-Old Detective," *Davar*, November 14, 1962.

25. Cited in "The 9-Year-Old Detective"; B. Adler, "The War on Intoxicating Drugs," *Ha-Tzofeh*, November 8, 1954.

26. Yigal Lev, "A Negro in the Dead of the Night," *Ma'ariv*, November 8, 1961.

27. Shlomo Giv'on, "The Shirts Were Too Inflated," *Ma'ariv*, May 23, 1962.

28. Ibid.

29. Lev, "Negro in the Dead of the Night."

30. Ibid.

31. Nomi Levenkron, "Between the Manifest and the Hidden: Historiography of Israel Police in the First Decade" (in Hebrew), *Mishtara ve-Historia* 1 (2019): 36.

32. Israel Police, *Annual Report for 1955*, in Hebrew (Tel Aviv, 1956), 58.

33. "The Situation of Criminality in the Country" (in Hebrew), *999* 2 (March 1954): 6; Israel Police, *Annual Report for 1951*, in Hebrew (Tel Aviv, 1952), 46.

34. Baruch Kimmerling, *Immigrants, Settlers, Natives: The Israeli State and Society between Cultural Pluralism and Cultural Wars*, in Hebrew (Tel Aviv: 'Am 'Oved, 2004), 283.

35. Israel Police, *Annual Report for 1951*, 38. See also Yosef Magen, "The Young Ones" (in Hebrew), *999* 1 (February 1953): 15; Israel Police, *Annual Report for 1958*, in Hebrew (Tel Aviv, 1959), 50, 67.

36. Kaufman, "Dangerous Drugs," 15. See also Philip Robins, *Middle East Drugs Bazaar: Production, Prevention and Consumption* (New York: Oxford University Press, 2016), 101.

37. Drapkin and Landau, "Drug Offenders in Israel," 382. See also ISA, HZ-5/2633, National Headquarters of the Israel Police, CID, Memorandum of Illicit Drug Trafficking, October 1963.

38. Elisha, Gleser, and Reiter, "Patterns, Policies, and Treatment Strategies of Substance Abuse in Israel, in *Drug Problems*.

39. Jonathan Lewy, "The Drug Policy of the Third Reich," *Social History of Alcohol and Drugs* 22 (2008): 145.

40. "A Significant Increase in the Number of Drug Addicts in Israel," *Ha-Aretz*, August 31, 1960 (italics mine). The *Ha-Aretz* report reproduced this excerpt from the following article penned by Avraham Turnau: "The Problem of Drug Addicts in Israel" (in Hebrew), in Hebrew, *Ha-Hevra* 4 (August 1960): 10–11.

41. ISA, G-12/5102, Report of the Government of Israel for the Calendar Year of 1958 on the Working of the International Treaties on Narcotic Drugs; ISA, G-3/2906, Report of the Government of Israel for the Calendar Year of 1964 on the Working of the International Treaties on Narcotic Drugs.

42. ISA, HZ-12/2613, Kahany to Ministry of Foreign Affair's UN Department, Intoxicating Drugs: Number of Addicts in Israel, September 8, 1960.

43. ISA, HZ-12/2613, Drug Addicts in Israel, October 25, 1960.

44. ISA, HZ-12/2613, Tel Aviv District Health Bureau to Director-General of Health Ministry, Intoxicating drugs: Number of Addicts in Israel, n.d.

45. ISA, HZ-12/2613, Yehuda Kaufman to International Organizations Division of the Israeli Ministry of Foreign Affairs, Drug Addicts in Israel, October 25,1960.

46. Natan Dunevitch, "In the Dens of Drug Smokers" (in Hebrew), *999* 7 (August 1953): 6.

47. Yitzhak White, "Drug Dealers Sold Hashish to Minors from an Institution Near Tiv'on," *Yedi'ot Ahronot*, February 3, 1963. See also Hava Novak, "A Crime with

No Prosecutor," *Davar*, May 26, 1960; Amos Carmeli, "Give Us Morphine or We Won't Talk," *Davar*, September 15, 1965.

48. The Jewish demographic turn—before 1948 the majority of immigrants to Israel migrated from Europe and America, whereas after 1948 immigrants from the Middle East and North Africa were a majority (51.6 percent compared with 48.4 percent)—may have concretized and dramatized these anxieties.

49. Ashley Wright, "Not Just a 'Place for the Smoking of Opium': The Indian Opium Den and Imperial Anxieties in the 1890s," *Journal of Colonialism and Colonial History* 18 (2017): doi:10.1353/cch.2017.0021. See also Marty Roth, "Victorian Highs: Detection, Drugs, and Empire," in *High Anxieties: Cultural Studies in Addiction*, ed. Janet Farrell Brodie and Mark Redfield (Berkeley: University of California Press, 2002), 85–93.

50. Cited in Yitzhak White, "The Government Is Distributing Dangerous Drugs to Every Addict," *Yedi'ot Ahronot*, June 29, 1956.

51. B. Adler, "War on Intoxicating Drugs," *Ha-Tzofeh*, November 8, 1954. See also Roman Frister, "Those Who Burn Incense," *'Al ha-Mishmar*, June 7, 1959; Eliyahu Segal, "Narcomaniacs," *Herut*, August 23, 1957.

52. Joshua Caspi, *Dangerous Drugs: Policy, Control, Enforcement and Trial*, in Hebrew (Haifa: Tamar, 1996), 131.

53. The Knesset, Protocol 26 of the Meeting of the Committee of Public Services, Bill for the Amendment of the Dangerous Drugs Ordinance, July 22, 1952, 8.

54. Daniel Monterescu, "The Bridled Bride of Palestine: Orientalism, Zionism, and the Troubled Urban Imagination," *Identities* 16 (2009): 647.

55. Shira Robinson, *Citizen Strangers: Palestinians and the Birth of Israel's Liberal Settler State* (Stanford, CA: Stanford University Press, 2013), 49.

56. Ibid., 34; Tom Segev, *One Palestine, Complete: Jews and Arabs under the British Mandate* (New York: Macmillan, 2000), 399.

57. Sharon Rotbard, *White City, Black City*, in Hebrew (Tel Aviv: Babel, 2005), 208.

58. Daniel Monterescu and Haim Hazan, *Twilight Nationalism: Politics of Existence at Life's End* (Stanford, CA: Stanford University Press, 2018), 191.

59. Rotbard, *White City, Black City*, 212. See also Daniel Monterescu, *Jaffa Shared and Shattered: Contrived Coexistence in Israel/Palestine* (Bloomington and Indianapolis: Indiana University Press, 2015), 80–84; and Mark LeVine, *Overthrowing Geography: Jaffa, Tel Aviv, and the Struggle for Palestine, 1880–1948* (Los Angeles: University of California Press, 2005), esp. 121–51. As Cyrus Schayegh maintains in *The Modern Middle East*, 286, the evolution of Jaffa as the antipode of Tel Aviv dates back to the city's founding in 1909, when it began to develop its own contrary urban identity in relation to "dirty," "violent," and "unmodern" Arab Jaffa.

60. Old Jaffa Development Company, http://www.oldjaffa.co.il/about-oldjaffa/ (accessed April 8, 2020).

61. Danny Raviv, "From 60th Street in Jaffa to Dizengoff Street," *Yediot Ahronot*, May 8, 1964.

62. Rotbard, *White City, Black City*, 219–20.

63. Tikva Weinstock, "We Came Down to Jaffa to Smoke Hashish," *Ma'ariv*, May 7, 1952; Yochanan Levi, "Hashish Dens in the Vicinity of Tel Aviv," *Yedi'ot Ahronot*, February 18, 1955.

64. Aharon Lahav, "A Routine Patrol in the Underworld," *Davar*, February 8, 1963. See also "There's Also Hope for Drug Addicts," *Ma'ariv*, October 24, 1963.

65. S. Itur, "In the Underground of Hashish Smokers," *Ma'ariv*, November 7, 1955; "The Thousand Golden Arms," *Ha-'Olam Ha-Zeh*, April 24, 1957; Menachem Talmi, "In the Den of Lost Illusions," *Ma'ariv*, May 11, 1962; Ze'ev Pilpel, "The Narcomaniacs," *Yedi'ot Ahronot*, January 11, 1965; Zvi Elgat, "Idleness in 60th Street," *Ma'ariv*, January 25, 1965.

66. Weinstock, "We Came Down to Jaffa"; Levi, "Hashish Dens"; Pilpel, "Narcomaniacs"; Shlomo Giv'on, "The Shirts Were Too Inflated," *Ma'ariv*, May 23, 1962.

67. ISA, HZ-9/1994, Police Report on the War on Intoxicating Drugs, March 1, 1955; Natan Dunevitch, "In the Dens of Drug Smokers," 6; Yagul, " Path of Hashish"; Yigal Lev, "Alcohol Is More Dangerous Than Hashish," *Ma'ariv*, December 27, 1964.

68. M. M., "A Tale about Ducks, Hashish and a Radio," *Ma'ariv*, March 29, 1953.

69. That is, at least until an Arab snitched on him to the police, returning Mahlul back to square one; ibid.

70. Haramati, "Theory of Autochthonous Zionism," 119.

71. Cited in Gidi Weitz, "The Protocols of the Wadi Salib Events: What Did the Founding Fathers of the State Really Think of the Mizrahim," *Ha-Aretz*, February 13, 2014. On the Wadi Salib riots, see, e.g., Yfaat Weiss, *A Confiscated Memory: Wadi Salib and Haifa's Lost Heritage* (New York: Columbia University Press, 2011); Henriette Dahan-Kalev, "The Wadi Salib Riots" (in Hebrew), *Te'oria u-Vikoret* 12 (1999): 149–57. A brief but valuable summary of the riot's causes, events, and aftermath can be found in Joseph Massad, "Zionism's Internal Others: Israel and the Oriental Jews," *Journal of Palestine Studies* 25 (1996): 59–61.

72. "The Risk of Intoxicating Drugs Increases," *Davar*, November 8, 1954; Israel Police, *Annual Report for 1954*, in Hebrew (Tel Aviv, 1955), 60, 76.

73. Adler, "War on Intoxicating Drugs."

74. ISA, HZ-9/1994, Police Report on the War on Intoxicating Drugs, March 1, 1955; Adler, "War on Intoxicating Drugs"; "Hashish Crops Discovered in the Vicinity of Ramla," *Ha-Tzofeh*, August 17, 1954.

75. Bashkin, *Impossible Exodus*, 50–51; Orit Rozin, "Food, Identity and Nation-Building in Israel's Formative Years," *Israel Studies Forum* 21 (2006): 52–80.

76. Bashkin, *Impossible Exodus*, 9. See also Roby, *Mizrahi Era of Rebellion*, 42. Shimon Ballas's *The Transit Camp*, discussed in the introduction, is replete with examples

of the reluctance on the part of state agencies—Israel's national emergency, medical, and ambulance services, as well as the police—to enter the transit camp. In rarer cases, though, Israeli police officers endorsed certain transit camps, settled in them, and helped immigrants with various issues such as fundraising campaigns. Levenkron, "Between the Manifest and the Hidden," 47.

77. Israel Police, *Annual Report for 1954*, 76; Dr. A. Foirstein, "Hashish Made in Israel," *Hayei Sha'ah*, September 9, 1954, 8.

78. ISA, HZ-10/1994, Report by the Government of Israel for the Calendar Year 1954 on the Traffic in Opium and Other Dangerous Drugs; ISA, HZ-9/1994, Police Report on the War on Intoxicating Drugs, March 1, 1955; ISA, HZ-9/1994, First Inspector Yehuda Kaufman to Ministry of Foreign Affairs, Memorandum on Dangerous Drugs, March 18, 1955; ISA, L-27/2480, Jerusalem District Police Headquarters, Economic Department, Report on Dangerous Drugs, May 22, 1956.

79. S. Avizemer, "Educating the Individual to Recognize Responsibility," *Davar*, September 10, 1954.

80. Kokhva, "'On 'Successes' in Hashish Growing," *'Al ha-Mishmar*, November 1, 1954. The murder sparked a vicious backlash against transit camp residents, as can be gleaned from "A Child from Ramat Gan Raped and Murdered," *Davar*, February 17, 1953; "2000 Investigated, 10 Arrested," *'Al ha-Mishmar*, February 18, 1953; "What Will We Tell Our Children?" *Davar*, February 27, 1953.

81. Roby, *Mizrahi Era of Rebellion*, 84.

82. Israel Police, *Annual Report for 1954*, 59; Adler, "War on Intoxicating Drugs."

83. Igal Sarna, *Yona Wallach*, in Hebrew (Jerusalem: Keter Books, 2009), 115–16. The line "the thrill of the first Hashish in a holy land" appears in Ginsberg's poem "Galilee Shore," which can be read in Robert Atwan and Laura Wieder, eds., *A Selection of Poetry in English Inspired by the Bible from Genesis through Revelation* (New York: Oxford University Press, 2000), 317–18.

84. Howard S. Becker, "Becoming a Marijuana User," *American Journal of Sociology*, 59 (1953): 235–42.

85. "The Hashashin," *Ha-'Olam Ha-Zeh*, March 11, 1964.

86. Becker, "Becoming a Marijuana User," 239.

87. "Hashashin."

88. Becker, "Becoming a Marijuana User," 239.

89. "Hashashin."

90. Ibid.

CONCLUSION

1. Rogel Alpher, "What Really Unites Israel's Right, Left and Center," *Ha-Aretz*, August 1, 2015, http://www.haaretz.com/opinion/.premium-what-really-unites-israels-right-left-and-center-1.5381876 (accessed October 13, 2019).

2. Yossi Harel-Fisch and Yaakov Ezrahi, *Psychoactive Drug Use among the Adult Population in Israel: National Epidemiological Survey of 2016*, in Hebrew (Jerusalem: Israel Anti-Drug Authority, 2017).

3. Yardena Schwartz, "The Holy Land of Medical Marijuana," *US News & World Report*, April 11, 2017, https://www.usnews.com/news/best-countries/articles/2017-04-11/israel-is-a-global-leader-in-marijuana-research (accessed April 9, 2020).

4. Flora K. Davidovitz, *The Use of Cannabis for Medical Purposes in Israel and Recognized Indications of Cannabis for Medical Purposes in Different Countries*, in Hebrew (Jerusalem: the Knesset Research and Information Center, 2015).

5. The Knesset Labor, Welfare, and Health Committee Discussion, January 9, 2017, http://main.knesset.gov.il/Activity/committees/Labor/News/Pages/first_090117.aspx (accessed April 9, 2020).

6. Kathryn Meyer and Terry Parssinen, *Webs of Smoke: Smugglers, Warlords, Spies, and the History of the International Drug Trade*, Kindle edition (Lanham, MD: Rowman & Littlefield, 2002), introduction. See also Philippe Bourmaud, "Turf Wars at the League of Nations: International Anti-Cannabis Policies and Oversight in Syria and Lebanon, 1919–1939," in *The League of Nations; Work on Social Issues: Visions, Endeavors and Experiments*, ed. Magaly Rodríguez García, Davide Rodogno and Liat Kozma (Geneva: United Nations Publications, 2016), 75–87.

7. James Tharin Bradford, *Poppies, Politics, and Power: Afghanistan and the Global History of Drugs and Diplomacy* (Ithaca, NY: Cornell University Press, 2019), 4. See also Alan Block, "European Drug Traffic and Traffickers between the Wars: The Policy of Suppression and its Consequences," *Journal of Social History* 23 (1989): 315.

8. Paul Knepper, "Dreams and Nightmares: Drug Trafficking and the History of International Crime," in *The Oxford Handbook of the History of Crime and Criminal Justice*, ed. Paul Knepper and Anja Johansen (New York: Oxford University Press, 2016), 216–17; Paul Gootenberg, "Talking about the Flow: Drugs, Borders, and the Discourse of Drug Control," *Cultural Critique* 71 (2009): 13–46.

9. Johan Mathew, *Margins of the Market: Trafficking and Capitalism across the Arabian Sea* (Oakland: University of California Press, 2016), 4.

10. Paul Gootenberg, "Talking about the Flow," 20.

11. David Courtwright, *Forces of Habit: Drugs and the Making of the Modern World* (Cambridge, MA: Harvard University Press, 2001), 44.

12. Phyllis Palgi, "The Traditional Role and Symbolism of Hashish among Moroccan Jews in Israel and the Effect of Acculturation," in *Cannabis and Culture*, ed. Vera Rubin (The Hague: Mouton, 1975), 214–15.

13. Zvi Lavi, "Gates Opened Also for Hashish Smugglers," *Ma'ariv*, November 15, 1967. The stockpiling of large quantities of hashish within Israel immediately after the war can be ascertained from the more than twenty-two-fold increase in hashish seizures during 1968 (3,865 kilograms) in comparison with the previous year (117 kilograms).

According to the *Police Annual Report for 1968*, in Hebrew (Tel Aviv: Planning and Operations Department, 1969), 91, "the quantities of drugs seized this year [1968] are unprecedented since the founding of the state."

14. In Israel at the time, the price of one kilogram of hashish was about $150; the price for the same quantity in the United States reached $2,500; Moti Argaman, *Cannabis, Marijuana and Hashish*, in Hebrew (Tel Aviv: Gal, 1997), 291–92; Nahum Pundak, "Sahara Number 1 Calling," *Davar*, November 22, 1968; Nahum Pundak, "Hashish with Everything," *Davar*, January 17, 1969. According to Raphael Patai, in *The Jewish Mind* (Detroit: Wayne State University Press, 1977), 453, "at one point, the price of hashish in Israel was one-tenth of its price in the U.S. and Canada."

15. ISA, GL-6/13824, Israel Police, Handling of Dangerous Drugs, January 28, 1969; ISA, G-3/2906, Health Ministry, Annual Report on International Supervision of Dangerous Drugs and the Problem of Drug Addicts for 1967, June 5, 1968.

16. Igal Sarna, *Yona Wallach*, in Hebrew (Jerusalem: Keter Books, 2009), 297.

17. Lavi, "Gates Opened."

18. Ibid.

19. Joseph Harrison, "Illegal Drug Use by Israeli Youth," *Addiction* 70 (1975): 336. A foreign student cited in "The Envelope Sent from the U.S. to Tel Aviv University Dormitories Contained Marijuana," *Yedi'ot Ahronot*, May 4, 1971, likewise argued that "you can go to Jerusalem to buy the drug like you buy cakes in a pastry shop." See also Dani Bloch, "Jerusalem of Problems," *Davar*, October 13, 1967.

20. Nachman Ben-Yehuda, "The Sociology of Moral Panics: Toward a New Synthesis," *Sociological Quarterly* 27 (1986): 499–500; Argaman, *Cannabis, Marijuana and Hashish*, 290.

21. Aharon Bachar, "Beware of the Brown Gold," *Yedi'ot Ahronot*, June 9, 1970. See also Ilan Cohen, "The Drug Problem Penetrating High Society and the Universities," *Yedi'ot Ahronot*, January 26, 1971; Yaakov Shoshan, "Greater Israel and the Drug Scene," *Yedi'ot Ahronot*, December 20, 1968.

22. See, e.g., Zvi Rimon, "'The Ugly Volunteer' Dropped Out of Sight," *Yedi'ot Ahronot*, June 21, 1968; Zvi Rimon, "Youngsters and the Drug Scene," *Yedi'ot Ahronot*, November 19, 1969.

23. Rory MacLean, *Magic Bus: On the Hippie Trail from Istanbul to India* (London: Penguin, 2006).

24. Don David, "The Hippies Come to Israel," *Israel Magazine* 3 (1970): 69–78.

25. Aviezer Golan, "Those Who Drug Themselves to Extremes," *Yedi'ot Ahronot*, May 8, 1964.

26. "Hashish Worth 20 Thousand Israeli Pounds Seized," *Davar*, November 5, 1965; "Eleven Suspects Arrested in a Hunt after Drug Smokers in Eilat," *Davar*, March 29, 1966; "Hashish Discovered on Drifters in Eilat," April 12, 1966.

27. Gil Shefler, "Finding New Life as a Cult Classic," *Forward*, January 26, 2011,

http://forward.com/culture/film-tv/134946/finding-new-life-as-a-cult-classic/ (accessed April 9, 2020).

28. The movie was thought to be lost until it was rediscovered in 2010 and was screened for the midnight movie circuit in Tel Aviv. "The movie [then] became so popular that audiences began yelling back to the screen, screaming out some of the film's ham-fisted dialogue in the same way that audiences in the 70s used to do the same at crowded midnight movie screenings of The Rocky Horror Picture Show." Bryan Thomas, "'An American Hippie in Israel': 'Man, I Feel Really Turned On!'" *Night Flight*, May 16, 2015, http://nightflight.com/an-american-hippie-in-israel-man-i-feel-really-turned-on/ (accessed April 9, 2020).

29. Eliyahu Amikam, "Dangerous Drugs Are on the Knesset's Agenda," *Yedi'ot Ahronot*, May 21, 1970. For hippies smuggling hashish to the United States directly from Lebanon at about the same time, see Richard Stratton, *Smuggler's Blues: A True Story of the Hippie Mafia* (New York: Arcade Publishing, 2016), 118–68.

30. Haim Noy, "Drug Smugglers Pose as Students," *Yedi'ot Ahronot*, April 13, 1969.

31. Bachar, "Beware of Brown Gold."

32. See, e.g. "Home Factory Producing Hashish Cans Revealed," *Davar*, November 4, 1968; "A Police Officer from Denmark to Investigate Hashish Shipments in Mail," *Davar*, November 18, 1968; "Young Tourists Suspected of Possessing and Smuggling Hashish," *Davar*, April 21, 1969; "International Network of Hashish Smugglers Revealed in Tel Aviv," *Davar*, October 26, 1969; "A Canadian Tourist Suspected of Trying to Smuggle Hashish via Mail," *Davar*, November 3, 1969; "An American Trying to Smuggle Hashish to the U.S. Arrested," *Davar*, December 12, 1969; "A Canadian Tourist Suspected of Trying to Smuggle Hashish via Mail," *Davar*, November 3, 1969.

33. Amos Carmeli, "Hashish Invasion from Sea and Land," *Davar*, September 15, 1967; Pundak, "Hashish with Everything"; Pundak, "Sahara Number 1 Calling"; Shoshan, "Greater Israel and the Drug Scene."

34. Bachar, "Beware of Brown Gold."

35. "The Hard Results of 'Hard' Drugs," *Dorban* (student weekly), June 30, 1970; Nitza Yissasharov, "Drug Use Permeated Broad Swaths of the Affluent Classes in Israel," *Yedi'ot Ahronot*, January 20, 1976.

36. Ben-Yehuda, "Sociology of Moral Panics," 500.

37. Menachem Barash, "Eighty-Three Percent of School-Going Adolescents Are Opposed to Drug Use," *Yedi'ot Ahronot*, February 23, 1972.

38. Palgi, "Traditional Role," 215.

39. Aharon Shamir, "The Drug Affliction," *Yedi'ot Ahronot*, January 23, 1976.

40. "A Network of Drugs Suppliers at the Hebrew University," *Davar*, January 14, 1969; "Students and Hashish," *Davar*, February 6, 1969.

41. "Police Action against Drug Use by Students," *Knesset Proceedings: The 373rd Session of the Sixth Knesset*, February 10, 1969, 1466–67; "Use of Intoxicating Drugs by

Hebrew University Students," *Knesset Proceedings: The 384th Session of the Sixth Knesset*, March 10, 1969, 1833.

42. "Rector Forbids Students to Use Drugs," *Davar*, January 21, 1969; "Use of Intoxicating Drugs by Hebrew University Students," *Knesset Proceedings: The 384th Session of the Sixth Knesset*, March 10, 1969, 1833.

43. For a version of this law in English, see ISA, G-3/2906, Dangerous Drugs Ordinance (Amendment no. 2) Law, 5728–1968.

44. Knesset Member Avraham Tiar, "Proposed Bill for Dangerous Drugs Ordinance Amendment–1967 (the First Reading)," *Knesset Proceedings: The 231st Session of the Sixth Knesset*, December 19, 1967, 478.

45. "Proposed Bill for Dangerous Drugs Ordinance Amendment–1967," *Knesset Proceedings: The 189th Session of the Sixth Knesset*, June 28, 1967, 2435.

46. Ibid.

47. "Details of Police Handling of Cases of the Use of Dangerous Drugs by Adolescents," in *Knesset Proceedings: The 148th Session of the Sixth Knesset*, February 13, 1969, 1244.

48. "Proposed Bill for Dangerous Drugs Ordinance Amendment–1967," *Knesset Proceedings: The 189th Session of the Sixth Knesset*, June 28, 1967, 2435.

49. KM Menachem Hacohen, "Proposed Bill for Dangerous Drugs Ordinance Amendment–1967 (the First Reading)," *Knesset Proceedings: The 231st Session of the Sixth Knesset*, December 19, 1967, 479. See also Shlomo Cohen-Tzidon, "The Knesset, Protocol 73 of the Meeting of the Committee of Public Services, Proposed Bill for the Amendment of the Dangerous Drugs Ordinance—1966," July 25, 1967.

50. Aryeh Arad, "Interview with Prof. Ezra Zohar," *Davar*, March 28, 1969. See also criminal lawyer Zvi Lidski, cited in Aharon Bachar, "Loophole in the Law Attracts Drug Dealers," *Yedi'ot Ahronot*, January 13, 1969; Hadassah Mor, "Rebellion of Youth: Danger to the Establishment?" *Yedi'ot Ahronot*, April 9, 1971.

51. Yoram Kaniuk, "Hashish, Hashish," *Davar*, August 28, 1970.

52. Avi Ashkenazi, "Fines Instead of Handcuffs: Cannabis Users' Non-Criminalization Reform, the Complete Guide," *Walla*, March 31, 2019, http://news.walla.co.il/item/3227773 (accessed April 9, 2020).

53. Ruth Margalit, "Closure of Israel's Border with Egypt Seeds a New Domestic Industry: Homegrown Pot," *Tablet*, February 18, 2014, http://www.tabletmag.com/jewish-news-and-politics/163130/israels-drug-drought (accessed April 9, 2020).

54. Alpher, "What Really Unites Israel's Right, Left and Center."

55. The clip can be accessed on YouTube at http://www.youtube.com/watch?v=CcT2Jy8aFPs (accessed April 9, 2020).

56. Talal Asad, *On Suicide Bombing* (New York: Columbia University Press, 2003).

57. Haggai Ram, *Iranophobia: The Logic of an Israeli Obsession* (Stanford, CA: Stanford University Press, 2009), 73–95.

BIBLIOGRAPHY

ARCHIVES

Central Zionist Archives, Jerusalem
Haganah Historical Archive, Tel Aviv (HHA)
IDF and Defense Establishment Archives, Kiryat Ono
Israel Police Heritage Center, Beit Shemesh
Israel State Archives, Jerusalem (ISA)
Knesset Archives, Jerusalem
League of Nations Archive, Geneva (LNA)
Middle East Center Archive, St. Antony's College, Oxford, UK
National Archives of the United Kingdom, London (NA [UK])
National Archives and Records Administration of the United States, Washington and
    College Park, MD (NA [US])
National Army Museum, London
National Library of Israel, Hebrew University of Jerusalem, Jerusalem

NEWSPAPERS

ARABIC

Al-Ahram (Cairo)
Al-Difa' (Jaffa)
Filastin (Jaffa)
Al-Hayat (Beirut)
Al-Karmil (Haifa)
Al-Khamis (Jaffa)
Mir'at al-Sharq (Jerusalem)
Al-Mukattam (Cairo)
Roz al-Yusuf (Cairo)
Umm al-Qura (Mecca)

ENGLISH

Forward (NYC)

The Times (London)

Los Angeles Times

New York Herald Tribune

Palestine Post (Jerusalem)

Tablet (NYC)

The Times (London)

US News & World Report (Washington)

FRENCH

Revue (Paris)

HEBREW

'Al ha-Mishmar (Tel Aviv)

Davar (Tel Aviv)

Do'ar ha-Yom (Jerusalem)

Ha-Aretz (Tel Aviv)

Herut (Jerusalem)

Ha-Mashkif (Tel Aviv)

Ha-'Olam Ha-Zeh (Tel Aviv)

Ha-Tzofeh (Tel Aviv)

Hayei Sha'ah (Tel Aviv)

'Iton Meyuhad (Tel Aviv)

Ma'ariv (Tel Aviv)

Yedi'ot Ahronot (Tel Aviv)

PUBLISHED SOURCES

Abd al-Hamid Ahmad, Mahsan. *Arab Security Collaboration and the Security Challenges* (in Arabic). Riyadh: Markaz al-dirasat wa-al-buhuth, 1999.

Abraham, Itty, and Willem van Schendel. "Introduction: The Making of Illicitness." In *Illicit Flows and Criminal Things: States, Borders, and the Other Side of Globalization*, edited by Willem van Schendel and Itty Abraham, 1–37. Bloomington: Indiana University Press, 2005.

Abu-Amr, Ziad. "Hamas: A Historical and Political Background." *Journal of Palestine Studies* 22 (1993): 5–19.

Abu-Rish, Ziad. "Review of Jonathan Marshall, *The Lebanese Connection: Corruption, Civil War, and the International Drug Traffic.*" *International Journal of Middle East Studies* 46 (2014): 414–16.

The Adventures of Gad Magen: Abdul Ma'ti's Emissary (in Hebrew). Tel Aviv: Hotza'a ha-Me'a ha-'Esrim, 1947.

The Adventures of Gad Magen: Gad Escapes Trouble (in Hebrew). Tel Aviv: Hotza'a ha-Me'a ha-'Esrim, 1947.

The Adventures of Gad Magen: Hashish and Murder (in Hebrew). Tel Aviv: Hotza'a ha-Me'a ha-'Esrim, 1947.

Afifi, Mohammed, Mahmoud Al-Zuheiri, Violet Fasheh, and Salah El-Sousi. "Drug Abuse: Problems, Policies, and Programs in Palestine." In *Drug Problems: Cross-Cultural Policy and Program Development*, Kindle edition, edited by Richard Isralowitz, Mohammed Afifi, and Richard Rawson. Westport, CT: Auburn House, 2002.

Alon, Yoav. "Bridging Imperial, National, and Local Historiographies: Britons, Arabs, and Jews in the Mandate Palestine Police," *Jerusalem Quarterly* 75 (2018): 62–77.

Alyagon, Orna Darr. *Plausible Crime Stories: The Legal History of Sexual Offences in Mandate Palestine.* Cambridge: Cambridge University Press, 2019.

"Animals: First-Rate Criminals" (in Hebrew). *999* 7 (1956): 8–9.

Anslinger, Harry J., and Courtney Ryley Cooper. "Marijuana: Assassin of Youth." *American Magazine*, July 1937, https://www.redhousebooks.com/galleries/assassin.htm. Accessed April 9, 2020.

Appadurai, Arjun. "Introduction: Commodities and the Political Value." In *The Social Life of Things: Commodities in Cultural Perspective*, edited by Arjun Appadurai, 3–63. Cambridge: Cambridge University Press, 1986.

Argaman, Moti. *Cannabis, Marijuana and Hashish* (in Hebrew). Tel Aviv: Gal, 1997.

Ariel, Y. "The Tricks of Concealment and Discovery" (in Hebrew). *Israel Police Quarterly* 5 (April 1957): 48–59.

Arnold, Guy. *The International Drugs Trade.* New York: Routledge, 2005.

Asad, Talal. *On Suicide Bombing.* New York: Columbia University Press, 2003.

Atwan, Robert, and Laura Wieder, eds. *A Selection of Poetry in English Inspired by the Bible from Genesis through Revelation.* New York: Oxford University Press, 2000.

Ayalon, Ami. *The Arabic Print Revolution: Cultural Production and Mass Readership.* Cambridge: Cambridge University Press, 2016.

Aynur, Hatice, and Jan Schmidt. "A Debate between Opium, Berş, Hashish, Boza, Wine and Coffee: The Use and Perception of Pleasurable Substances among Ottomans." *Journal of Turkish Studies* 31 (2007): 51–117.

Bailey, Clinton. *The Magic of Camel-Mares: Bedouin Poetry from Sinai to the Negev* (in Hebrew). Beit Berl, Israel: Institute for Israeli Arab Studies, 1993.

Ballas, Shimon. *In Front of the Wall: Stories* (in Hebrew). Ramat Gan, Israel: Massada, 1969.

——. *Tel Aviv East: Trilogy* (in Hebrew). Tel Aviv: Hakibbutz Hameuchad, 2003.

——. *The Transit Camp* (in Hebrew). Tel Aviv: 'Am 'Oved, 1964.

Banko, Lauren. "Keeping Out the 'Undesirable Elements': The Treatment of Communists, Transients, Criminals, and the Ill in Mandate Palestine." *Journal of Imperial and Commonwealth History* (2019): 1–28.

Bartels, Elizabeth. "Policing Politics: Crime and Conflict in British Mandate Palestine (1920–1948)." PhD diss., City University of New York, 2004.

Bashkin, Orit. *Impossible Exodus: Iraqi Jews in Israel.* Stanford, CA: Stanford University Press, 2017.

Becker, Howard S. "Becoming a Marijuana User." *American Journal of Sociology,* 59 (1953): 235–42.

Beckert, Sven. *Empire of Cotton: A Global History.* New York: Vintage, 2015.

Belgiojoso, Cristina. *Harems, Hashish, and Holy Men.* Kindle edition. Amazon Digital Services, [1858] 2012.

Benvenisti, Meron. *Sacred Landscape: The Buried History of the Holy Land since 1948.* Berkeley: University of California Press, 2002.

Ben-Yehuda, Nachman. "The Sociology of Moral Panics: Toward a New Synthesis." *Sociological Quarterly* 27 (1986): 495–513.

Bergman, Ronen, and Gil Meltzer. *The Yom Kippur War: Moments of Truth* (in Hebrew). Tel Aviv: Miskal-Yediot Ahronot Books, 2003.

Bernstein, Deborah. *Women on the Margins: Gender and Nationalism in Mandatory Tel Aviv* (in Hebrew). Jerusalem: Yad Ben Zvi, 2008.

Berridge, Virginia. "Drugs and Social Policy: The Establishment of Drug Control in Britain 1900–30." *Addiction* 79 (1984): 17–29.

———. *Opium and the People: Opiate Use and Drug Control Policy in Nineteenth- and Early Twentieth-Century England.* London: Free Association Books, 1999.

———. "Illicit Drugs and Internationalism: The Forgotten Dimension." *Medical History* 45 (2001): 282–88.

Blickman, Tom, Dave Bewley-Taylor, and Martin Jelsma. *The Rise and Decline of Cannabis Prohibition: The History of Cannabis in the U.N. Drug Control System and Options for Reform.* Amsterdam: Transnational Institute, 2014.

Block, Alan. "European Drug Traffic and Traffickers between the Wars: The Policy of Suppression and its Consequences." *Journal of Social History* 23 (1989): 315–27.

Blum, Benyamin. "The Hounds of Empire: Forensic Dog Tracking in Britain and Its Colonies, 1888–1953." *Law and History Review* 35 (2017): 621–65.

Boon, Marcus. *The Road of Excess: A History of Writers on Drugs.* Cambridge, MA: Harvard University Press, 2002.

Booth, Martin. *Opium: A History.* New York: St. Martin's Griffin, 1996.

Bourmaud, Phillipe. "Turf Wars at the League of Nations: International Anti-Cannabis Policies and Oversight in Syria and Lebanon, 1919–1939." In *The League of Nations' Work on Social Issues,* edited by Magaly Rodríguez García, Davide Rodogno, and Liat Kozma, 75–87. Geneva: United Nations Publications, 2016.

Boyarin, Daniel. *Unheroic Conduct: The Rise of Heterosexuality and the Invention of the Jewish Man*. Berkeley: University of California Press, 1997.

Bradford, James Tharin. *Poppies, Politics, and Power: Afghanistan and the Global History of Drugs and Diplomacy*. Ithaca, NY: Cornell University Press, 2019.

Broadhurst, Joseph F. *From Vine Street to Jerusalem*. London: Stanley Paul, 1936.

Buchman, Yael. *Pashas, Fellahs, and Pirates: A Window to the Ways of Life in the Land of Israel from the 16th to the 18th Centuries* (in Hebrew). Sde Ilan, Israel: Yeda ha-Aretz, 2013.

Çaksu, Ali. "Janissary Coffee Houses in Late Eighteenth-Century Istanbul." In *Ottoman Tulips, Ottoman Coffee: Leisure and Lifestyle in the Eighteenth Century*, edited by Dana Sajdi, 117–32. London: I. B. Tauris, 2007.

Camporesi, Piero. *Bread of Dreams: Food and Fantasy in Early Modern Europe*, translated by David Gentilcore. Chicago: University of Chicago Press, 1996.

Campos, Isaac. *Home Grown: Marijuana and the Origins of Mexico's War on Drugs*. Chapel Hill: University of North Carolina Press, 2012.

———. "Mexicans and the Origins of Marijuana Prohibition in the United States: A Reassessment." *Social History of Alcohol and Drugs* 32 (2018): 6–37.

Campos, Michelle U. *Ottoman Brothers: Muslims, Christians, and Jews in Early Twentieth-Century Palestine*. Stanford, CA: Stanford University Press, 2011.

Carlson, John Roy. *Cairo to Damascus*. New York: Knopf, 1951.

Carnwath, Tom, and Ian Smith. *Heroin Century*. London and New York: Routledge, 2002.

Caspi, Joshua. *Dangerous Drugs: Policy, Control, Enforcement and Trial* (in Hebrew). Haifa: Tamar, 1996.

Chawla, Sandeep, and Thomas Pietschmann. "Drug Trafficking as a Transnational Crime." In *Handbook of Transnational Crime and Justice*, edited by Philip Reichel, 160–81. Thousand Oaks, CA, and London: Sage, 2005.

Chouvy, Pierre-Arnaud. *Opium: Uncovering the Politics of the Poppy*. London: I. B. Tauris, 2009.

Chouvy, Pierre-Arnaud, and Kenza Afsahi. "Hashish Revival in Morocco," *International Journal of Drug Policy* 25 (2014): 416–23.

Cleveland, William L., and Martin Bunton. *A History of the Modern Middle East*, sixth edition. Boulder, CO: Westview Press, 2016.

Cockburn, Alexander, and Jeffrey St. Clair. *Whiteout: The CIA, Drugs, and the Press*. London: Verso, 1998.

Cohen, Amnon. "Al-Nabi Musa: An Ottoman Festival (*Mawsim*) Resurrected." In *Mamluks and Ottomans: Studies in Honour of Michael Winter*, edited by David Wasserstein and Ami Ayalon, 44–54. London: Routledge, 2013.

Cohen, Arik. "Hashish and Hashishniks in Acre" (in Hebrew). *'Avaryanut ve-Hevra* 3 (1968): 34–39.

Cohen, Hillel. *Good Arabs: The Israeli Security Agencies and the Israeli Arabs, 1948–1967*, translated by Haim Watzman. Berkeley: University of California Press, 2011.

———. *Year Zero of the Arab Israeli Conflict, 1929*, translated by Haim Watzman. Lebanon, NH: Brandeis University Press, 2015.

Cohn, Bernard S. *Colonialism and Its Forms of Knowledge: The British in India*. Princeton, NJ: Princeton University Press, 1996.

Conrad, Sebastian. *What Is Global History?* Princeton, NJ: Princeton University Press, 2016.

Cotterell, Paul. *The Railways of Palestine and Israel*. Abingdon, UK: Tourret Publishing, 1984.

Courtwright, David. *Forces of Habit: Drugs and the Making of the Modern World*. Cambridge, MA: Harvard University Press, 2001.

Cowan, Brian. *The Social Life of Coffee: The Emergence of the British Coffeehouse*. New Haven, CT: Yale University Press, 2008.

Crowdy, Terry. *French Soldier in Egypt, 1798–1801: The Army of the Orient*. Oxford: Osprey Publishing, 2003.

Daftary, Farhad. "'Order of the Assassins': J. von Hammer and the Orientalist Misrepresentations of the Nizari Ismailis." *Iranian Studies* 39 (2006): 71–82.

Dahan-Kalev, Henriette. "The Wadi Salib Riots" (in Hebrew). *Te'oria u-Vikoret* 12 (1999): 149–57.

"Dangerous Drugs Ordinance 1925." *Palestine Gazette* 140 (June 1925): 249–52.

Davenport-Hines, Richard. *The Pursuit of Oblivion: A Global History of Narcotics*. New York: W. W. Norton, 2003.

David, Don. "The Hippies Come to Israel." *Israel Magazine* 3 (1970): 69–78.

Davidovitz, Flora K. *The Use of Cannabis for Medical Purposes in Israel and Recognized Indications of Cannabis for Medical Purposes in Different Countries* (in Hebrew). Jerusalem: Knesset Research and Information Center, 2015.

De Monfreid, Henry. *Hashish: A Smuggler's Tale*. London: Penguin, 2007 [1935].

D'Erlanger, Baron Harry. *The Last Plague of Egypt*. London: L. Dickson and Thompson, 1936.

Dikötter, Frank, Lars Peter Laamann, and Zhou Xun. *Narcotic Culture: A History of Drugs in China*. Chicago: University of Chicago Press, 2004.

Dirks, Nicholas B. Foreword to *Colonialism and Its Forms of Knowledge*, by Bernard S. Cohn. Princeton, NJ: Princeton University Press, 1996.

Drapkin, Israel, and Simha F. Landau. "Drug Offenders in Israel: A Survey." *British Journal of Criminology* 6 (1966): 376–90.

"Drug Trafficking in Palestine." In *The King's Royal Rifle Corps Chronicles, 1936*. Winchester, UK: Warren & Son, 1937.

Duff, Douglas V. *Galilee Galloper*. London: John Murray, 1935.

———. *Sword for Hire: The Saga of a Modern Free-Companion*. London: John Murray, 1934.

Dufton, Emily. *Grass Roots: The Rise and Fall and Rise of Marijuana in America*. New York: Basic Books, 2017.

Dunevitch, Natan. "In the Dens of Drug Smokers (in Hebrew)." *999* 7 (August 1953): 5–7, 24.

Dykmann, Klaas. "How International Was the Secretariat of the League of Nations?" *International History Review* 37 (2015): 721–44.

Edwards, Martin. *The Golden Age of Murder: The Mystery of the Writers Who Invented the Modern Detective Story*. London: HarperCollins, 2015.

Ehrenreich, Barabara. *Blood Rites: Origins and History of the Passions of War*. London: Virago, 1997.

Elisha, David, Jorge Gleser, and Michael Reiter. "Patterns, Policies, and Treatment Strategies of Substance Abuse in Israel: Past and Present." In *Drug Problems: Cross-Cultural Policy and Program Development*, Kindle edition, edited by Afifi Isralowitz and Richard Rawson. Westport, CT: Auburn House, 2002.

Ergut, Ferdan. "Policing the Poor in the Late Ottoman Empire." *Middle Eastern Studies* 38 (2002): 149–64.

Eyal, Gil. *The Disenchantment of the Orient: Expertise in Arab Affairs and the Israeli State*. Stanford, CA: Stanford University Press, 2006.

Fabris, Antonio, ed. *Cristina Trivulzio Di Belgiojoso: An Italian Princess in the 19th C. Turkish Countryside*. Venice: Filippi Editore Venezia, 2010.

Feldman, Ilana. *Police Encounters: Security and Surveillance in Gaza under Egyptian Rule*. Stanford, CA: Stanford University Press, 2015.

Fletcher, Robert S. G. *British Imperialism and "the Tribal Question": Desert Administration and Nomadic Societies in the Middle East*. Oxford: Oxford University Press, 2015.

Floor, Willem. "The Art of Smoking in Iran and Other Uses of Tobacco." *Iranian Studies* 35 (2002): 47–85.

Foster, Zachary. "Are Lod and Ramla the Drug Capitals of Israel and Palestine?" *Palestine Square*, December 30, 2015, https://palestinesquare.com/2015/12/30/are-lod-and-ramla-the-drug-capitals-of-israel-and-palestine/. Accessed April 9, 2020.

———. "Illicit Drug Trafficking and Use in British Mandatory Palestine." Unpublished paper, 2010.

Friedland, Roger, and Richard Hecht. "The Nebi Musa Pilgrimage and the Origins of Palestinian Nationalism." In *Pilgrims and Travelers to the Holy Land*, edited by B. F. Le Beau and M. Mor, 89–118. Omaha: Creighton University Press, 1996.

Gelper, Shlomo. *The Blue Crosses: The Tales of Hashish Smugglers* (in Hebrew). Tel Aviv: Ha-Balash, 1932.

Gelvin, James. "The League of Nations and the Question of National Identity in the Fertile Crescent." *World Affairs* 158 (1995): 35–43.

———. *The Modern Middle East: A History*. New York: Oxford University Press, 2005.

———. "Was There a Mandates Period? Some Concluding Thoughts." In *The Routledge*

Handbook of the History of the Middle East Mandates, edited by Cyrus Schayegh and Andrew Arsan, 420–32. New York: Routledge, 2015.

Ghiabi, Maziyar, "Deorientalizing Drugs in the Modern Middle East. In *OUP Handbook of Global Drug History*, edited by Paul Gootenberg. Oxford: Oxford University Press, forthcoming.

———. *Drug Politics: Managing Disorder in the Islamic Republic of Iran*. Cambridge: Cambridge University Press, 2019.

———. "Drugs and Revolution in Iran: Islamic Devotion, Revolutionary Zeal and Republican Means." *Iranian Studies* 48 (2015): 139–63.

Ghiabi, Maziyar, Masoomeh Maarefand, Hamed Bahari, and Zohreh Alavi. "Islam and Cannabis: Legalization and Religious Debate in Iran." *International Journal of Drug Policy* 56 (2018): 121–27.

Gilman, Sander. *The Jew's Body*. New York: Routledge, 1991.

Gingeras, Ryan. *Heroin, Organized Crime, and the Making of Modern Turkey*. Oxford: Oxford University Press, 2014.

Gluzman, Michael. *The Zionist Body: Nationalism, Gender and Sexuality in Modern Hebrew Prose* (in Hebrew). Tel Aviv: Hakibbutz Hameuchad, 2007.

Goodman, Jordan. *Tobacco in History: The Cultures of Dependence*. London and New York: Routledge, 2005.

Gootenberg, Paul. *Andean Cocaine: The Making of a Global Drug*. Chapel Hill: University of North Carolina Press, 2008.

———. "Talking about the Flow: Drugs, Borders, and the Discourse of Drug Control." *Cultural Critique* 71 (2009): 13–46.

Gootenberg, Paul, and Isaac Campos. "Toward a New Drug History of Latin America: A Research Frontier at the Center of Debates." *Hispanic and American Historical Review* 95 (2015): 1–35.

Green, Nile. "Breaking the Begging Bowl: Morals, Drugs, and Madness in the Fate of the Muslim Faqīr." *South Asian History and Culture* 5 (2014): 226–45.

Grehan, James. "Smoking and 'Early Modern' Sociability: The Great Tobacco Debate in the Ottoman Middle East (Seventeenth to Eighteenth Centuries)." *American Historical Review* 111 (2006): 1352–77.

Guba, David A. "Antoine Isaac Silvestre de Sacy and the Myth of the Hachichins: Orientalizing Hashish in 19th-Century France." *Social History of Alcohol and Drugs* 30 (2016): 50–74.

Guo, Li. "Paradise Lost: Ibn Dāniyāl's Response to Baybars' Campaign against Vice in Cairo." *Journal of the American Oriental Society* 121 (2001): 219–35.

Gürsoy, Özgür Burçak. "The Opium Problem in Turkey, 1930–1945." MA thesis, Boğaziçi University, 2007.

Hadka, A. "Forty Years of the Campaign against Narcotic Drugs in the United Arab Republic." *Bulletin on Narcotics* 17 (1965): 1–12.

Halpern, Yirmiyahu. *The Revival of Hebrew Shipping* (in Hebrew). Tel Aviv: Hadar, 1960.

Haramati, Michal. "The Theory of Autochthonous Zionism in Political Discourse in Israel, 1961–1967." *Journal of Spatial and Organizational Dynamics* 6 (2018): 112–39.

Harel-Fisch, Yossi, and Yaakov Ezrahi. *Psychoactive Drug Use among the Adult Population in Israel: National Epidemiological Survey of 2016* (in Hebrew). Jerusalem: Israel Anti-Drug Authority, 2017.

Hari, Johann. *Chasing the Scream: The First and Last Days of the War on Drugs*. New York: Bloomsbury, 2015.

Harouvi, Eldad. *Palestine Investigated: The CID in Eretz Yisrael, 1920–1948* (in Hebrew). Tzur Yigal, Israel: Porath Publishing, 2011.

Harrison, Joseph. "Illegal Drug Use by Israeli Youth." *Addiction* 70 (1975): 335–37.

Harwich, A. E. "A Method of Detecting Hashish," *Palestine Police Magazine* 1 (1933): 14–16.

Hasan, Manar. *Hidden from View: Women and Palestinian Cities* (in Hebrew). Tel Aviv: Van Leer and Hakibbutz Hameuchad, 2017.

Hattox, Ralph. *Coffee and Coffeehouses: The Origins of a Social Beverage in the Medieval Near East*. Seattle: University of Washington Press, 1985.

Helman, Anat. *Young Tel Aviv: A Tale of Two Cities*, translated by Haim Watzman. Waltham, MA: Brandeis University Press, 2010.

Heshbaya, Aryeh. "Infiltration by Sea" (in Hebrew). *999* 9 (October 1953): 9–10.

Hever, Hannan. *Producing the Modern Hebrew Canon: Nation Building and Minority Discourse*. New York: New York University Press, 2002.

———. "Yitzhak Shami: Ethnicity as an Unresolved Conflict." *Shofar* 24 (2006): 124–39.

Hever, Hannan, and Yehouda Shenhav. "Shimon Ballas: Colonialism and *Mizrahiyut* in Israel" (in Hebrew). *Teòria u-Vikoret* 20 (2002): 289–303.

Hillard, Charles, ed. *Selection of 19th-Century British Press Cuttings on the Subject of Cannabis*. Kindle edition. Self-publication, 2011.

Himmelstein, Jerome L. "From Killer Weed to Drop-Out Drug: The Changing Ideology of Marihuana." *Contemporary Crises* 7 (1983): 13–38.

Hirsch, Dafna. "'Hummus Is Best When It Is Fresh and Made by Arabs': The Gourmetization of Hummus in Israel and the Return of the Repressed Arab." *American Ethnologist* 38 (2011): 617–30.

Hobsbawm, Eric. *Nations and Nationalism since 1780: Program, Myth, Reality*. Cambridge: Cambridge University Press, 1990.

Hod, Elie, and Erella Shadmi. *History of Israel Police, Vol. 1: The Foundation Stage, 1948–1958* (in Hebrew). Jerusalem: Israel Police Human Resources Division, History Department, 2004.

Hopshteter, Ephraim. "International Police and Israel Police" (in Hebrew). *999* 3 (April 1953): 23–24.

Horne, Edward. *A Job Well Done (Being a History of the Palestine Police Force 1920–1948)*. Essex, UK: Anchor Press, 1982.

Ilany, Ofri. "'An Oriental Vice': Representations of Homosexuality in the Hebrew Press of the British Mandate Era." In *Sexuality in Transregional Perspective: The Homophobic Argument*, edited by Achim Rhode, Christina von Braun, and Stefanie Schüler-Springorumm, 107–20. New York: Routledge, 2017.

The Imperial Ottoman Penal Code, translated and annotated by John A. Strachey Bucknill and Haig Apisoghom S. Utidjian. London: Oxford University Press, 1913.

Israel Police. *Annual Report for 1948* (in Hebrew). Tel Aviv, 1949.

———. *Annual Report for 1949* (in Hebrew). Tel Aviv, 1950.

———. *Annual Report for 1951* (in Hebrew). Tel Aviv, 1952.

———. *Annual Report for 1953* (in Hebrew). Tel Aviv, 1954.

———. *Annual Report for 1954* (in Hebrew). Tel Aviv, 1955.

———. *Annual Report for 1955* (in Hebrew). Tel Aviv, 1956.

———. *Annual Report for 1957* (in Hebrew). Tel Aviv, 1958.

———. *Annual Report for 1958* (in Hebrew). Tel Aviv, 1959.

———. *Annual Report for 1960* (in Hebrew). Tel Aviv, 1961.

———. "The First Decade of Israel Police" (in Hebrew). *Annual Report for 1957*. Tel Aviv, 1958.

———. "Twenty Years of Israel Police" (in Hebrew). *Annual Report for 1968*. Tel Aviv: Yefet Publishing, 1969.

Jacobson, Abigail. "Sephardim, Ashkenazim and the 'Arab Question' in Pre-First World War Palestine: A Reading of Three Zionist Newspapers." *Middle Eastern Studies* 39 (2003): 105–30.

———. *From Empire to Empire: Jerusalem between Ottoman and British Rule*. Syracuse, NY: Syracuse University Press, 2011.

———. "Practices of Citizenship and Loyalty to Empire: The Movement of Ottomanization as a Case Study" (in Hebrew). In *Zionism and Empires*, edited by Yehouda Shenhav, 159–82. Tel Aviv: Van Leer and Hakibbutz Hameuchad, 2015.

Jacobson, Abigail, and Moshe Naor. *Oriental Neighbors: Middle Eastern Jews and Arabs in Mandatory Palestine*. Waltham, MA: Brandeis University Press, 2016.

Jarvis, C. S. "Sinai," *Journal of the Royal Central Asian Society* 22 (1935): 32–51.

Jay, Mike. *Emperors of Dreams: Drugs in the Nineteenth Century*. Sawtry, UK: Dedalus, 2000.

Kafadar, Cemal. "A History of Coffee," *The XIIIth Congress of the International Economic History Association (IEHA)*, 2002.

Kamieński, Łukasz. *Shooting Up: A Short History of Drugs and War*. New York: Oxford University Press, 2016.

Karababa, Emınegül, and Gülız Ger. "Early Modern Ottoman Coffeehouse Culture and the Formation of the Consumer Subject." *Journal of Consumer Research* 37 (2011): 737–60.

Karamustafa, Ahmet T. *God's Unruly Friends: Dervish Groups in the Islamic Later Middle Period, 1200–1550*. Salt Lake City: University of Utah Press, 1994.

Kaufman, Yehuda. "Dangerous Drugs" (in Hebrew). *999* 4 (May 1953): 14–15.

Kaufman, Yehuda, and David Ginsburg. "Smuggling Dangerous Drugs" (in Hebrew). *999* 6 (July 1955): 12.

Keire, Mara L. "Dope Fiends and Degenerates: The Gendering of Addiction in the Early Twentieth Century." *Journal of Social History* 31 (1998): 809–22.

Keller, Richard C. *Colonial Madness: Psychiatry in French North Africa*. Chicago: University of Chicago Press, 2007.

Kelly, Matthew Kraig. *The Crime of Nationalism: Britain, Palestine, and Nation-Building on the Fringe of Empire*. Oakland, CA: University of California Press, 2017.

Kendell, Robert. "Cannabis Condemned: The Proscription of Indian Hemp." *Addiction* 98 (2003): 143–51.

Khairallah, Shereen. *Railways in the Middle East, 1856–1948: Political and Economic Background*. Beirut: Librairie Du Liban, 1991.

Khalifa, Ahmad M. "Traditional Patterns of Hashish Use in Egypt." In *Cannabis and Culture*, edited by Vera Rubin, 195–205. The Hague: Mouton, 1975.

Khater, Akram Fouad. "'House' to 'Goddess of the House': Gender, Class, and Silk in 19th-Century Mount Lebanon." *International Journal of Middle East Studies* 28 (1996): 325–48.

Khazzoom, Aziza. "The Great Chain of Orientalism: Jewish Identity, Stigma Management, and Ethnic Exclusion in Israel." *American Sociological Review* 4 (2003): 481–510.

Khoury, Elias. *Bundle of Secrets* (in Arabic). Beirut: Dar al-Adab, 1994.

Kia, Mehrdad. *Daily Life in the Ottoman Empire*. Santa Barbara, CA: Greenwood Press, 2011.

Kimmerling, Baruch. *Immigrants, Settlers, Natives: The Israeli State and Society between Cultural Pluralism and Cultural Wars* (in Hebrew). Tel Aviv: 'Am 'Oved, 2004.

Kirli, Cengiz. "Coffeehouses: Leisure and Sociability in Ottoman Istanbul." In *Leisure Cultures in Urban Europe, c. 1700–1870: A Transnational Perspective*, edited by Peter Borsay and Jan Hein Furnée, 161–81. Manchester, UK: Manchester University Press, 2016.

Klein, Menachem. *Lives in Common: Arabs and Jews in Jerusalem, Jaffa and Hebron*. Oxford: Oxford University Press, 2014.

Knepper, Paul. "Dreams and Nightmares: Drug Trafficking and the History of International Crime." In *The Oxford Handbook of the History and Crime and Criminal Justice*, edited by Paul Knepper and Anja Johansen, 208–25. Oxford: Oxford University Press, 2016.

———. *International Crime in the Twentieth Century: The League of Nations Era, 1919–1939*. London: Palgrave, 2011.

Knight, John. "The Successful Failure of Reform: Police Legitimacy in British Palestine." In *The Routledge Handbook of the History of Middle East Mandates*, edited by Cyrus Schayegh and Andrew Arsan, 198–211. New York: Routledge, 2015.

Kolinsky, Martin. *Law, Order and Riots in Mandatory Palestine, 1928–35*. London: St. Martin's Press, 1993.

Koren, Yeshayahu. *Those Who Stand at Night* (in Hebrew). Tel Aviv: Hakibbutz Hameuchad, 1992.

Korf, Dirk J. "Dutch Coffee Shops and Trends in Cannabis Use." *Addictive Behaviors* 27 (2002): 851–56.

Kozma, Liat. "Cannabis Prohibition in Egypt, 1880–1939: From Local Ban to League of Nations Diplomacy." *Middle Eastern Studies* 47 (2011): 443–60.

———. *Global Women, Colonial Ports: Prostitution in the Interwar Middle East*. Albany: State University of New York Press, 2017.

———. "The League of Nations and the Debate over Cannabis Prohibition." *History Compass* 9 (2011): 61–70.

———. "White Drugs in Interwar Egypt: Decadent Pleasures, Emaciated Fellahin, and the Campaign against Drugs." *Comparative Studies of South Asia, Africa and the Middle East* 33 (2013): 89–101.

Kramer, John C. "Opium Rampant: Medical Use, Misuse and Abuse in Britain and the West in the 17th and 18th Centuries." *British Journal of Addiction* 74 (1979): 377–89.

Lane, Edward William. *An Account of the Manners and Customs of the Modern Egyptians*. The Hague and London: East-West Publications, 1989 [1836].

"Lebanon-Israel Drug Connection." *Journal of Palestine Studies* 13 (1984): 169.

Legg, Stephen. "'The Life of Individuals as Well as of Nations': International Law and the League of Nations' Anti-Trafficking Governmentalities." *Leiden Journal of International Law* 25 (2012), 647–64.

Lepore, Jill. *These Truths: A History of the United States*. New York and London: W. W. Norton, 2018.

Levenkron, Nomi. "Between the Manifest and the Hidden: Historiography of Israel Police in the First Decade" (in Hebrew). *Mishtara ve-Historia* 1 (2019): 17–49.

LeVine, Mark. *Overthrowing Geography: Jaffa, Tel Aviv, and the Struggle for Palestine, 1880–1948*. Los Angeles: University of California Press, 2005.

Lev Tov, Boaz. "Leisure and Popular Cultural Patterns of Eretz Israeli Jews in the Years 1882–1914 as a Reflection of Social Changes" (in Hebrew). PhD dissertation, Tel Aviv University, 2009.

Levy-Aksu, Noémi. *Ordre et désordres dans l'Istanbul ottoman, 1879–1909*. Paris: Karthala, 2012.

Levy, Lital. "Reorienting Hebrew Literary History: The View from the East." *Prooftexts* 29 (2009): 127–72.

Lewy, Jonathan. "The Drug Policy of the Third Reich." *Social History of Alcohol and Drugs* 22 (2008): 144–67.

Lincoln, Bruce. "An Early Moment in the Discourse of 'Terrorism': Reflections of a Tale from Marco Polo." *Comparative Studies in Society and History* 48 (2006): 242–59.

Lockman, Zachary. *Comrades and Enemies: Arab and Jewish Workers in Palestine, 1906–1948*. Berkeley: University of California Press, 1996.

Maalouf, Amin. *The Crusades through Arab Eyes*. New York: Schocken Books, 1987.

MacLean, Rory. *Magic Bus: On the Hippie Trail from Istanbul to India*. London: Penguin, 2006.

Magen, Yosef. "The Young Ones" (in Hebrew). *999* 1 (February 1953): 15, 31.

Mamdani, Mahmood. *Good Muslim, Bad Muslim: America, the Cold War, and the Roots of Terror*. New York: Pantheon Books, 2004.

Manganaro, Elise Salem. "Voicing the Arab: Multivocality and Ideology in Leon Uris' *The Haj*," *MELUS* 15 (1988), 3–13.

Marshall, Jonathon. *The Lebanese Connection: Corruption, Civil War, and the International Drug Traffic*. Stanford, CA: Stanford University Press, 2012.

Marx, Emanuel. "Hashish Smuggling by Bedouin in South Sinai." In *Organized Crime: Culture, Markets and Policies*, edited by Dina Siegel and Hans Nelen, 29–37. New York: Springer, 2008.

Massad, Joseph. "Zionism's Internal Others: Israel and the Oriental Jews." *Journal of Palestine Studies* 25 (1996): 53–68.

Mathew, Johan. *Margins of the Market: Trafficking and Capitalism across the Arabian Sea*. Oakland: University of California Press, 2016.

———."Smoke on the Water: Cannabis Smuggling, Corruption and the Janus-Faced Colonial State," *History Workshop Journal* 86 (2018): 67–89.

Matthee, Rudi. *The Pursuit of Pleasure: Drugs and Stimulants in Iranian History, 1500–1900*. Princeton, NJ: Princeton University Press, 2005.

———. "Tobacco in Iran." In *Smoke: A Global History of Smoking*, edited by Sander L. Gilman and Zhou Xun, 58–67. London: Reaktion Books, 2004.

McAllister, William B. *Drug Diplomacy in the Twentieth Century*. London: Routledge, 2000.

McClintock, Anne. *Imperial Leather: Race, Gender, and Sexuality in the Colonial Contest*. New York: Routledge, 1995.

Meyer, Kathryn, and Terry Parssinen. *Webs of Smoke: Smugglers, Warlords, Spies, and the History of the International Drug Trade*. Lanham, MD: Rowman & Littlefield Publishers, 2002.

"The Middle East Narcotics Survey Mission (September–October 1959) of the UN." *UNODC*, January 1, 1960, https://www.unodc.org/unodc/en/data-and-analysis/bulletin/bulletin_1960-01-01_4_page006.html. Accessed April 8, 2020.

Mikhail, Alan. "The Heart's Desire: Gender, Urban Space and the Ottoman Coffee House." In *Ottoman Tulips, Ottoman Coffee: Leisure and Lifestyle in the Eighteenth Century*, edited by Dana Sajdi, 133–70. London: I. B. Tauris, 2014.

Mills, James H. *Madness, Cannabis and Colonialism: The "Native Only" Lunatic Asylums of British India, 1857–1900*. London: Palgrave, 2000.

——. *Cannabis Britannica: Empire, Trade, and Prohibition*. Oxford: Oxford University Press, 2003.

——. "Colonial Africa and the International Politics of Cannabis: Egypt, South Africa and the Origins of Global Control." In *Drugs and Empires: Essays in Modern Imperialism and Intoxication, c. 1500–c. 1930*, edited by James H. Mills and Patricia Barton, 165–84. London: Palgrave, 2007.

——. *Cannabis Nation: Control and Consumption in Britain, 1928–2008*. Oxford: Oxford University Press, 2013.

Mishani, Dror. "Why the Mizrahim Should Return to 'The Transit Camp'" (in Hebrew). *Mi-Ta'am* 3 (2005): 91–98.

Mitchell, Timothy. "The World as Exhibition." *Comparative Studies in Society and History* 31 (1989), 217–36.

Monterescu, Daniel. "The Bridled Bride of Palestine: Orientalism, Zionism, and the Troubled Urban Imagination." *Identities* 16 (2009): 643–77.

——. *Jaffa Shared and Shattered: Contrived Coexistence in Israel/Palestine*. Bloomington and Indianapolis: Indiana University Press, 2015.

Monterescu, Daniel, and Haim Hazan. *Twilight Nationalism: Politics of Existence at Life's End*. Stanford, CA: Stanford University Press, 2018.

Moore, Sally Falk. "Explaining the Present: Theoretical Dilemmas in Processual Ethnography." *American Ethnologist* 14 (1987): 727–36.

Morgan, H. Wayne. *Drugs in America: A Social History, 1800–1980*. Syracuse, NY: Syracuse University Press, 1981.

Morris, Benny. *The Birth of the Palestinian Refugee Problem Revisited*. Cambridge, UK: Cambridge University Press, 2004.

——. *Israel's Border Wars, 1949–1956: Arab Infiltration, Israeli Retaliation, and the Countdown to the Suez War*. Oxford: Oxford University Press, 1993.

Musari, R. "Criminal Way of Life under the Naguib Regime" (in Hebrew)." *999* 6 (July 1953): 23–24.

Nahas, Gabriel. "Hashish and Drug Abuse in Egypt during the 19th and 20th Centuries." *Bulletin of the New York Academy of Medicine* 61 (1985): 428–44.

——. "Hashish in Islam 9th to 18th century." *Bulletin of the New York Academy of Medicine* 58 (1982): 814–31.

Nasasra, Mansour. "Bedouin Tribes in the Middle East and the Naqab: Changing Dynamics and the New State." In *The Naqab Bedouin and Colonialism: New Perspectives*, edited by Mansour Nasasra, Sophie Richter-Devroe, Sarab Abu-Rabia-Queder and Richard Ratcliffe, 35–56. New York: Routledge, 2015.

——. *The Naqab Bedouins: A Century of Politics and Resistance*. New York: Columbia University Press, 2017.

Osterhammel, Jürgen. *The Transformation of the World: A Global History of the Nineteenth Century*. Princeton, NJ: Princeton University Press, 2014.

Palgi, Phyllis. "The Traditional Role and Symbolism of Hashish among Moroccan Jews in Israel and the Effect of Acculturation." In *Cannabis and Culture*, edited by Vera Rubin, 207–16. The Hague: Mouton, 1975.

Pappé, Ilan. *The Forgotten Palestinians: A History of the Palestinians in Israel*. New Haven, CT: Yale University Press, 2011.

Patai, Raphael. *The Jewish Mind*. Detroit: Wayne State University Press, 1977.

Paz, Omri, "Crime, Criminals, and the Ottoman State: Anatolia between the Late 1830s and the Late 1860s." PhD dissertation, Tel Aviv University, 2011.

Pedersen, Susan. "Back to the League of Nations: Review Essay." *American Historical Review* 112 (2007): 1091–1117.

Peele, Stanton. *The Meaning of Addiction: An Unconventional View*. New York: Lexington Books, 1985.

Péri, Benedek. "'It Is the Weed of Lovers': The Use of Cannabis among Turkic Peoples up to the 15th Century." *Acta Orientalia Academiae Scientiarum Hung* 69 (2016): 139–55.

Petersen, Andrew. "A Preliminary Report of Three Muslim Shrines in Palestine." *Levant* 28 (1996): 97–113.

Phillips, Norman. *Guns, Drugs and Deserters: The Special Investigation Branch in the Middle East*. London: Werner Laurie, 1954.

Piccato, Pablo. *A History of Infamy: Crime, Truth, and Justice in Mexico*. Oakland: University of California Press, 2017.

Pinhas, Shira, "Road, Map: Partition in Palestine from the Local to the Transnational." *Journal of Levantine Studies* 10, forthcoming.

Police Annual Report for 1968 (in Hebrew). Tel Aviv: Planning and Operations Department, 1969.

Poroy, Ibrahim I. "Expansion of Opium Production in Turkey and the State of Monopoly of 1828–1839." *International Journal of Middle East Studies* 13 (1981): 191–211.

Rabinowitz, Dan. *Overlooking Nazareth: The Ethnography of Exclusion in Galilee*. Cambridge: Cambridge University Press, 1997.

Radai, Itamar. "The Collapse of the Palestinian-Arab Middle Class in 1948: The Case of Qatamon," *Middle East Journal* 43 (2007): 961–82.

——. "The Rise and Fall of the Palestinian-Arab Middle Class under the British Mandate, 1920–1939," *Journal of Contemporary History* 51 (2016): 487–506.

Ram, Haggai. *Iranophobia: The Logic of an Israeli Obsession*. Stanford, CA: Stanford University Press, 2009.

——. "Middle East Drug Cultures: The Long View." In *OUP Handbook to Global Drug History*, edited by Paul Gootenberg. New York: Oxford University Press, forthcoming.

——. "On Sleuth Literature, Border-Crossings, and Crime in Mandatory Palestine" (in Hebrew). *Jama'a* 21 (2015): 119–31.

———. "Travelling Substances and Their Human Carriers: Hashish-Trafficking in Mandatory Palestine." In *A Global Middle East: Mobility, Materiality and Culture in the Modern Age, 1880–1940*, edited by Liat Kozma, Avner Wishnitzer, Cyrus Schayegh London, 201–28. I. B. Tauris, 2014.

Razin, Raphael. "Helping the Investigator with Police Dogs" (in Hebrew). *Israel Police Quarterly* 20–21 (December 1965): 23–26.

Regavim, Ram B. "The Most Sovereign of Masters: The History of Opium in Modern Iran, 1850–1955." PhD dissertation, University of Pennsylvania, 2012.

Robins, Philip. "Drugs of Choice, Drugs of Change: Egyptian Consumption Habits since the 1920s," *Third World Quarterly* 39 (2018), 248–60.

———. *Middle East Drugs Bazaar: Production, Prevention and Consumption.* Oxford: Oxford University Press, 2016.

Robinson, Shira. *Citizen Strangers: Palestinians and the Birth of Israel's Liberal Settler State.* Stanford, CA: Stanford University Press, 2013.

Roby, Bryan K. *Mizrahi Era of Rebellion: Israel's Forgotten Civil Rights Struggle, 1948–1966.* Syracuse, NY: Syracuse University Press, 2015.

Rodríguez-García, Magaly, Davide Rodogno, and Liat Kozma. Introduction to *The League of Nations' Work on Social Issues: Visions, Endeavors and Experiments*, edited by Magaly Rodríguez-Garcia, Davide Rodogno, and Liat Kozma, 13–38. Geneva: United Nations Publications, 2016.

Rogan, Eugene. *The Fall of the Ottomans: The Great War in the Middle East, 1914–1920.* London: Penguin, 2015.

———. "The Palestine Police Oral History Project." *CBRL Bulletin* 2 (2007): 35–40.

Rolo, J. V. "Russell, Sir Thomas Wentworth (1879-1954)." *Oxford Dictionary of National Biography.* Oxford: Oxford University Press, 2004, https://www.oxforddnb.com/view/10.1093/ref:odnb/9780198614128.001.0001/odnb-9780198614128-e-35886;jsessionid=918EB24AE0425EA0E7F5EEE4B0C0A624. Accessed April 7, 2020.

Rosenthal, Franz. *The Herb: Hashish versus Medieval Muslim Society.* Leiden: Brill, 1971.

Rotbard, Sharon. *White City, Black City* (in Hebrew). Tel Aviv: Babel, 2005.

Roth, Marty. "Victorian Highs: Detection, Drugs, and Empire." In *High Anxieties: Cultural Studies in Addiction*, edited by Janet Farrell Brodie and Marc Redfield, 85–93. Berkeley: University of California Press, 2002.

Rozin, Orit. "Food, Identity, and Nation-Building in Israel's Formative Years." *Israel Studies Review* 21 (2006): 52–80.

———. "Infiltration and the Making of Israel's Emotional Regime in the State's Early Years." *Middle Eastern Studies* 52 (2016): 448–72.

———. *The Rise of the Individual in 1950s Israel: A Challenge to Collectivism.* Waltham, MA: Brandeis University Press, 2011.

Russell Pasha, Thomas. *Egyptian Service, 1902–1946.* London: J. Murray, 1949.

Ryzova, Lucie. *The Age of the Efendiyya: Passages to Modernity in National-Colonial Egypt*. Oxford: Oxford University Press, 2014.

Said, Edward W. *Orientalism*. New York: Vintage, 1978.

Salt, Jeremy. "Fact and Fiction in the Middle Eastern Novels of Leon Uris." *Journal of Palestine Studies* 14 (1985): 54–63.

Sariyannis, Marinos. "Law and Morality in Ottoman Society: The Case of Narcotic Substances." In *The Ottoman Empire, the Balkans, and the Greek Lands: Toward a Social and Economic History*, edited by Elias Kolovos, Phokion Kotzageorgis, Sophia Laiou, and Marinos Sariyannis, 307–21. Istanbul: Isis Press, 2007.

Sarna, Igal. *Yona Wallach* (in Hebrew). Jerusalem: Keter Books, 2009.

Saunier, Pierre-Yves, and Akira Iriye. "Introduction: The Professor and the Madman." In *The Palgrave Dictionary of Transnational History from the Mid-19th Century to the Present Day*, edited by Akira Iriye and Pierre-Yves Saunier, xviii–xx. New York: Palgrave, 2009.

Scott, Peter Dale. *American War Machine: Deep Politics, the CIA Global Drug Connection, and the Road to Afghanistan*. Lanham and Boulder: Rowman & Littlefield, 2014.

Segev, Tom. *Palestine under the British* (in Hebrew). Jerusalem: Keter, 1999.

———. *One Palestine, Complete: Jews and Arabs under the British Mandate*. New York: Macmillan, 2000.

Schayegh, Cyrus. "The Many Worlds of 'Abud Yasin; or, What Narcotics Trafficking in the Interwar Middle East Can Tell Us about Territorialization." *American Historical Review* 116 (2011): 273–306.

———. *The Middle East and the Making of the Modern World*. Cambridge, MA: Harvard University Press, 2017.

Schayegh, Cyrus, and Andrew Arsan. Introduction to *The Routledge Handbook of the History of Middle East Mandates*, edited by Cyrus Schayegh and Andrew Arsan, 1–23. New York: Routledge, 2015.

Schivelbusch, Wolfgang. *Tastes of Paradise: A Social History of Spices, Stimulants, and Intoxication*. New York: Vintage Books, 1993.

Shahak, Israel. "The Real Israeli Interests in Lebanon." *Washington Report on Middle East Affairs* (July 1996), http://www.bintjbeil.com/E/occupation/shahak2.html. Accessed April 8, 2020.

Shechter, Relli. *Smoking, Culture and Economy in the Middle East: The Egyptian Tobacco Market, 1850-2000*. London and New York: I. B. Tauris, 2006.

Shami, Yitzhak. *Life's Mill* (in Hebrew), edited with an epilogue by Yigal Schwartz and Joseph Zernik. Or Yehuda, Israel: Kinneret Zmora-Bitan Dvir, 2015.

———. *Vengeance of the Fathers* (in Hebrew). Jerusalem: Mitzpeh, 1927.

Shamir, Ronen, and Daphna Hacker. "Colonialism's Civilizing Mission: The Case of the Indian Hemp Drug Commission." *Law & Social Inquiry* 26 (2001): 435–61.

Shavit, Yaakov, and Zohar Shavit. "History of the Hebrew 'Crime Story' in the Land of Israel" (in Hebrew). *HaSafrut* 18–19 (1974): 30–73.

Sheetrit, Bechor Shalom. "The Police and the Merging of Exiles" (in Hebrew). *999* 2 (March 1953): 4.

Shenhav, Yehouda, ed. *Zionism and Empires*. Tel Aviv: Van Leer and Hakibbutz Hameuchad, 2015.

Sherratt, Andrew. "Introduction: Peculiar Substances." In *Consuming Habits: Drugs in History and Anthropology*, edited by Jordan Goodman, Paul E. Lovejoy, and Andrew Sherratt, 1–10. London and New York: Routledge, 1995.

Shimoni, Batya. "From Babylon to the Ma'abarah: Iraqi Jewish Women in the Mass Immigration of the 1950s" (in Hebrew). *Sugiyot Hevratiyot be-Israel* 14 (2012): 9–33.

———. *On the Threshold of Redemption: The Story of the Ma'abarah, First and Second Generation* (in Hebrew). Or Yehuda, Israel: Kinneret Zmora-Bitan Dvir, 2008.

Shlaim, Avi. *The Iron Wall: Israel and the Arab World*. New York: W. W. Norton, 2001.

Simon, Reeva S. *Spies and Holy Wars: The Middle East in 20th-Century Crime Fiction*. Austin: University of Texas Press, 2010.

"The Situation of Criminality in the State [of Israel]" (in Hebrew). *999* 2 (March 1954): 6–7.

Sloman, Larry. *Reefer Madness: The History of Marijuana in America*. Indianapolis: Bobb-Merrill, 1979.

Smith, Woodruff D. "From Coffeehouses to Parlour: The Consumption of Coffee, Tea and Sugar in North-Western Europe in the Seventeenth and Eighteenth Centuries." In *Consuming Habits: Drugs in History and Anthropology*, edited by Jordan Goodman, Paul Lovejoy, and Andrew Sherratt, 149–64. London: Routledge, 1995.

Speaker, Susan L. "'The Struggle of Mankind against Its Deadliest Foe': Themes of Counter-Subversion in Anti-Narcotic Campaigns, 1920–1940." *Journal of Social History* 34 (2001): 591–610.

Stoler, Ann L. *Carnal Knowledge and Imperial Power: Race and the Intimate in Colonial Rule*. Berkeley: University of California Press, 2002.

Stratton, Richard. *Smuggler's Blues: A True Story of the Hippie Mafia*. New York: Arcade Publishing, 2016.

Svirski, Marcelo, and Ronnen Ben-Arie. *From Shared Life to Co-Resistance in Historic Palestine*. London: Rowman & Littlefield, 2018.

Swedenburg, Ted. *Memories of Revolt: The 1936–1939 Rebellion and the Palestinian National Past*. Minneapolis: University of Minnesota Press, 1995.

———. "Sa'ida Sultan/Danna International: Transgender Pop and the Polysemiotics of Sex, Nation, and Ethnicity on the Israeli-Egyptian Border." In *Mass Mediations: New Approaches to Popular Culture in the Middle East and Beyond*, edited by Walter Armbrust, 88–119. Berkeley: University of California Press, 2000.

Tagliacozzo, Eric. *Secret Trade, Porous Borders: Smuggling and States along a Southeast Asian Frontier, 1865–1915*. New Haven, CT: Yale University Press, 2005.

Taha, Ibrahim. "Duality and Acceptance: The Image of the Outsider in the Literary Work of Shimon Ballas." *Hebrew Studies* 38 (1997): 63–87.

Talmon-Heller, Daniella "Job (Ayyūb), al-Husayn, and Saladin in Late Ottoman Palestine: The Memoirs of Nu'mān al-Qasāṭlī, the Arab Scribe of the PEF Team," In *Exploring the Holy Land: 150 Years of the Palestine Exploration Fund*, edited by David Gurevich and Anat Kidron, 124–51. Sheffield, UK: Equinox, 2019.

Tam, Alon. "Cairo's Coffeehouses in the Late 19th and Early 20th Centuries: An Urban and Socio-Political History." PhD dissertation, University of Pennsylvania, 2018.

Tamari, Salim. "Ishaq al-Shami and the Predicament of the Arab Jew in Palestine." *Jerusalem Quarterly File* 21 (2004): 10–26.

———. *Mountain against the Sea: Essays on Palestinian Society and Culture*. Berkeley: University of California Press, 2008.

———. "Wasif Jawhariyyeh's Jerusalem." In *The Storyteller of Jerusalem: The Life and Times of Wasif Jawhariyyeh, 1904–1948*, edited by Salim Tamari and Issam Nassar, Kindle edition. Northampton, MA: Olive Branch Press, 2014.

"Ten Years (in Hebrew)." *Israel Police Quarterly* 7–8 (April 1958).

Thomas, Bryan. "'An American Hippie in Israel': 'Man, I Feel Really Turned On!'" *Night Flight*, May 16, 2015, http://nightflight.com/an-american-hippie-in-israel-man-i-feel-really-turned-on/. Accessed April 9, 2020.

Tidhar, David. *Crime and Criminals in Palestine*. Jerusalem: the Kahane Press, 1924.

———. *Criminals and Crime in the Land of Israel* (in Hebrew). Jerusalem: Tzion, 1924.

Treadway, Walter Lewis. "The Abusive Use of Narcotic Drugs in Egypt." *Public Health Reports* 45 (1930): 1239–41.

Türker, Ebru A. "Alternative Claims on Justice and Law: Rural Arson and Poison Murder in the 19th-Century Ottoman Empire." PhD dissertation, Boğaziçi University, 2011.

Turnau, Avraham. "The Problem of Drug Addicts in Israel" (in Hebrew). *Ha-Hevra* 4 (August 1960): 10–11.

Uris, Leon. *Exodus*. London: Corgi Books, [1958] 1983.

———. *The Haj*. London: Book Club Associates, 1984.

Velmet, Aro. "From Universal Relaxant to Oriental Vice: Race and French Perceptions of Opium Use in the Moment of Global Control." In *Prohibitions and Psychoactive Substances in History, Culture and Theory*, edited by Susannah Wilson, 33–50. New York and London, Routledge, 2019.

Veracini, Lorenzo. "The Other Shift: Settler Colonialism, Israel, and the Occupation." *Journal of Palestine Studies* 42 (2013): 26–42.

Walton, Stuart. *Intoxicology: A Cultural History of Drink and Drugs*. London: Dean Street Press, 2016.

Wasserstein, Bernard. *On the Eve: The Jews of Europe before the Second World War*. London: Profile Books, 2012.

Warnock, John. "Insanity from Hasheesh." *Journal of Mental Science* 49 (1903): 96–110.

———. "Twenty-Eight Years' Lunacy Experience in Egypt (1895–1923)." *British Journal of Psychiatry* 70 (1924): 579–612.

Watenpaugh, Heghnar Z. "Deviant Dervishes: Space, Gender, and the Construction of Antinomian Piety in Ottoman Aleppo." *International Journal of Middle East Studies* 37 (2005): 546, 551.

Weiss, Yfaat. *A Confiscated Memory: Wadi Salib and Haifa's Lost Heritage.* New York: Columbia University Press, 2011.

Winder, Alex. "Abu Jilda, Anti-Imperial Antihero: Banditry and Popular Rebellion in Palestine." *The Routledge Handbook of the History of the Middle East Mandates,* edited by Cyrus Schayegh and Andrew Arsan, 308–20. New York: Routledge, 2015.

Wolfe, Patrick. "Settler Colonialism and the Elimination of the Native." *Journal of Genocide Research* 8 (2006): 387–409.

Wright, Ashley. "Not Just a 'Place for the Smoking of Opium': The Indian Opium Den and Imperial Anxieties in the 1890s." *Journal of Colonialism and Colonial History* 18 (2017): doi:10.1353/cch.2017.0021.

Yazbak, Mahmoud. "The Muslim Festival of Nabi Rubin in Palestine: From Religious Festival to Summer Resort." *Holy Land Studies* 10 (2011): 169–98.

Yiftachel, Oren. *Ethnocracy: Land and Identity Politics in Israel/Palestine.* Philadelphia: University of Pennsylvania Press, 2006.

Zarinebaf, Fariba. *Crime and Punishment in Istanbul, 1700–1800.* Los Angeles: University of California Press, 2010.

Zieger, Susan. *Inventing the Addict: Drugs, Race, and Sexuality in Nineteenth-Century British and American Literature.* Amherst: University of Massachusetts Press, 2008.

INDEX

Abbasiyya Mental Asylum, 95

Abraham, Itty, 34

addiction: class and, 6, 67, 75, 94, 97; conditions of, 23, 157; as contagion, 136–37; drug trade and, 23–25; Egypt and, 20; epidemic levels of, 3; formation of, 190n68; French soldiers and, 20; gender and, 6; League of Nations on, 84; legalization and, 158; low levels of, 75; military use of, 118–25; Mizrahim and, 134–35, 141, 213n40; Orient and, 84, 92–99; as principal pleasure, 19; race and, 6; riffraff and, 133–43; statistics on, 134–36; symptoms of, 19; trafficking and, 113, 118–19, 123, 126; underworld and, 63, 65–68, 75

Al-Ahram newspaper, 120, 122

Aigner, Arthur, 39

alcohol, 22, 69, 71, 74, 99, 138

Aleh Yarok (Green Leaf) Party, 159

Algiers School of Psychiatry, 94

alienation, 10–11, 31, 80, 83, 127, 151

Altman, Nathan, 39

American Hippie in Israel, An (film), 154, 219n28

Anslinger, Harry J., 25, 37, 92, 97, 118, 171n62, 197n45

Appadurai, Arjun, 10–11, 31, 34

al-Aqsa, 159

Arabian Sea, 150

Arab-Israeli Wars, 6, 100, 103, 110, 135, 152–55

Arab Jews, 2–3

Arab League, 103–5, 119–23

Arabs: backwardness of, 144; Balfour

Declaration and, 4; Britain and, 5, 176n13; cannabis and, 3, 20, 36, 49, 62, 69, 76, 84, 89, 91, 95, 98, 120–21, 125, 128, 141, 150–52, 160; coffeehouses and, 13, 131, 153; culture of, 2–3, 13–14, 61–67, 77, 82, 89, 128, 141, 145; drug trade and, 20, 25; expulsion of, 15; gangs and, 14; Mashriq and, 5, 64; Mizrahim and, 128–31, 134–41, 144–45, 147; normalization and, 150–55, 160; Orient and, 79–91, 95, 99–100; Palestine and, 2–8, 11, 15, 35–36, 38, 40, 44–45, 49, 53–54, 58–69, 73, 75–89, 100, 103–6, 128–29, 137, 150–51; smuggling and, 35–41, 44–45, 49, 53–54, 58–59; source materials of, 11; state for, 4, 77, 104, 130; trafficking and, 101–10, 119–25; underworld and, 61–69, 73–78; Zionists and, 2, 8

arms smuggling, 27, 39–40, 45, 52, 55, 126, 178n34

Arsan, Andrew, 163n18

Artificial Paradises (Baudelaire), 119

Ashkenazi: class and, 2, 65, 128, 135, 151, 155; crime and, 133; ideology of, 2; middle class and, 135, 155–56; Mizrahim and, 135–37, 144; normalization and, 151, 155; Orient and, 14; over-Levantization and, 128, 151; transit camps and, 2; underworld and, 65, 78

assassination, 52, 80, 86–88, 91, 158–59, 195n24

attorneys, 38, 122, 132

austerity measures (*tzena*), 106, 112, 141

Australia, 152, 154

The authorized representative in the EU for product safety and compliance is:
Mare Nostrum Group
B.V Doelen 72
4831 GR Breda
The Netherlands

www.ingramcontent.com/pod-product-compliance
Lightning Source LLC
Chambersburg PA
CBHW030355270326
41926CB00009B/1111